D0265258

WITHDRAWN

WITHDRAWN

In for a Penny

BY THE SAME AUTHOR

The Art of Botanical Illustration
Pietro's Pilgrimage
A Persian Spring
Of Flowers and a Village
Cockerell
Isfahan
The Dream King
The Compleat Naturalist
John Christie of Glyndebourne
The Golden Road to Samarkand
On Wings of Song
'England's Michelangelo'
The Ark in the Park

Wilfrid Blunt

In for a Penny

A Prospect of Kew Gardens:
their Flora, Fauna and Falballas

So sits enthroned in vegetable pride
Imperial KEW by Thames's glittering side.

The Botanic Garden,
Erasmus Darwin, 1791

HAMISH HAMILTON
in association with
THE TRYON GALLERY

ST. PAUL'S SCHOOL

Class 914·2 13

Accession M4840.

WALKER LIBRARY

First published in Great Britain 1978
by Hamish Hamilton Ltd
90 Great Russell Street London WC1B 3PT
in association with The Tryon Gallery
41–42 Dover Street London W1X 3RB

Copyright © 1978 by Wilfrid Blunt

British Library Cataloguing in Publication Data

Blunt, Wilfrid
   In for a penny
   1. Royal Botanic Gardens, Kew—History
   I. Title
   580′.744′42195   QK73.G72K4
   ISBN 0-241-89823-4

Filmset by BAS Printers Limited, Over Wallop, Hampshire
Printed in Great Britain by
Ebenezer Baylis & Son Ltd, The Trinity Press,
Worcester, and London

Contents

Colour Illustrations

Black and White
Illustrations

Acknowledgements

I WISH to acknowledge my gratitude to the Director of Kew, Mr J. P. M. Brenan, for kindly allowing me to make use of the Herbarium's world-famous and admirably organized botanical Library, and to its Librarian, Mr V. D. H. Parry, and his colleagues for much assistance. Mr Desmond Meikle, a member of the Herbarium staff, saved me from a number of those botanical errors and other pitfalls that so easily ensnare the amateur; Mr Ray Desmond, Mr Parry's predecessor as Librarian, gave me much help on the historical side, and Miss Sandra Raphael kept a watchful eye where bibliography was concerned. My old friend Mr John Holmstrom offered shrewd criticism and also tidied up a hundred little stylistic inelegancies. I am further indebted for information of various kinds to Lady Audrey Morris, Mrs Ann Leaney, Dr David Mabberley, Mr Anthony Huxley and Mr Peter Taylor.

Miss Caroline Tonson Rye once again took charge, with her customary efficiency, of the provision of my illustrations, and I am also indebted to Mr John Freeman and Mr Jeremy Marks for photography. Miss Raphael, who compiled the splendid index for Blanche Henrey's monumental *British Botanical and Horticultural Literature before 1800*, has kindly provided one for my much humbler work. Sir Colville Barclay, Miss Susan Radcliffe and Mr Ray Desmond transported me on various occasions to and from Kew by car, thus sparing an old man some of the all too familiar horrors of public transport in the 1970s.

This is my indebtedness to the living; to the dead—to George Frederic Watts and his wife Mary—I continue to owe the good fortune of having a house large enough to contain my substantial library, and the leisure and peace in which to write.

Crown copyright material is reproduced by permission of the Controller, Her Majesty's Stationery Office, and the Director, Royal Botanic Gardens, Kew, and three drawings in the Royal Library, Windsor Castle, and two extracts from Queen Victoria's Diaries are included by gracious permission of Her Majesty the Queen. I also gratefully acknowledge permission to quote as follows: *The Hookers of Kew* by Mea Allan (Michael Joseph Ltd.); *The Journal of Beatrix Potter* (Frederick Warne & Co.); *Queen Charlotte* by Olwen Hedley (John Murray Ltd.); *The Royal Botanic Gardens, Kew* by Dr W. B. Turrill (Herbert Jenkins Ltd), and the *Kew Guild Journal* (Mr Richard Ward, editor 1976/7).

Finally, may I ask my friends the botanists to forgive a little gentle badinage at their expense? They are kind and delightful people and (unlike specialists in certain other fields into which I have perhaps too rashly strayed) wonderfully tolerant towards the amateur. But they live in a rather rarefied atmosphere, and it is surely no less than a duty for an outsider with a fresh eye to make constructive criticism where he feels it might prove useful; in particular, there seems to me to be some dead wood in the Kew museums that calls for pruning. I was born within three miles of Kew Gardens; I have known and loved them all my life, and they are magnificent: but nothing in this world is perfect.

W.J.W.B.

Foreword

THE TITLE of this book hardly calls for explanation: 'In for a Penny'—for at least a pound's-worth of pleasure. Kew Gardens are the best value for money in all England.

As for the sub-title—Flora also, I think, speaks for herself: she is what the visitor to Kew goes principally to see, though he may also envisage a family outing at smallish expense in what might almost be mistaken—in bluebell time near the Queen's Cottage, at all events—for 'the country'.

By Fauna I do not mean the wild life—the tufted duck and crested grebe that eager ornithologists will search for by the Lake; the grey squirrels, so rashly introduced from Woburn in 1908, which showed their gratitude by using the leaden labels as tooth-sharpeners—but rather these men and women who, over the years, have combined to create a paradise that is the envy of foreigners hardly able to believe that they are actually allowed *to walk on the grass!* Among the Fauna, last but not least must also be included the scientific workers behind the scenes who study the roots (as it were) of the flower that is all that the public sees.

And Falballas (the *O.E.D.* prefers 'falbalas', but however you spell it you must stress the first syllable)? Now here, for the sake of alliteration, I have cheated a bit. 'Follies', admittedly, would have served almost as well, but it has offensive overtones. Sir William Chambers's orientalia in the Gardens were dismissed by a contemporary as 'unmeaning falballas of Turkish and Chinese chequerwork',[1] but I intend the word to apply to all those temples, pavilions, and indeed the famous Pagoda itself, which, though now sadly reduced in number, add character and period charm to the Gardens. 'Falbala' means 'flounce' or 'trimming': these falbalas may be nothing more than frills, yet they are a link with the past and so make Kew something that Wisley, for all its recent architectural embellishment, can never become in our lifetime. Stourhead and Stowe, for example, have the necessary architectural features, but they lack the botanical and scientific ingredients. So Kew remains unique.

I ought also to make it clear that my approach to my subject is personal, capricious, irreverent. And perhaps even prejudiced, for I have always had a

---

[1] Quoted in the *D.N.B.* without mention of the author's name. Every effort to discover it, including a letter in *The Times Literary Supplement*, has failed.

kind of love-hate relationship with the botanists. I do not intend my book as a guide. It is something to be consumed in advance of a visit: an aperitif to the feast that Kew provides, not a meal to be eaten in the Gardens. Nor does it set out to give a balanced *botanical* account, and any who wish for such fare should turn to Dr W. B. Turrill's scholarly *The Royal Botanic Gardens, Kew*, published by Herbert Jenkins in 1959. This offers a very filling repast—by page 11 we are already knee-deep in *Cryptogamae, Spermatophyta* and *Angiospermae*—and I think that the layman may prefer (if he can get hold of it) W. J. Bean's similarly-titled and eminently readable book or Madeleine Bingham's neat little *The Making of Kew* (Michael Joseph, 1975). Ronald King's copiously illustrated *The World of Kew* (Macmillan, 1976) deals chiefly with various groups of plants that interest its author, only one of its thirteen chapters being to any great extent concerned with Kew. There is a handy, popular *Souvenir Guide*, purchasable in the Gardens and provided with an excellent map that enables the visitor to find his way around; it is an indispensable adjunct to my book.

I have also made extensive use of Mea Allan's *The Hookers of Kew* (Michael Joseph, 1967)—a most helpful work, though I feel she has on occasions mistaken Sir Joseph for *St* Joseph. I am told that its sales in America have been affected—though in what way I was not informed—by the unfortunate ambiguity of its title.[1] In addition to the above-mentioned books I have consulted so many others that I have funked compiling a bibliography. Where I considered it either courteous or necessary I have given the source of a quoted passage in a footnote; but I think it inappropriate in a 'popular' work of this kind to make a parade of what an innocent reader might mistake for 'scholarship'. There still remains great need of a full-length, official and definitive history of an institution which had such a tremendous impact on the economic affairs of the Empire and of the world; I understand that Mr Ronald King, a former Secretary of Kew, has prepared just such a work, and I hope that before too long it may find a publisher.

---

[1] In America a 'hooker' is, of course, a prostitute.

Introduction

'A great green book, whose broad pages are
illuminated with flowers, lies open at the feet
of Londoners. This volume, without further preface,
lies ever open at Kew Gardens . . .'
                    Richard Jefferies, *Nature near London*, 1883

SINCE THE material in this book does not follow a strict chronological sequence, I have thought it best (though it will involve some repetition) to begin with a brief survey of the rather confusing early development of Kew Gardens. The reader may find it convenient to read, and perhaps even digest this before embarking upon the main text, which should then be easier to follow.

Kew Gardens, as we know them today, were formed by the fusion of two distinct properties, both royal but with entirely different histories. The western (or riverside) half, known as the Richmond (Lodge) Gardens, was part of the grounds of Richmond (or Ormonde) Lodge which once stood in the Old Deer Park; the eastern half corresponded roughly to the grounds of Kew House ('The White House'), situated near the present Kew Palace ('The Dutch House') but demolished in 1802. The properties were separated by Love Lane, an ancient bridle-road between Richmond and Brentford Ferry.

About 1730 Queen Caroline, wife of George II, when occupying Richmond Lodge built Merlin's Cave and other 'follies' in the Richmond Gardens, but these also did not long survive. At the same time their son Frederick, Prince of Wales, leased the White House and developed the existing garden. After his marriage in 1736 he was helped and encouraged in this by his wife, Augusta; but it was not until 1760, nine years after Frederick's death, that his widow, with the assistance of Lord Bute, began to convert some nine acres into an 'exotick' (i.e., botanic) garden and arboretum of scientific intent. These, which were gradually increased till their size was approximately doubled, were later to become the nucleus of the present Royal Botanic Gardens. William Aiton was appointed superintendent of the Dowager Princess's garden and William Chambers her architect, Bute being director in all but name. To Chambers we owe the Pagoda, Orangery, and much else besides that has for the most part vanished.

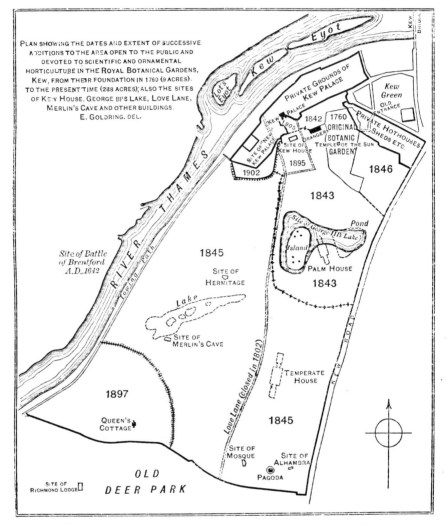

PLAN SHOWING THE DATES AND EXTENT OF SUCCESSIVE
ADDITIONS TO THE AREA OPEN TO THE PUBLIC AND
DEVOTED TO SCIENTIFIC AND ORNAMENTAL
HORTICULTURE IN THE ROYAL BOTANICAL GARDENS,
KEW, FROM THEIR FOUNDATION IN 1760 (9 ACRES).
TO THE PRESENT TIME (288 ACRES); ALSO THE SITES
OF KEW HOUSE, GEORGE III'S LAKE, LOVE LANE,
MERLIN'S CAVE AND OTHER BUILDINGS.
E. GOLDRING. DEL.

Plan of Kew Gardens showing the dates and extent of successive additions

George III, when at Kew, first occupied Richmond Lodge, where he employed Lancelot ('Capability') Brown to remodel the grounds. But on the death in 1772 of Augusta he purchased the White House, thus becoming the owner of the two estates which now constitute Kew Gardens; the inconvenience of their being separated by a public right of way was later overcome by the closure of Love Lane. In 1781, the King also acquired the red-brick Dutch House. After Augusta's death, Bute's position as unofficial director had been taken over by young (Sir) Joseph Banks, who was largely responsible for sending collectors to all parts of the world to get plants for Kew. In 1793, Aiton was succeeded by his son, W. T. Aiton, as 'Gardener to His Majesty'.

With the death in 1820 of both the King and Banks, Kew languished for nearly two decades. In 1838 a Committee was appointed to report on the condition of the Gardens; but for a time no action was taken, and their fate hung in the balance. When, however, it was learned that someone in high places was proposing to disperse the botanical collections and turn the greenhouses into vineries, pressure was brought to bear on Parliament and at the eleventh hour the disaster averted. In 1841 the botanic garden and arboretum were placed under public control, and Sir William Hooker appointed Kew's first official Director.

William Hooker died in harness in 1865 and was succeeded by his son Joseph, who ruled the Gardens for twenty years. In less than a half-century these two remarkable and dedicated men, Sir William in particular, were to extend a small botanic garden to create the miracle that is Kew today! *Si monumentum requiris, circumspice!* But Kew is far more than its gardens and greenhouses, and the casual visitor, as he wanders through them admiring the pretty flowers, can hardly be expected to appreciate that what he sees is no more than the iceberg tip of a vast and world-famous scientific institution.

Joseph Hooker was succeeded in 1885 by his son-in-law, Sir William Thiselton-Dyer, who carried the Hooker torch into the present century. Subsequent Directors, under whom Kew continued to go forward steadily, were:

1905–22	Sir David Prain
1922–41	Sir Arthur Hill
1941–43	Sir Geoffrey Evans, acting Director
1943–56	Sir Edward Salisbury
1956–71	Sir George Taylor
1971–76	Professor John Heslop-Harrison
1976–	Mr J. P. M. Brenan

I

Queen Caroline

I<small>T IS</small> customary—indeed only proper—to begin a book about Kew Gardens by stating that 'Kew' may be spelt in a dozen or more different ways (Kayhoo, Kai-ho, etc.), most of which look at least as Chinese as its famous Pagoda, and that it may or may not mean 'the quay of the howe, or hough'—whatever that may mean. There usually follows mention of the fact that William Turner, the 'Father of English Botany', when physician to Protector Somerset at Sion, had a garden of his own somewhere (though no one knows where) in Kew, and the general observation that Richmond and Kew have had royal associations since Norman times.

As will later be told, the origins of Kew Gardens date back to the seventeenth century; but for the moment we may turn to the year 1704 when James, second Duke of Ormonde, built in Richmond Old Deer Park an elegant and fairly substantial house, known variously as Ormonde Lodge or Richmond Lodge,[1] to replace a Tudor building that had been occupied by Cardinal Wolsey after his fall from power in 1530. The property, leased from the Crown, was extensive, stretching as far as Richmond Green to the south, and northwards to include roughly the riverside half of what is now Kew Gardens. After the Duke's impeachment in 1715 his estates were forfeited; but six years later the lease of the Richmond property was restored to his brother, the Earl of Arran, who immediately disposed of it to George Augustus, Prince of Wales—the future George II.

The Prince, and more particularly his wife, Caroline of Anspach, soon grew very fond of this 'sweet villa'; for Caroline the chief attraction was the rural charm of an estate so near to London, and the scope the ground afforded her to indulge in the latest fashionable pursuit: landscape gardening.

On the afternoon of 14 June 1727, George Augustus was sleeping soundly after his customary gigantic dinner when two horsemen galloped up to the gates of Richmond Lodge and demanded an immediate audience with the Prince; they were curtly informed that it was impossible for him to be disturbed. But the stouter of the two riders, forcing his way past the

---

[1] And even, occasionally, as Richmond Palace. It stood about two hundred yards to the south-west of the present Gardens (see plan), and is not to be confused with the Tudor Richmond Palace on Richmond Green, of which only a brick gatehouse survives.

Ormonde (or Richmond) Lodge.
Watercolour drawing by T. Sandby, c. 1778

protesting pages and frightened ladies, burst into the Prince's bedroom, where he found himself in the presence of an irate little man who greeted him with a shower of Anglo-German oaths; for George Augustus recognised in his unwelcome visitor Sir Robert Walpole, the Prime Minister and his bitterest enemy.

However, the news that he brought was as unexpected as it was agreeable: 'I have the honour to announce to Your Majesty,' said Walpole, falling on his knees, 'that your royal father, King George I, died at Osnabrück on Saturday last, the 12th instant.'

'*Dat is one big lie!*'[1] roared his disbelieving Majesty King George II in his guttural, imperfect English. But it was not, as the despatch from Osnabrück confirmed. His hated father was indeed dead, and the new King, as he struggled into his breeches, had the huge satisfaction of giving the first command of his reign: when Walpole asked for the royal instruction, he was told to go to Sir Spencer Compton, the Royal Treasurer, and take *his* orders!

'Queen Caroline,' wrote Horace Walpole, 'made great pretentions to Learning and Taste, with not much of the former and none of the latter.' Nevertheless, it is happily with the Queen, rather than with her boorish and lecherous spouse, that we are here chiefly concerned; for though the rustic poet Stephen Duck (of whom more in a moment) wrote that it was 'Royal George and heav'nly Caroline' who 'bid nature in harmonious Lustre shine'

[1] Thackeray, *The Four Georges*. The actual words are no doubt Thackeray's, but they will serve.

in the gardens of Richmond Lodge, the King's interest in his wife's horticultural activities began with contempt for their absurdity and ended with indignation at her extravagance.

The opening years of the eighteenth century witnessed the decline of the formal garden in favour of what Pope, established in his Villa just across the Thames at Twickenham, called 'Nature unadorned'. William Kent, said Horace Walpole, was 'the first to leap the fence and show that the whole of Nature is a garden', and Charles Bridgeman, though not (as is often stated) the inventor of the 'ha-ha', did at all events popularise this ingenious device for concealing the boundaries of a garden and letting it appear to merge into

Queen Caroline, wife of George II.
Mezzotint after a painting by
Sir Godfrey Kneller

the surrounding countryside. Pope ridiculed in the *Guardian* the excesses of 'verdant sculpture'—his imaginary sale of topiary work such as 'Adam and Eve in yew—Adam a little shaken by the fall of the Tree of Knowledge', and so on—and in his *Epistle to Lord Burlington* satirised the dreariness of formality and symmetry:

> No pleasing intricacies intervene,
> No artful wildness to perplex the scene;
> Grove nods at grove, each alley has a brother,
> And half the platform just reflects the other. . . .

Addison also objected to 'trees rising in cones, globes and pyramids', and considered that 'an orchard in flower looked infinitely more delightful than all the little labyrinths of the most finished parterre'.

Caroline employed Bridgeman and Kent to convert the grounds of Richmond Lodge into the kind of garden then fashionable. All that she created has now vanished, but we know something of what it must have been like in 1761 from the Diary[1] of Baron Friedrich Kielmansegge, a German who visited England in 1761, and we have exact knowledge of its two famous 'follies' — Merlin's Cave and the Hermitage — which will be discussed in the chapter that follows. There is also a valuable plan of the Richmond and Kew Gardens, made by J. Roque in 1736.

'Though the palace [i.e., Richmond Lodge] is unsuitable to the dignity of a King of England,' wrote Kielmansegge, 'the gardens are extremely fine . . . In short, almost everything here has an agreeable wildness, and a pleasing irregularity, that cannot fail to charm all those who are in love with nature' — and he goes on to describe the Dairy — 'a neat but low building, to which there is an ascent by a flight of steps; in the front is a handsome angular pediment. The walls on the inside are covered with stucco, and the house is furnished suitably to a royal dairy, the utensils for the milk being of the most beautiful china.' A canal led to a domed temple with Tuscan columns, and near the river was 'a wood, which you enter by a walk terminated by the Queen's pavilion, a neat elegant structure, wherein is seen a beautiful chimney piece' after a design by Palladio.

There is mention also of two summerhouses dating from the Duke's time; one of them, which stood on the terrace, was 'a light small building, with very large lofty windows, to give a better view of the country, and particularly of that noble seat called Sion House. In this edifice are two good pictures, representing the taking of Vigo, by the Duke of Ormonde'. Then follows a description of Merlin's Cave, leaving which 'seat of contemplation

> you pass through fields clothed with grass; through corn fields, and a wild ground interspersed with broom and furze, which afford excellent shelter for hares and pheasants; and here there are great numbers of the latter very tame. From this pleasing variety, in which nature appears in all her forms of cultivation and barren wildness, you come to an amphitheatre formed by young elms, and a diagonal wilderness through which you pass to the forest walk, which extends about half a mile, and passing through a small wilderness, you leave the gardens. . .

Such was Caroline's paradise — 'the prettiest place in the world'. When, in 1772, George III acquired the White House, whose grounds now constitute the other half of Kew Gardens, Richmond Lodge was demolished

---

[1] *The Royal Magazine*, March 1765, pp. 114–15.

and at a later date the two estates were united. But their character has always remained distinct, the Richmond Gardens retaining their wildness and the 'Pleasure Grounds' of the White House being more elaborately landscaped.

In 1728 Caroline had also leased the Dutch House (or 'Kew Palace' — opposite the White House), which was bought by George III in 1781 and occupied at one time or another by various members of the royal family.

2

Thresher Duck

ONE OF the strangest inhabitants of Kew Gardens at that time was Stephen Duck (1705–56), pet poet and the tame hermit of Queen Caroline; it was the age of tame hermits and of the discovery of rustic genius.

'Thresher' Duck —as he was called —was born at Charlton St Peter in the Vale of Pewsey, Wiltshire, of parents 'remarkable only for their honesty and industry'. After a short term at the village school, he was withdrawn (before he had even reached his 'Syntaxis') by mutual agreement between master and parents, the former having made the unusual complaint that his pupil 'took his learning too fast', which made the Ducks fear that their over-eager duckling might develop into 'too fine a gentleman'. So at the age of fourteen, Stephen, a copy of *Paradise Lost* tucked into his capacious pocket, found himself driving the plough (for four shillings and sixpence a week) over the broad Wiltshire downs, day-dreaming of poetry and glory.

Stephen Duck.
Miniature, c. 1740, attributed to Bernard Lens

Stephen Duck.
Frontispiece of his Poems on
Several Subjects, *1733*

The years passed. With the help of a 'dear friend' of similar tastes who had been a footman in London, Stephen gradually managed to acquire a few books: volumes of the *Spectator*, an English dictionary (much needed for Milton), several of Shakespeare's plays and some of the Latin classics. These he studied with his friend, or alone through long nights after tiring days in the fields; and soon he was trying his own hand at versification. At nineteen he married a young woman—an unamiable creature with no real understanding of her husband's talents or ambition—who provided him with three children in rapid succession.

At the christening of Stephen's third child an ancient crone who was present at the ceremony took it into her head to inform the officiating priest—'a dignify'd Person in the University of Oxford'—that Duck was 'a

Man of great Learning, and had Wit enough to be a Parson; for that he could make Verses . . . as good as ever she had heard'. The clergyman set Duck the theme for a poem, perused the result and advised him to burn it. After this setback, poor Duck consigned manuscript after manuscript to the flames.

To make matters worse, his wife had come to the conclusion that her husband was possessed by the devil—an opinion she did not have the discretion to keep to herself. However, good was to come out of her gossiping, for it gave the poet a notoriety which 'at length began to rouze the Wits of Wiltshire to some consideration of him'. Before long he found himself invited to the tables of the local gentry, and even to recite his poems to Lady Hertford in her famous grotto[1] under the Mound at Marlborough. It was now that he composed his first considerable surviving works: *On Poverty*, *The Thresher's Labour* (which earned him his sobriquet), and *The Shunammite*. These were 'handed about the Country with great Applause, in Manuscript', and a copy of them was sent to Lord Tankerville at Windsor, where it chanced to fall into the hands of Mrs Clayton (afterwards Lady Sundon), a lady-in-wating to the Queen. Thus it came about that on Friday 11 September 1730, the verses of the humble ploughman were read by Lord Macclesfield to Queen Caroline herself, who graciously rewarded the poet with a house at Richmond and a pension of thirty guineas a year:

> O DUCK! preferr'd by bounteous Queen
> To cackle Verse on *Richmond Green*. . .

Mrs Duck, never the right wife for a poet, tactfully selected this moment of his triumph to die, leaving the unsorrowing widower to bask unencumbered in the immediate rays of his royal patroness. The Queen, as happy as a child with a new toy, now proceeded to advance her protégé's cause, and the three poems, entitled *Poems on Several Subjects* and dedicated to Her Majesty, were hurried through the presses. One of the first copies, its opening pages sewn together to conceal the author's name and condition, was immediately sent by Caroline to Pope with a request for his opinion. Not for a moment deceived, Pope replied that 'he supposed most villages could supply verses of the same force'. He acted, however, with generosity: learning that Duck was an amiable and unassuming man (and no doubt satisfied that he could not conceivably damage his own reputation), he visited him several times and did what he could to help him. Lesser poets, however, were soon jealous of the preferential treatment accorded to the 'Phenomenon of Wiltshire', and even Swift, who did not enjoy the advantages of royal patronage, dipped his pen into vitriol to write a withering epigram:

---

[1] When I last saw it, it was being used by the College authorities to store swedes.

The thresher Duck could o'er the Queen prevail;
The proverb says 'no fence against a flail':
From threshing corn he turns to thresh his brains,
For which her Majesty allows him grains:
Tho' 'tis confest that those who ever saw
His poems, think them all not worth a straw.
Thrice happy Duck! employed in threshing stubble,
Thy toil is lessened, and thy profits double.

Duck had become a ten-days' wonder. Edition after edition of the *Poems* was called for, and when Eusden, the poet Laureate, died in 1730, it was widely, though erroneously, predicted that the Queen's favourite would be chosen to succeed him. In 1733, Duck was made a Yeoman of the Guard and—a happy coincidence?—keeper of Duck Island in St James's Park, and in the same year he further consolidated his position at court by marrying Sarah Big, the Queen's housekeeper at Richmond Lodge. Two years later he was appointed librarian of the famous 'Merlin's Cave', while his wife was entrusted with the care of the adjacent Hermitage.

The little gothic 'folly' known as Merlin's Cave[1] was built for the Queen in 1735, the architect probably being William Kent. We know from an engraving made in 1754 that it was a kind of glorified lath-and-plaster summerhouse and consisted of three rooms, the central one entered by a Tudor doorway and each crowned with a conical thatched roof that recalled at once a beehive and the hut of a Basuto chieftain. It was approached 'through several fine walks and agreeable labyrinths (the ground being most beautifully laid out)', and contained a small library and what Horace Walpole dubbed an 'unintelligible puppet show'—a table round which were

Merlin's Cave.
Engraving by T. Bowles

[1] Its site was close to or beneath the waters of the Lake made by Sir William Hooker in 1856.

seated life-sized figures of the Welsh prophet Merlin; Queen Elizabeth and her nurse; Elizabeth, Queen of Henry VII who had built Richmond Palace; a queen of the Amazons, and so on. 'The incongruity of this gathering,' says Bean, 'is explained by the supposition that the queens were there as clients of the magician.' Courtiers posed for these portraits, which were modelled in wax by the then celebrated Mrs Salmon. The library, to judge from two satirical couplets in Pope's *Epistle to Colonel Cotterell*, seems to have been meagrely stocked with books:

> Lord! how we strut through Merlin's Cave to see
> No poets there, but Stephen, you and me.

> How shall we fill a library with wit,
> When Merlin's Cave is half unfurnished yet.

The Hermitage or Grotto, built two or three years earlier than Merlin's Cave, and also portrayed in an eighteenth-century engraving, is believed to have stood about three hundred yards to the north of it—that is to say, not far from the present azalea garden. Though seemingly more like the entrance to Reading Gaol or a Piranesi ruin, it was in fact described as 'very gothique, being a heap of stones thrown into very artful disorder, and curiously embellished with moss and shrubs, to represent rude nature'. The 'venerable look', we are told, was improved by a 'solemn grove behind and a little turret on the top with a bell, to which you may ascend by a winding walk'. Three conifers were planted on the summit of the mound.

Within was an octagonal room, hung with some of the famous Holbein drawings recently discovered by the Queen in a bureau in Kensington Palace and furnished with niches containing marble busts (by Michael Rysbrack and Guelfi) of Robert Boyle, John Locke, Sir Isaac Newton, William Wollaston (the philosopher) and Dr Samuel Clarke. All of these except Clarke were dead, and Pope considered the inclusion of the Doctor, who regularly frequented the Court, particularly absurd:

> Ev'n in an ornament its place remark,
> Nor in an Hermitage set Dr Clarke.[1]

The *Gentleman's Magazine* invited 'all the fine Genii of the two Universities, and the schools of Eaton and Winchester, and all the Learned whatsoever', to produce Latin verses on the building, and many in both English and Latin, some far from complimentary, were published in its pages.

These two follies were erected and furnished with money provided by Robert Walpole from the Treasury, though the King—who had firmly refused to look at Caroline's plans, announcing that 'he did not care to see

---

[1] *Moray Essays* IV 77–78, 1732. The busts are now in Kensington Palace.

The Hermitage.
Engraving after a drawing by J. Gravelot, 1736

how she flung away her own revenue' (Horace Walpole)—was under the impression that the country was put to no expense. When the editor of an opposition newspaper, the *Craftsman*, ridiculed Merlin's Cave, the King observed to his wife, 'I am very glad of it. You deserve to be abused for such childish silly stuff, and it is the first time I ever knew the scoundrel to be in the right.'

In 1736, the year after Duck's appointment as librarian, a special edition of his works, now entitled *Poems on Several Occasions* and prefaced by a 'Life' from the pen of Pope's friend Joseph Spence, was published in a fine quarto volume. But a fickle society was already beginning to tire of its pet: no longer could Pope have written, as he had done in 1730, that a certain duchess would be thought 'insensible to all bright qualities and exalted geniuses, in court and country alike', if she did not succeed in enticing the poet to her house. Then in 1737 came the *coup de grâce*—the death of the Queen.[1]

There is little record of Duck's doings during the next nine or ten years. In 1746 he was ordained priest; five years later he became a preacher at Kew Chapel, and in 1752 he was appointed Rector of Byfleet. But the shadows were beginning to fall about him, and before long his mind gave way. In 1756, in a fit of depression, he drowned himself in a trout stream 'behind the Black Lion Inn' at Reading.

Merlin's Cave and the 'much-sung grotto of the Queen' did not long survive Duck's death, and about the year 1770 'Capability' Brown was ordered to demolish them. Perhaps, however, they survived just long enough for the eldest sons of George III to have seen them (in 1770 the future George IV was eight, his brothers Frederick and William seven and five respectively), for we are told that with the help of a bricklayer the King's 'boyish sons' built a 'rockery with a small stone house and an underground cellar' which may well have been inspired by their great-grandmother's grotto. It was demolished in 1822 'for the sake of its materials'.

Traces of Merlin's Cave and the Hermitage remained until 1840, but today not even an inscription records the sites:

> Lo! from his melon-ground the peasant slave
> Has rudely rush'd and level'd *Merlin's Cave*,
> Knocked down the *waxen wizard*, seized his wand,
> Transform'd to lawns what late was fairy land;
> And marr'd with impious hand each sweet design
> of *Stephen Duck* and good QUEEN CAROLINE.[2]

[1] O Death, where is thy sting,
   To take the Queen and leave the King?
      (Found posted at the Royal Exchange.)
[2] William Mason, *Heroic Epistle to Sir William Chambers*, 1773.

According to Sir Leslie Stephen, 'Lord Palmerston gave a piece of land [now known as Duck's Acre] to provide an annual feast at Charlton in commemoration of the poet. The rent in 1869 was £2. 9s. 9d.[1] This was the first Viscount Palmerston, great-grandfather of the Prime Minister, and it is pleasant to learn that these dinners continue to be held regularly each 1st of June at the Cat Inn, where various relics—the Duck glass, Duck hat, and a copy of his *Poems on Several Occasions*—are still preserved.[2] Duck himself must have attended at least one of these feasts, for he mentions that at them 'all eat enough, and many drink too much'; and fearing that in time to come some youngster might not appreciate what was being commemorated, he added:

> Some grateful Father, partial to my Fame,
> Shall thus describe from whence, and how it came:
> Thus shall Tradition keep my Fame alive;
> The Bard may die, the Thresher still survive.

---

[1] *D.N.B.*

[2] For further details see *Country Life*, 4 June 1964, and *Country Life Annual* for 1970. For the information of any who may wish to inspect the relics over a pint, I should mention that the Cat does not open its doors of an evening until 6.45.

3

Frederick and Augusta

'MY DEAR first-born is the greatest ass, and the greatest liar, and the greatest *canaille*, and the greatest beast, in the whole world, and I most heartily wish he were out of it': such was to be Caroline's considered opinion of her son Frederick, Prince of Wales (1707–51). The King thought the same, calling him 'a monster and the greatest villain that ever was born'. 'Popularity always makes me sick,' said the Queen on another occasion, adding that Frederick's popularity made her 'vomit'. It was therefore unfortunate that Frederick, two or three years after his arrival in 1728 from Hanover (where he had been left behind when his parents came to England), should have leased the White House at Kew, thus finding himself separated there from his parents by no more than the inappropriately named Love Lane.[1]

The White House belonged to the Capel (or Capell) family. Evelyn, recording in his Diary on 27 August 1678 a visit to 'my worthy friend Sir Henry Capel' (later Lord Capel), mentions that his garden has 'certainly the choicest fruite of any plantation in England, as he is the most industrious and understanding in it'. On another visit five years later he mentions that 'the two great greenhouses for oranges and myrtles communicating with the rooms below, are very well contrived. There is a cupola made with pole-work between two elms at the end of a walk, which being covered by plashing the trees to them is very pretty.' Later still, in 1688, he found 'the Orangerie and Myrtetum . . . most beautiful and perfectly well kept', and added that Capel 'was contriving very high palisadoes of reeds to shade his orange trees during the summer, and painting these reeds in oil'.

A fuller account of Capel's garden was given by J. Gibson in 1691:

> Sir Henry Capell's garden at Kew has curious greens, and is as well kept as any about London. His two lentiscus[2] trees (for which he paid forty pounds to Versprit) are said to be the best in England, not only of their kind, but of greens. He has four white striped hollies, about four feet

---

[1] In 1765 Parliament conditionally approved the closure of Love Lane, and in April 1774 'upwards of four hundred labourers' demolished the walls on each side of it. The actual amalgamation did not take place until some years later.

[2] The mastic, *Pistacia lentiscus*, introduced from southern Europe in 1664. 'Greens' are, of course, 'evergreens'.

*Frederick, Prince of Wales and his sisters (with whom he was not on speaking terms)
making music in the gardens of the White House. In the background is the
Dutch House.
Oil painting by Philip Mercier, 1733*

above their cases, kept round and regular, which cost him five pounds a
tree this last year, and six laurustinuses he has, with large round equal
heads, which are very flowery and make a fine shew. His orange trees and
other choicer greens stand out in summer in two walks about fourteen feet
wide, enclosed with a timber frame about seven feet high, and set with
silver firs hedge-wise, which are as high as the frame, and this is to secure
them from wind and tempest, and sometimes from the scorching sun.

His terrace walk, bare in the middle, and grass on either side, with a
hedge of rue on one side next a low wall, and a row of dwarf trees on the
other, shews very fine, and so do from thence his yew hedges with trees of
the same at equal distance, kept in pretty shapes with tonsure. His flowers
and fruit are of the best, for the advantage of which two parallel walls,
about fourteen feet high, were now raised and almost finished. . . .[1]

[1] *Archaeologia 12* (1796): 184–5.

The White House—Frederick, Prince of Wales's residence at Kew.
Engraving by W. Woollett after a drawing by Joseph Kirby. From Chambers's
monograph on Kew

On the death in 1721 of Capel's widow the 'old timber house' passed to his great-niece Lady Elizabeth Capel, who had married Samuel Molyneux—a keen gardener, too, but an even more enthusiastic astronomer. Molyneux attached an observatory to the eastern end of the house, and with the assistance of James Bradley, the Astronomer Royal, constructed there the Newtonian telescope and made the observations of the star γ Draconis that led to Bradley's important discovery of the aberration of light (1727); the spot where the observatory stood is now marked by a sundial. Molyneux died in 1728 and his widow followed him to the grave two years later; they left no children, and it was thus that Frederick was able to rent the property from the cousin who had inherited it.

He found the house in a terrible state and infested with rats: one day John Hampshire, the 'Rat Physician', caught more than five hundred, which he carried alive to Leicester House to demonstrate his prowess to the Prince. Frederick immediately engaged the services of William Kent to modernise the building both internally and externally, and to design furniture for the principal rooms—furniture which, to Kent's dismay, was later to be ruined by indoor 'baseball' which the whole family, male and female, used to play in the drawing-room after dinner.[1] The construction was not completed until about 1736.

Frederick, while still in Hanover, had wanted to marry Wilhelmine, daughter of King Friedrich Wilhelm I of Prussia. The plan of a double

[1] W. Neville, *Royal Residences of Great Britain*, Barrie and Rockliffe, 1960.

alliance, with Frederick's sister Amelia marrying Wilhelmine's brother, the future Frederick the Great, had indeed been promoted long since by George I; but later the relations between England and Prussia deteriorated, and though Frederick persisted and even plotted, nothing came of what might today be described as this 'package deal'. Wilhelmine married the Margrave of Bayreuth; she was an enthusiastic gardener, as Frederick's eventual wife was to become, so that Kew might in any case have had a Princess of Wales who played an important part in preparing the way for the Royal Botanic Gardens as we know them today.

It was certainly high time that Frederick settled down. Since the age of sixteen there had been a succession of mistresses, the first, according to some accounts, having been Madame d'Elitz, who had in her day served in the same capacity both his father and his grandfather—a sexual hat-trick that surely deserves a place in the *Guinness Book of Records* and which 'inspired the eighteenth-century wit George Selwyn with one of his most-quoted *bons mots*. In discussing the loves of Madame d'Elitz, a friend remarked, "There's nothing new under the sun." "Or under the grandson," added Selwyn.'[1]

Where marriage was concerned, the trouble was that eligible Protestant princesses were thin on the ground and for the most part plump and plain. Several were looked over, only to be rejected as too old, too young, too ugly, or not of the stuff of which a queen of England might eventually be made. Meanwhile Frederick was much in the arms of Jane, third wife of Lord Archibald Hamilton and already the mother of ten children. In 1735 the King set out for Hanover to vet a girl, Princess Augusta of Saxe-Gotha, of whom he had received favourable reports; apparently she was almost the only candidate not known to have insanity in the family, and as the King is reported to have said, 'I did not think ingrafting my half-witted coxcomb upon a madwoman would mend the breed'.

Augusta, though no great beauty and pitted, as were most people at that time, with smallpox,[2] seemed amiable and was approved. The following year she arrived in England, where she so charmed Frederick that he told his mother, 'If I had myself to look all Europe over I should have pitched my choice upon Augusta'. The girl even found some favour with the Queen, who observed that her hair was 'almost the same shade as the Duchess of Devonshire's but rather more of a sheep's colour'. The marriage ceremony took place on 27 April 1736 in the Chapel of St James's Palace; the bridegroom was twenty-nine, the bride seventeen.

It cannot be denied that Frederick was in many ways a pretty dreadful young man, soon made yet more unpleasant by the company he kept: Lord

[1] *The Royal Griffin* by John Walters, Jarrolds, 1972.
[2] Convention ordained that portrait-painters should omit the ravages of smallpox.

Princess Augusta.
Detail of oil painting
by Allan Ramsay, c. 1758.
(The charming portrait by Liotard
reproduced on p. 12 of Ronald
King's The World of Kew *is not,*
as there stated, of this Princess,
but of her daughter.)

Hervey's *Memoirs*, even after allowing for his malice, leaves us in no doubt. Yet there was a better side to his nature. Whereas his father hated 'bainting and boetry', Frederick took some interest in both, befriending Pope[1] who crossed the Thames to dine with him. He dabbled in astronomy. He was musical, as was his father, and after he had taken up the 'cello would sing French and Italian songs 'to his own playing for an hour or two together', his audience being 'all the underling servants and rabble of the Palace'; but this taste in common merely divided father and son still further, the former patronising Handel and the latter (to annoy him) Bononcini in the greatest musical feud of the century. Frederick's enthusiasm for gardening was also serious, and he is not always given sufficient credit for what he achieved.

When the Prince was in London he would be rowed up the Thames to Kew in his superb royal barge, designed for him by Kent and now in the Maritime Museum at Greenwich, to see what progress had been made in his absence by John Dillman, his 'Master Gardener'. Dillman had been appointed in 1730 with a salary of £50 a year; and he must have given satisfaction, for by the time he came to retire in 1752, a year after Frederick's death, it had been raised to £700. He was succeeded by Robert Greening, who contracted 'to keep and maintain the pleasure gardens at Kew, supplying his own labourers' tools, and buy at his own expense sufficient

---

[1] Frederick presented Pope with some ornaments for his Villa, and, as is well known, Pope gave the Prince a dog with a collar inscribed:

> I am his Highness' dog at Kew;
> Pray tell me, sir, whose dog are you?

flock of sheep to feed the lawn, and find and provide all seeds for raising flowers, etc.'. For these services he was paid 300 guineas a year and given fifty-four acres of farmland for his own use.

From the pen of George Vertue, the engraver and antiquary, we have a picture of the Prince in action at the White House:

> After our chocolate we were conducted into the Garden where his Hig^ss was directing the works & workmen with great diligence & activity. . . . His intention was to make an aquaduct thro his Gardens at Kew and the earth thrown up was to make a mount which he intended to adorn with the Statues or Busts of . . . philosphers, and to represent the mount parnassus. . . . He was planting about his Gardens also many curious & forain Trees exotic. . . .

The Prince's last order to Vertue was to collect drawings of ancient and modern philosophers from which these busts could be made.

Vertue also mentions that in 1750 a large number of men were working on the Prince's 'new Chinesia Summer hous, painted in their stile & ornaments the Story of Confucius & his doctrines etc.'. This 'House of Confucius' was the first of the innumerable 'follies' designed by William Chambers for Kew.[1] In all this we see that much though Frederick disliked his mother (who, to his undisguised satisfaction, had died in 1737), he was still to some extent under her influence where garden design was concerned.

Frederick and Augusta suffered from what Lord Chesterfield called *'furor hortensis'*. Everyone who came to Kew was made to lend a hand in the gardens, and each of the royal children had his or her own small plot there. Poor fat Bubb Dodington, not built for manual labour, noted in his diary for 27 February 1750: 'Worked in the new walk at Kew,' and again the following day, 'All of us, men women & children, worked at the same place—a cold supper'. That cold supper must have been the last straw. At the end of the same year, which seems to have been one of great horticultural and botanical activity at Kew, Frederick was also beginning the erection of a vast hothouse which was completed after his death by his widow:

> The Prince of Wales is now about preparation for building a stove three hundred feet in length, for plants and not pines [i.e., pineapples]; and my Lord Bute has already seatled a correspondance in Asia, Africa, America, Europe, and every where he can; as, to be shure, my Lord is the most knowing of any in this kingdome by much of any in it; such is his great abilitys therein; and he is the person as has prompted the young prince; and from such, what may not be expected? And next spring it will rise and grow apase, as all glasse and frams will be ready. . . .[2]

---

[1] See p. 30.
[2] Thomas Knowlton, 13 November 1750. For Lord Bute see pp. 23ff.

The House of Confucius from Chambers's monograph on Kew

Gardening hastened—may, indeed, have been the immediate cause of—Frederick's death on 20 March 1751. As John Mitchell wrote to John Bartram, the earliest native-born American botanist, on 30 March of that year:

> We have had two great losses, lately, in Planting and Botany in England, which will hardly be repaired, I am afraid. . . . The Duke of Richmond, and the Prince of Wales, are suspected both to have lost their lives by it, by being out in their gardens, to see the work forwarded, in very bad weather. The Prince of Wales . . . manifestly lost his life by this means. He contracted a cold, by standing in the wet to see some trees planted (through a sort of obstinacy against any sort of precautions of that kind, which it seems the whole family are blamed for), which brought on a pleurisy, that he died of, lately. . .

The proximate cause of the Prince's death, however, was the breaking of a large abscess, the result of a blow on the chest from a ball while playing 'what they call Prison-Bars' at Cliveden, several years earlier.

The following epitaph, obviously written by a Jacobite, has often been quoted:

> Here lies poor Fred
> Who was alive and is dead:
> Had it been his father,
> I had much rather;
> Had it been his brother,
> Still better than another;
> Had it been his sister,
> No one would have missed her;
> Had it been the whole generation,
> Still better for the nation;
> But since 'tis only Fred
> Who was alive and is dead
> There's no more to be said.

But Frederick was not quite the nonentity that this doggerel suggests, and the gardening world genuinely mourned his death. In another letter to Bartram, written on 24 April 1751 by the distinguished naturalist and antiquarian Peter Collinson, we read:

... The death of our late excellent Prince of Wales has cast a great damp over all the nation. Gardening and planting have lost their best friend and encourager; for the prince had delighted in that rational amusement, a long while; but lately, he had a laudable and princely ambition to excel all

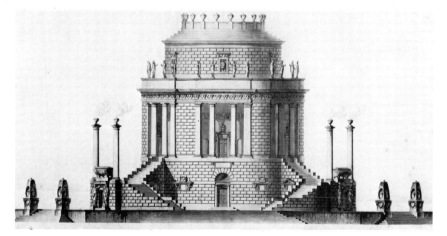

Mausoleum for Frederick, Prince of Wales, engraving by John Yenn after a design by Sir William Chambers, c. 1752. One of several projects, none of which was executed

others. But the good thing will not die with him: for there is such a spirit and love of it amongst the nobility and gentry, and the pleasure and profit that attends it will render it a lasting delight. . . .

Frederick's eldest son, the thirteen-year-old future George III, when told of his father's death turned pale and, laying his hand on his chest, said: 'I feel something here, just as I did when I saw the two workmen fall from the scaffold at Kew.'

*   *   *

'The Royal Gardens, Kew, were started, as is well known, by Princess Augusta . . . in 1759–60'; so their Director, Sir Arthur Hill, informed *The Times* in the spring of 1937, and was immediately, and very properly, corrected by a local historian, H. M. Cundall. The correspondence continued for some weeks, but Hill refused to admit what was indisputable: that the *royal* gardens dated from about 1730, when George II and Caroline took possession of Richmond Lodge and Frederick of the White House. Gardens in grounds that are now a part of the Royal Botanic Gardens had, as we have already seen, been established in the seventeenth century.[1] An earlier Director, Sir William Thiselton-Dyer, showed much better understanding when he wrote that 'to Sir Henry Capel, an ardent cultivator of plants . . . may be fairly ascribed the genesis of Kew as a horticultural, if not a botanical, centre'. On another occasion, taking as his starting-point the year in which the Gardens became the property of the nation, he referred to Kew's 'Jubilee' in 1891, and that same year produced an excellent little booklet entitled *Historical Account of Kew to 1841* (H.M.S.O, price twopence.)

By 1750, at all events, Lord Bute was beginning (as Knowlton's letter makes plain) to obtain interesting plants from all over the world. This greater emphasis on the scientific side of the gardens of the White House was undoubtedly increased when in 1759 William Aiton was appointed and a year later an 'exotick garden' established. It is of course convenient to fix a definite date of birth, and the alleged bi-centenary was celebrated with some pomp in 1959; in any case this ought really to have been 1960.[2] So far as I am aware, the 'centenary' in 1859 or 1860 passed wholly unnoticed, as did that alternative centenary in 1941 when in any case we were at war.

---

[1] It is absurdly claimed in Flückinger and Hanbury's *Pharmacographia* (2nd ed., 1879, p. 767) that 'the foundation of Kew gardens' was attributable to William Turner in the sixteenth century'. (See p. 1)

[2] 'The physic or exotic garden was not begun, before 1760.' Chambers, *Plans . . . of the Gardens and Buildings at Kew . . .*, 1763. It is, however, possible to maintain that it was *founded* in 1759.

4

Augusta, Bute, and George

ONE DAY in the year 1747, Frederick was attending the races at Egham when a sudden shower obliged him to seek cover in his pavilion. To pass the time he proposed a game of whist; but a fourth player was needed, and since someone had noticed the Earl of Bute on the course, an equerry was sent in search of him. The game eventually at an end, the Earl found himself stranded; for to save expense (at that time he was still far from well off) he had accepted a lift in the chariot of a friend who, tired of waiting, had left without him. When Frederick was told what had happened, he graciously carried Bute back to Cliveden with him for the night. Thus began a friendship with the Prince and Princess that was to change the course of Bute's life and, incidentally, the future of Kew Gardens.

'The life of a fly would be as interesting,' Lord Thurlow is said to have observed when told that someone intended writing a biography of Lord Bute. Nevertheless, the bare bones of it must be given here.

John Stuart, third Earl of Bute (1713–92), was a proud, vain and outstandingly handsome young man, reputed to have 'the most elegant legs in London'. After leaving Eton he had spent some time in Holland, partly at Leyden, world-famous as a botanical centre, where his interest in the subject had been fostered. In 1741 he and his wife, the daughter of Lady Mary Wortley Montagu, abandoned London to live more economically for the next five years on his Scottish island at the mouth of the Firth of Clyde. Here he devoted his time and energies to botanical and other scientific pursuits; but he must have remained in touch with leading botanists both in England and on the Continent, for during these years of voluntary exile Linnaeus named the lovely *Stuartia malacodendron*,[1] newly introduced into Europe from Carolina, in honour of 'a Lord of Iland Bute in Scotland'. It was only a year after the Butes had decided to take the plunge and settle permanently in England that the meeting at Egham had taken place.

[1] Linnaeus wrote 'Stewartia'. See Alice M. Coats, 'Scots wha ha'e', *Gardeners' Chronicle*, 18 May 1966, for a discussion on the correct spelling. 'The stuartia flowered for the first time in the Princess of Wales' Garden at Kew, which is the Paradise of our world, where all the plants are found, that money or interest can procure' (Collinson to John Bartram, 21 August 1766).

There is also a genus of tropical trees named *Butea* — 'the aristocracy, with its plurality of titles', having 'an unfair advantage in plant nomenclature'.

*John Stuart, 3rd Earl of Bute,
by Allan Ramsay, 1758.
This portrait was commissioned by
the Prince of Wales*

Frederick, charmed by Bute at first sight, introduced him into his 'little, idle, frivolous and dissipated court' at Leicester House and appointed him Lord of the Bedchamber. Augusta too was captivated. Certainly a love of gardening drew the three together; but it was soon being rumoured that Bute and the Princess shared interests other than horticulture. Frederick, when he wanted to be alone with his latest conquest, Lady Middlesex, would (said Walpole) 'bid the Princess walk with Lord Bute'; and he added slyly, 'As soon as the Prince was dead, they walked more and more, in honour of his memory'. It was widely believed that the Princess was Bute's mistress, and some four hundred cartoons and broadsheets satirising the alleged affair between the 'Jack-boot' (John Bute) and the 'Petticoat' have survived, together with a famous—or infamous—political squib by Horne Tooke, entitled *The Petition of an Englishman* . . ., published anonymously in 1765 and illustrated with an engraving showing how Bute could have slipped unobserved through the garden gate of his houses[1] on Kew Green to reach the White House. The truth will never be known: that Bute was very happily married is not conclusive evidence of the innocence of their relationship. What is, however, certain is that soon after Frederick's death the young Prince of Wales (the future George III) became infatuated with Bute.

[1] To his house he added a second, now a part of Cambridge Cottage, 'to study in'.

'A View of Lord Bute's Erections at Kew. . .'
'A House [extreme left] built for Lord Bute (TO STUDY IN,) and where none of
his Family resides and kept for him by one C. . . ., a German, who is Brother to the
Ps of W's WOMAN . . . [and] now HOUSEKEEPER to Lord Bute. By means of
which LUCRATIVE post he is at present become a man of considerable Property and
Fortune.'

The engraving, first published in Horne Tooke's The Petition of an Englishman . . .
(1765), is intended to show how Bute could have visited the White House (A) from
his study (I) through a garden gate (L) unobserved from the house (H) in which he
and his family lived.

'The loaded Boot or Scotch preferment in Motion . . .'
A cartoon satirising the alleged affair between the Dowager Princess of Wales and Lord
Bute. 3 November 1762

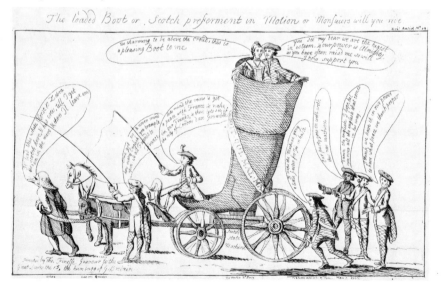

George III.
Studio of Allan Ramsay, c. 1767

At the age of seventeen the Prince—'a tall, handsome boy with light auburn hair and blue eyes, generally regarded as backward, but innately kind, courageous and honest'[1]—was put under the tutorship of Bute, who with the Princess watched over him and guarded him from all other influences. 'None but their immediate and lowest creatures,' wrote Chesterfield, 'were suffered to approach him.' A year later, when George came of age and was given an establishment of his own, his first act was to make his mentor 'Groom of the Stole', thus insuring a continuation of Bute's dominion over him.

The letters written over the next few years by the susceptible youth to this 'father-figure' are moving and pathetic. The thought of ever losing his 'dearest friend' put him 'on the rack . . . 'tis too much for mortal man to bear', and should Bute ever desert him he would refuse the crown and take refuge in solitude. 'I will with the greatest affection and tenderness be yours till death separates us,' he wrote. Even Kew seemed a desert without him; and when Bute hinted that their relationship would inevitably alter after George married, the latter wrote, 'I shall never change in that, nor will I ever bear to be in the least depriv'd of your company'. In 1759, the Prince fell

[1] Olwen Hedley, *Queen Charlotte*, John Murray, 1975.

'A View of the Palace [the White House] from the North side of the Lake, the Green House, & the Temple of Arethusa . . .'
The Swan Boat was built by John Rich, manager of Covent Garden, and presented to the Prince of Wales (George III) on his seventeenth birthday, 4 June 1755. It was 18 ft. high, could hold ten passengers, and was propelled by four feet 'artfully contrived as to supply the place of oars.' One is again reminded of Ludwig II—the 'Swan King'. Engraving by William Elliott after a drawing by William Woollett, from Chambers's monograph on Kew

head-over-ears in love with a fourteen-year-old Irish girl, Lady Sarah Lennox, and asked Bute's *permission*—for that is what it amounted to—to propose to her. Bute replied:

> . . . think, Sir . . . who you are, what is your birth right, what you wish to be, and prepare to hear the voice of truth, for such alone shall come from me, however painful the office duty and friendship and a thousand other ties, commands me, and I will obey tho' death looked me in the face.

George unhesitatingly accepted the advice. 'If I must lose my friend or my love,' he answered sadly, 'I will give up the latter, for I esteme your friendship above every earthly joy.'[1]

It is interesting to compare the relationship of Bute and George with that of Wagner and Ludwig II of Bavaria. In each case the younger partner was about eighteen when the friendship began—Ludwig just a King, George soon to become one. Wagner was in his fifties, Bute only in his forties. The intensity of the infatuation was not dissimilar, though its nature was rather different: Ludwig worshipped a god, whereas George—backward, lonely

---

[1] *Letters from George III to Lord Bute, 1756–66*, edit. by Romney Sedgwick, Macmillan, 1939.

and unloved by his mother (who far preferred his brother Edward) — cried out for affection, for a 'guide, philosopher and friend'. If George was ever 'in love' with Bute, it was only a passing phase of adolescence; Ludwig was, of course, homosexual, though he can hardly have been physically attracted to his ageing, battle-scarred hero. Ludwig said he would lay down his crown if Wagner wished him to, George that he would refuse to accept one if Bute abandoned him; yet both reigned, and the lives of both ended tragically. But how differently their lives developed! Wagner, genius but cad, came near to ruining the trusting youth who risked everything for him. George, within six years of ascending the throne, was to outgrow his infatuation, abandon his mentor, and settle down to a life of boring domesticity.

When the old King died in 1760, Bute found himself pitched into the political maelstrom, was showered with honours and in 1762 made Prime Minister. Chesterfield later spoke of George and Bute as 'the King and his Anointed'. But poor Bute — a mountaineer with no head for heights — never stood a chance of surviving at such dizzy altitudes. According to the sardonic Bishop Warburton he was trebly unsuited to be a Prime Minister of England. First he was a Scot (and it is hard for us to realise today how Scots were hated at that time in England). Then he was the royal favourite. And lastly, he was 'an honest man'. Warburton might have added that he

Sir William Chambers.
Oil painting by Reynolds.

had no sense of humour—something essential when dealing with men such as John Wilkes and Henry Fox. Fox had proclaimed his intention to make Bute 'the most hated man in England'; within a year he had succeeded, and forced his resignation. The pretext—'a great relaxation of my bowels of many years standing'—cannot be accepted as its cause.[1]

Losing the emoluments of his office did not trouble Bute, whose wife, on the death of her father in 1771, had inherited considerably more than a million pounds.[2] His fall from royal favour, which occurred soon after the King's first bout of porphyria in 1765, was due in part to the waning of that affection which George had sworn would endure 'till death separates us', in part to the intrigues of politicians. But during those halcyon years when Bute and Augusta had 'walked more and more' in honour of Frederick's memory in Kew Gardens and George was still bewitched by Bute, a little miracle had been taking place in those very Gardens. It began with the appointment in 1757 of William Chambers as Architect to the Dowager Princess of Wales, and continued with that soon afterwards of William Aiton as her Gardener.

---

[1] I am an author with no head for politics, or for wars; the reasons for Bute's political fall must therefore be read elsewhere. See, for example, the brief but admirable *Lord Bute* by Alice Coats, Lifelines No. 27, Shire Publications, 1975, of which I have made much use.
[2] For what Bute achieved later, see chapter 6.

5

William Chambers

SIR WILLIAM Chambers, who was now to scatter upon the green sward of Kew Gardens a whole host of temples and other 'follies', was born in 1723 in Sweden, where his father was a partner in the mercantile firm of Chambers and Pierson. The firm had lost a good deal of money through supplying the armies of that notoriously bad payer, King Charles XII; William, therefore, after a schooling in England, did not join the family business but became at seventeen a supercargo to the Swedish East India Company. During the next nine years he sailed to India and twice to China, and while in Canton made a number of architectural drawings which were later to serve him for his *Designs of Chinese Buildings* (1757). On his return to Sweden he decided that architecture must be his career; he was now twenty-six.

In the autumn of 1749 he again visited England where, thanks no doubt to some high-powered introductions, he was presented to Frederick, Prince of Wales, for whom he designed the first of his buildings at Kew, the already mentioned House of Confucius.[1] But Chambers knew that he needed to study seriously, and most of the next six years were spent in Rome, where he married the woman who for some time past had been his mistress. On Frederick's death in 1751, Chambers immediately set to work in Rome on a number of designs, in the grandest of grand Franco-Roman neo-classical manners, for a Mausoleum intended for Kew. It is sad, though perhaps not surprising, that the project, which was uninvited, never left the drawing-board, and that what he was in fact to erect at Kew were for the most part little more than agreeable trifles.

After his return to London in 1755, one or two commissions successfully accomplished led to Chambers's renewed contact with Princess Augusta and her son George, and to the friendship and patronage of Lord Bute. All this was a singular piece of good fortune for the still little-known young man, who two years later was appointed not only architect to the Princess but also architectural tutor to her son, for whose instruction he wrote his valuable *Treatises on Civil Architecture* (1759). Chambers's jobs were no

---

[1] This was moved by Chambers in 1758 to another part of the Gardens and subsequently moved again, for in 1849 it was reported as being in a meadow near Richmond Bridge; it no longer exists. Chambers apparently became ashamed of this youthful folly, alleging later that it was 'built I believe to the designs of Mr Goupy'!

sinecures, for the Princess had five establishments to supervise, and coaching the painstaking princeling consumed three mornings a week; but their prestige value was enormous, and soon his hands were more than full with commissions for the greatest in the land.

At Kew, within the space of five or six years (1757–62), Chambers designed and executed some two dozen miscellaneous buildings, in styles ranging from sober classical to wildest oriental, for the embellishment of the Gardens.[1] The designs were published in 1763, at George III's expense, in a well-illustrated folio entitled *Plans, Elevations &c, of the Gardens and Buildings at Kew.*

Chambers later built an Observatory, in the Old Deer Park near Richmond Lodge, to enable George III to watch the Transit of Venus on 3 June 1769; this was the same event that Captain Cook, accompanied by Joseph Banks, sailed in the *Endeavour* to observe in Tahiti.[2] The building still stands and is now used by the Meteorological Office. He also designed, and erected near the Observatory, a temporary Pavilion ('surrounded with a broad fosse to keep out the populace') for the reception of King Christian IV of Denmark on 24 September 1769.

Thus royally launched, Chambers soon became both rich and famous, his finest and best-known work being Somerset House in London. In 1771, in gratitude for a set of drawings of Kew Gardens, he was created by Gustav III of Sweden a knight of the Polar Star and, like Sir John Hill[3] who soon afterwards received the Order of Vasa, allowed by George III to assume the style and title of a knight; perhaps the Swedes, though now ruled by a different dynasty, had a rather guilty conscience where the Chambers family was concerned.

On the morning of 10 March 1796 Chambers died: or rather, he 'resigned his earthly post to sing hallelujahs' in Paradise and, no doubt, to enliven its

---

[1] John Harris, in his *Sir William Chambers* (Zwemmer, 1970), lists his buildings for Augusta at Kew as follows: 'Bridge or sub-structure to House of Confucius (1757); Gallery of Antiques (1757); Orangery (1757–61); Temple of Pan (1758); Temple of Arethusa (1758); Alhambra (1758); Garden seats (1758); Porter's Lodge (1758); Stables (1758); Temple of Victory (1759); Ruined Arch (1759); Theatre of Augusta (1760); Temple of Bellona (1760); Menagerie (1760); Exotic Garden (1760); Mosque (1761); Temple of the Sun (1761); Pagoda (1761–62); Temple of Peace (1763, uncompleted); Temple of Eolus, Temple of Solitude, Palladian Bridge (all before 1763); Dairy, and alterations to Kew House for George III, (1772).' Of all these, only six survive today: the Orangery, Ruined Arch and Pagoda, and the rebuilt (or resited) Temples of Bellona, Eolus (Aeolus) and Arethusa.

[2] A transit of Venus, which occurs only four times in 243 years, was studied from several suitably situated places in order to calculate the distance of the Sun from the Earth. George III was interested in astronomy, and it is related that one day at a very early hour he dragged from his bed the distinguished German physicist Georg Lichtenberg, his guest at Kew, to ask him whether or not the moon was inhabited.

[3] See p. 47.

outmoded gardens with a fresh crop of his fashionable falballas. Of the many epitaphs written on him, that by Lord Charlemont may be quoted:

> To
> Sir William Chambers, Knight, Etc.,
> Fellow of the Royal Academy,
> And Professor of Architecture,
> The Best of Men, and the First of English Architects,
> Whose Buildings, Modelled From His Own Mind,
> Elegant, Pure and Solid,
> Will Long Remain the Lasting Monuments
> Of That Taste,
> Whose Chastity Could Only Be Equalled
> By The Immaculate Purity of The Author's Heart,
> James Earl of Charlemont, His Friend,
> From Long Experience of His Worth and Talents,
> Dedicates This Inscription
> To Him and Friendship.

*   *   *

When Chambers found himself invited by Princess Augusta to embellish her 'gardens' at Kew, he surveyed the unpromising acres of level fields and saw that his task would be a difficult one. Six years later, the work accomplished to his own satisfaction, he wrote:

> The Gardens at Kew are not very large. Nor is their situation by any means advantageous; as it is low, and commands no prospects. Originally the ground was one continued dead flat: the soil was in general barren, and without either wood or water. With so many disadvantages it was not easy to produce anything even tolerable in gardening: but princely munificence, guided by a director equally skilled in cultivating the earth, and in the politer arts, overcame all difficulties. What was once a Desert is now an Eden.

Not everyone agreed. 'There is little invention or taste shown,' wrote Horace Walpole in 1760—admittedly at a time when Chambers's project was only half completed. 'Being on a flat, Lord Bute raised hillocs to diversivy the ground, & carried Chambers the Architect thither, who built some temples, but they are all of wood and very small.' He lists what had so far been carried out, adding that 'the bridge & the round Temple were each erected in a night's time to surprise the Princess'.

Adverse criticism also came from the author of an article in the *London Magazine* (August 1774) entitled, 'On GARDENS, and the FALSE TASTE thereof, particularly of KEW and RICHMOND': 'The Harlequin temples of Confucius, and the Sun, are mere baubles, and seem calculated for citizens to take their tea in ... The mosques are false in their construction, the letters ill made, and no Mussulman ever saw the basha's tails hung thereon as trophies to Mahomet.'

But John Harris, writing two centuries later, is more generous: 'This transformation is a tribute to [Chambers], William Aiton the gardener, Bute himself a renowned botanist, the Princess with her Privy Purse, and George, Prince of Wales, the future King.' William Aiton, who was not yet thirty when in 1759 he came from the Chelsea Physic Garden to Kew, was concerned only with the nine acres of the botanic garden and arboretum. Bute was the 'principal manager', while Chambers combined the duties of architect and landscape gardener.

Of the concrete expression of Chambers's dalliance with the Orient, from Moslem Spain (which he had never visited) to China, one alone of his 'unmeaning falballas of Turkish and Chinese chequerwork' still stands: his famous one-hundred-and-sixty-foot-high Pagoda.

The charmingly absurd *Drang nach Osten*, which swept Europe in the eighteenth century, produced some remarkable whimsicalities inspired by the often undisciplined reports of travellers of the wonders of the East. At Schwetzingen, for example, there was a Chinese garden and temple, 'Indian' pagodas and, incidentally, a little town for dwarfs which, because of a local scarcity of them, had to be peopled by children. At Hennegau in Belgium there was a Tartar village, with a mosque that concealed a dairy and whose minarets served as dovecotes. At Pillnitz, Nymphenburg and Sans Souci, *chinoiseries* were obligatory. In England there was the Verneys' house, Claydon; a Chinese temple at Woodside, Old Windsor; and later Sezincote, the Brighton Pavilion and Alton Towers.[1]

The craze was satirised by Peacock in his *Headlong Hall*, where Squire Headlong's new gardener, Mr Milestone, advocates the complete reconstruction of his master's garden:

My dear Sir—accord me your permission to wave the wand of enchantment over your grounds. The rocks shall be blown up, the trees shall be cut down, the wilderness and all its goats shall vanish like mist. Pagodas and Chinese bridges, gravel walks and shrubberies, bowling green, canals, and clumps of larch, shall rise upon its ruins. . . .[2]

Though pleasant enough as the termination of a vista, the Pagoda at Kew does not stand up to closer inspection; for it is really little better than a cheap travesty—it is said to have cost £12,000—of the genuine article, hurriedly

[1] See O. Siren, *China and the Gardens of Europe in the 18th Century*, New York, 1950, and John Harris, *op. cit.* pp. 147–8.

[2] Quoted by Hugh Honour, 'Pagodas for the Park', *Country Life*, 29 January 1959.

'*A View of the Wilderness with the Alhambra, the Pagoda, & the Mosque, in the Royal Gardens at KEW*' *from Chambers's monograph on Kew*

though sturdily built in stock brick in 1761–62.[1] An unofficial guide to the Gardens (1904) spoke of it 'rearing its ungainly form' and Moncrieff[2] of its 'towering intrusiveness'. In its defence it must, however, be remembered that it has long since been stripped of the eighty glittering dragons, bell in mouth, that once projected from the corners of its ten roofs, and that the multicoloured varnished iron plates that covered these roofs have been replaced by dreary slate. If Joseph Hooker is right in saying that the dragons were sold by George IV 'to pay his debts', this presumably happened in the 1820s. At the same time extensive repairs had to be carried out; and the work must have been well done, for when, more than a hundred years later, the Germans scattered a handful of bombs dangerously close to it, the Pagoda did not wince.

Chambers, when in China, seems to have got no further than Canton, though he was probably familiar with engravings of the famous Porcelain Pagoda at Nanking[3] and one or two others elsewhere. Perhaps the model he chiefly had in mind when designing his Pagoda was the Wa-tap (or Flowery

---

[1] Bean states that it was not begun until the *autumn* of 1761; but Horace Walpole, writing to Lord Strafford on 5 July 1761, says, 'We begin to perceive the tower of Kew from Montpellier Row [Twickenham]; in a fortnight you will see it in Yorkshire.'

[2] A. R. Hope Moncrieff, *Kew Gardens*, A. & C. Black, 1908.

[3] First figured in John Nieuhoff's *An Embassy . . . to the Grand Tartar Cham, Emperour of China*, 1669.

The Porcelain Pagoda, Nanking.
Engraving from John Nieuhoff's An Embassy . . . to the Grand Tartar Cham . . ., 1669

Pagoda) in Canton. But the sixth-century Wa-tap was built in golden stone and to the glory of Buddha, not in cheap brick and a great hurry for the amusement of an impatient Princess. Moreover, had Chambers been able to travel more extensively; had he been able to see, for example, the Lung-hua Pagoda near Shanghai or any of those whose 'irregular wavy roofs almost look like trees frozen rigid', he might have produced something less phallic and more in harmony with its vegetable surroundings.

Chambers's *Designs for Chinese Buildings* came too late to have much influence in England; its effect was far greater on the Continent, which had lagged behind in discovering the fatal charms of *chinoiseries*. But it was undoubtedly Kew Pagoda that inspired Britain's only other extant pagoda,[1] the much smaller but much wittier one at Alton Towers, built by Robert Abraham in imitation of the Canton To-ho.

This was one of the innumerable follies (they include an 'imitation cottage for a blind harper') designed in the 1820s for Charles, 15th Earl of Shrewsbury, for his fantastic garden near Uttoxeter in Staffordshire. Though intended to have been about half the height (88 ft.) of that at Kew, at the time of the Earl's death in 1827 it had risen only to one storey above

---

[1] One erected in St James's Park for the Victory celebrations on 1 August 1814 caught fire and fell into the water that same night. The so-called 'pagoda' at Cliveden, first shown at the Great Exhibition of 1851, is hardly more than a pavilion.

Pagoda, Alton Towers.
As originally designed by
Robert Abraham, c. *1826*

the surface of the pool in which it stands; it was completed later in a reduced, three-storey version. We know, however, from Loudon's *Encyclopaedia of Gardening* what it should have looked like. Its forty 'highly enriched Chinese lamps' were to have been fed from a 'gasometer fixed in the lower storey', and grotesque monsters projecting over the angles of the canopies would have spouted water 'from their eyes, nostrils, fins, tails, &c,' while a jet from the summit rose a further seventy or eighty feet into the air.

Loudon is pretty bitter about the Earl—a man 'abounding in wealth . . . but with much more fancy than sound judgment' who 'consulted almost every artist, ourselves among the number', but apparently 'only for the purpose of avoiding whatever that artist might recommend'. However, Lord Shrewsbury had unwittingly provided the perfect basic ingredients for the Amusement Park that his gardens have now become; they required only the addition of dodgems, giant slides, candy-floss stalls and other such horrors to make it, for those who like such things, the funniest fun-fair in all England.

The most recent Guide to Kew Gardens states that its Pagoda 'is not and never has been open to the public'; an earlier Guide, however, denies this and attributes its closure to the *graffiti* that defiled its walls and stairs, and I have elsewhere seen it suggested that so open an invitation to suicide from the summit also played its part. In any case, it could not be made accessible to the great crowds who now visit Kew in the summer. During the Second World War, planks were removed from the various landings to allow experiments in ballistics to be made.

The Stationery Office publishes an excellent little Guide to the Orangery—together with the Pagoda the most important of Chambers's surviving buildings at Kew.

Its author, Ronald King, begins with an interesting account of the earliest cultivation of the orange in England, probably in Elizabethan times on the Carew estate at Beddington, near Croydon, or at Burghley House near Wimbledon. By 1691 there was an orangery more than 200 feet long at Beddington, with trees up to thirteen feet tall that are said to have produced ten thousand oranges in the previous year (is that possible?). But the Beddington Orangery was a very ramshackle affair: a 'Tabernacle of boards and stoves, removable in summer', wrote Evelyn, who had reported so favourably in 1688 on Sir Henry Capel's 'Orangerie and Myrtetum' at Kew.[1]

Chambers's Orangery is a substantial classical building in what appears to be stone but which slight damage at one corner reveals as brick surfaced with his particular brand of stucco; it is 145 feet long, 30 feet wide and 25 feet high, and was formerly heated by a hypocaust. But, handsome though it undoubtedly is, it proved from the first far too dark for its intended purpose, and even glass doors added at each end in 1842[2] availed little; rough-and-ready removable covering, as used at Beddington, was far more suitable. So, over the years, the Orangery has proved something of a white elephant and has been put at one time or another to a variety of uses.

In 1841, when the Gardens became national property, the orange trees were removed to Kensington Palace and replaced by Australian and New

---

[1] 'When the hook-nosed William arrived from Holland [in 1688], anything was used of orange colour in honour of him; many ladies went so far as to "tataowe" themselves that frightful colour. . . . It was then our gardeners exerted their talents to compliment this new Dutch Prince with extensive orangeries. . . .' 'Harlequin' in the *London Magazine*, 1774.
[2] The *Guide* states that the letter 'A' in the two escutcheons over these doors is a tribute to Princess Augusta. As was pointed out (by S. T. Dunn) more than sixty years ago, in fact—and oddly enough—it stands for Adelaide, Queen of William IV, who died in 1849.

Zealand plants also doomed to languish in that perpetual twilight. Twenty-two years later these were transferred to the new Temperate House, and the Orangery, 'long condemned as utterly unsuited to the cultivation of plants', fitted up to receive a 'magnificent collection of Timbers, Cabinet and Furniture Woods' in search of a home when the Great Exhibition of 1862 closed its doors.

Other bric-à-brac was added from time to time. I recall a collection of about a million walking-sticks, and what looked like a huge renaissance marble tomb—in fact an Indian Shrine containing a Burmese prayer-chest; it can be seen in a photograph on p. 11 of the current Orangery Guide. A more appropriate exhibit was a life-sized wax model of *Rafflesia arnoldii*,[1] the largest and one of the most malodorous flowers in the world, discovered in 1818 in Sumatra by Sir Stamford Raffles' botanist companion, Dr Joseph Arnold. This extraordinary parasite, whose mottled pink and yellow flower is a yard in diameter and weighs about fifteen pounds, fascinated me as a child, and the model would surely still fascinate even the sophisticated young of today. But where is it now? Disintegrated? Melted down? No—hidden away, I am informed, on that first floor of the General Museum to which the public is no longer admitted.

But there was, for a time, something far stranger on the ceiling of the Orangery; a life-sized drawing of *Amorphophallus titanum*—an immense aroid which Kew was the first to flower in captivity. This obscene-looking plant was discovered in 1878, by an Italian named Beccari, also in the mountains of Sumatra, where it grows to a height of seventeen feet and makes a load for a dozen porters. The plant which flowered at Kew in 1890[2] and was 'one of the sensations of the London season' was a mere dwarf, less than seven feet tall; but its stench—'a mixture of rotten fish and burnt sugar'—soon drove the curious out of the Orchid House and into the fresh air. Poor Miss Matilda Smith, instructed to draw this 'giant stinker' for the *Botanical Magazine* (1891; Plates 9153–5), must have held her nose with one hand as she drew it with the other. What has happened to the monster drawing, 18 ft. long and 15 ft. 6 in. wide, which Signor Beccari so generously presented to Kew? If Puritans contrived its removal, surely in

---

[1] It must have been there for a considerable time, for a little volume of dreadful verse by J. Hunt Cooke, published in 1877 and entitled *Thought Blossoms, gathered in Kew Gardens*, contains a poem on *Rafflesia arnoldii* which begins:

> What strange gigantic flower is here
> That shows its lonesome pallid face
> Where neither stems nor leaves appear?

Other vegetables thus immortalised include *Fourcroya gigantea* (*Furcraea foetida*), *Stipa spartea* and the extraordinary *Welwitschia mirabilis* (now *W. bainesii*)—of which more later.

[2] *Amorphophallus titanum* is rarely to be seen in flower at Kew, but a plant obliged in May 1940 for the exiled King Zog and Queen Geraldine of Albania, who were deeply impressed.

Amorphophallus titanum
flowering at Kew

this permissive age it could be reinstated—though perhaps in some other Museum in the Gardens.

The year 1959, as we have already said, was considered to be the bicentenary of Kew Gardens. The Director, Sir George Taylor, decided that one feature of the celebrations should be the rehabilitation of the Orangery, so elegant a building deserving a better fate than that of a repository for acres of unloved timber. He therefore had its contents transferred to Cambridge Cottage or put into store, removed a hideous Victorian balcony, redecorated the interior with taste, procured some sculpture, re-introduced orange trees and so restored the whole to something of which Chambers would have approved. The renovated building was reopened by the Queen.

Unhappily, in spite of additional lighting and other favoured treatment, the orange trees again sulked. But worse was to follow: in 1960, extensive dry rot was discovered, and the blame for it laid on the moisture produced by the watering of the trees. So the Orangery was closed, the trees once again expelled, and the woodwork stripped down and treated. In 1971 Professor John Heslop-Harrison had to find a different use for this unhappy building. Acoustic difficulties having (allegedly) ruled out concerts of chamber music, he decided to convert it into a bookstall-cum-'orientation area' designed to

The Temple of the Sun designed by Sir William Chambers, 1761

instruct the visitor in the history of the Gardens and the scientific work — cytology, cell physiology, biochemistry and so on — carried on behind the scenes. In the circumstances, this was possibly as good a solution as could be found; but the ghost of Sir William Chambers must, I think, wander unhappily among all those higgledy-piggledy screens which give the whole a makeshift appearance that suggests a large village hall temporarily partitioned for the reception of blood donors. Here, surely, is a case for the employment of a real expert in the art of display.

It is generally agreed that the Temple of the Sun, which Chambers erected in the middle of Augusta's Botanic Garden, was the most successful of all his Classical pleasure pavilions. It was a circular, domed building, supported by eight fluted columns and ornamented with a rich entablature; internally, the roof was decorated with a sunburst above a frieze showing the signs of the zodiac. The model for it was that very elegant little temple at Baalbek which had just been brought to the attention of the West by Chambers's friend, Robert Wood; and which was also copied at Stourhead.

Near to the Temple — too near, as things turned out — was planted a cedar

The Temple of the Sun after the storm on 28 March 1916

of Lebanon from the garden at Whitton of the Duke of Argyll—dubbed by
Horace Walpole the 'tree-monger'.[1] 'The conjunction,' wrote Bean in 1908,
'has proved a most happy one, the dark straight limbs of the cedar and the
curving lines of the white temple affording an admirable contrast'. It was
not, however, quite so happy a juxtaposition as he thought: only a few years
later, during a violent storm on 28 March 1916, that 76-foot-tall tree fell on
the Temple and demolished it!

According to the *Kew Bulletin*, the falling tree 'swept it off its pedestal,
and reduced it to a shapeless mass'. Being of a suspicious nature, I had always
wondered whether the damage was really as irreparable as was alleged. We
were, of course, at war: the Battle of Verdun was at its height, and more
important things were falling at that moment than this little bauble, whose
passing might in any case hardly have caused the shedding of a botanist's
tear. The overworked Director of Kew, Sir David Prain, was an economic
botanist endlessly importuned at that time by the Government about ways

[1] The tree was raised from seed sown by the Duke in 1725. In the spring of 1762, after the
Duke's death, his finest trees and shrubs were moved to Kew.

The Temple of Aeolus in spring

of increasing the nation's food supplies. Nor was the little temple to be his greatest loss: his only son was killed in the War. But I found that I had done him an injustice, for a photograph shows that what had seemed a solid stone building, like its prototype at Baalbek, was in fact shoddy lath-and-plaster that the tree's fall had completely flattened. But it must have been a very pretty pastiche all the same.

The site of the Temple of the Sun is marked by a ginkgo[1] planted one foggy November day in 1923 by Queen Mary. 'Her Majesty, *using an ordinary garden spade* [my italics], placed several spits of earth on the roots of the tree', which has now reached a height of about twenty-five feet.

The Temple of Aeolus is just inside the (now closed) Cumberland Gate. It was built by Chambers on a mound which, like all those at Kew, is artificial, and originally sheltered 'a large semi-circular nich, serving as a seat, which revolves on a pivot, and may with great ease be turned by one hand to any exposition, notwithstanding its size'. These agreeable

[1] Or maidenhair tree. I wonder how many botanists know that Goethe wrote a little allegorical poem, 'Gingo biloba' (*Westöstliche Divan*), about the cleft, fan-shaped leaf of this remarkable Chinese tree—sole survivor of an ancient race.

contrivances—common enough in their modern equivalent, the revolving summerhouse, but no doubt at that time very much of a novelty—enable, of course, the sitter to opt for sun or shade, to court or shun such winds as Aeolus sees fit to provide.

It seems that the Temple of Aeolus gradually fell into decay, and we owe a debt of gratitude to Sir William Hooker who, instead of regarding it as an eyesore or a convenient quarry and demolishing it,[1] had the taste and sound sense to commission Decimus Burton to rebuild it. This was in 1845, only four years after he had taken over control of the Gardens. But charming as this little open, domed pavilion is, it is really the setting that makes it so enchanting; for here 'wild' gardening, inspired by pioneers such as William Robinson and Gertrude Jekyll, is seen at its best and most imaginative. Nothing could be more delightful than the mound in spring, with a million daffodils starring the grass beneath the light shade of magnolias and other early-flowering trees. I fear, however, that the flora here must, from a botanist's point of view, be commonplace—just ordinary daffodils and 'easy' trees and shrubs—for Dr Turrill sweeps past with barely a nod of recognition. He does, however, paint in the tenth chapter of his book on Kew a brave picture of spring in the Gardens as a whole, when Nature wakens the first 'geophytes'—to you and me the snowdrops, crocuses, daffodils, and so on—from their long winter sleep.

In 1761, John Smeaton, the most celebrated civil engineer of his day,[2] constructed near the Temple of Aeolus an 'engine for raising water' which continued in use until 1850. Chambers, who gives a diagram of it in his book, said that 'it answers perfectly well, raising upwards of 3,600 hogshead [about 190,000 imperial gallons] of water in twelve hours'.

The Temple of Bellona now stands (for it has been moved from its original site) on a small artificial mound near the Victoria Gate. Passing through a Doric portico, we enter a rather stuffy little room with an oval ceiling gaily painted blue and ornamented with a golden sunburst. Below are stucco festoons and medallions with the names of British and Hanoverian regiments which distinguished themselves in the Thirty Years' War. Like the Museums, it is useful as a refuge from a sudden downpour.

And so is the rather dreary Temple of Arethusa, dismissed by Bean as 'simply a covered garden-seat of classic design'. It would make a very adequate Athenian bus-stop shelter; perhaps the Greeks, who are always (and with some reason) clamouring for the return of the Elgin Marbles, would accept it instead. In it is a memorial to Kew gardeners killed in the two World Wars.

---

[1] Moncrieff mentions rockeries made 'by the destruction of one or more of those fanciful structures of the Georgian age'.
[2] He had just built the third Eddystone Lighthouse, which survived until 1877.

The Ruined Arch. Designed by Sir William Chambers, 1759. Engraved by
W. Woollett after a drawing by Joseph Kirby. From Chambers's monograph on Kew

Last of Chambers's unobliterated fantasies is the Ruined Arch. I fear that 'shoddy' is the only appropriate adjective to apply to this fake ruin, though it did in its day at least serve the practical purpose of a carriage-way across what is now Kew Road. Time, shedding the stone facing, has left it even shoddier, and it is best remembered as shown in an eighteenth-century engraving and an oil-painting by Richard Wilson.

Of those of Chambers's buildings that have disappeared, the Mosque and a corner of the Alhambra are shown in the engraving of the Pagoda (page 34), and in another we see the pretty little water-borne Chinese Pavilion and its bridge in the (old) Menagerie. The latter, probably the humblest of zoos, was somewhere in Augusta's botanic garden. Designs for or engravings of a few more of these fripperies by Chambers or other architects—especially Muntz,[1] who sometimes collaborated with him—are recorded in Chambers's folio on Kew.

Finally there is of this period a picturesque little thatched cottage, known as the Queen's Cottage, which stands in thirty-seven acres of woodland in the remotest south-west corner of the Gardens. Built by George III for Queen Charlotte, probably in 1772, for royal picnicking and innocent

[1] Johann Muntz, a Swiss, who was responsible for a Gothic cathedral and also for the first design for the Alhambra.

The Old Menagerie and its Pavilion. From Chambers's monograph on Kew

junketing, the cottage together with its grounds was the last substantial addition to the gardens: a Diamond Jubilee gift from Queen Victoria, who asked that its sylvan glades—once the game preserve of Ernest, Duke of Cumberland—should be left for all time untamed.

Who designed this romantic but ludicrous Hansel-and-Gretel building is not known for certain; according to the *London Magazine* (1774), however, the Queen was said to have been her own architect. Since I have never succeeded in setting foot inside the Cottage—it was long inaccessible to the public, and is now (1977) again closed for 'major renovation'—I must rely on the account of one who was more fortunate:

> There is a pretty sitting room on one side of the hall and on the other a staircase leading up to the tea-parlour. Although the parlour has at either end a tall, transomed window with a carved and gilded pediment surmounted by a crown, its appearance is that of a pavilion on bamboo frames wreathed with convolvulus. The painted decorations are said to have been designed by Princess Elizabeth in 1805. . . .
>
> On either side of the fireplace a door leads to a landing from which another staircase descends to two little red-flagged kitchens, each with its hob-grate and cupboards. The door on the left has a peculiarity. Silken skirts vanished through it, hands pressed against it an inner door lined with thick felt and then closed an outer door, also lined with felt and so contrived that the occupant alone could release herself. The sanctum was a close-stool room *en petit*, the most ingenious imaginable. . . .[1]

[1] Olwen Hedley, *op. cit.*, p. 308.

The Queen's Cottage. Lithograph after a drawing by G. E. Papendiek, c. 1840

A leaflet published by the Ministry of the Environment[1] gives an account of some of the parties held in the Queen's Cottage in former days:

Here the royal family often took tea, at times breakfast and occasionally dinner. Indeed in 1806, on the last Sunday that King George III stayed at Kew with his family, the Princess Elizabeth . . . arranged for the King to have dinner there at one o'clock, after he had walked through the gardens from morning service at Kew Church; heavy rain, however, caused the project to be abandoned. The Princesses in particular were frequent visitors to the cottage, for it was near the New Menagerie[2] where some of their pets were kept. One of the last great tea-parties there was that which took place on 11 July 1818, the day of the double marriage of the Duke of Clarence and the Duke of Kent at the present palace.[3] After the wedding-banquet all the royal party (except the dying Queen Charlotte and the Duke and Duchess of Clarence) drove to the cottage for tea, headed by the Prince Regent.

[1] The Gardens are now under the Ministry of Agriculture, the buildings under that of the Environment.
[2] See p. 58.
[3] See p. 73.

6

The Exotick Garden and Arboretum

CHAMBERS'S WORK at Kew, with the exception of some part that he played in alterations to the White House in 1772, had been completed by 1763, and in that same year Catherine the Great of Russia sent an architect and some gardeners there to get ideas for the improvement of the grounds of her palace at Peterhof. Bute, though deserted by the King, continued for a time to assist Augusta and William Aiton in the development of the Arboretum and Botanic Garden; on Augusta's death in 1772, however, he resigned from his position of unofficial Director of Kew Gardens, his place being taken by Sir Joseph Banks.

But Bute still worked with unabated energy to promote botany in England.[1] He created a superb garden at Luton Hoo, where he assembled an extensive collection of pictures, a great library (destroyed by fire in 1771), and a vast number of herbarium specimens and botanical drawings by Ehret, Simon Taylor (who drew for him the latest plants at Kew) and others. Collinson described Bute as 'the only great man that encourages ingenious men in painting botanical rarities', and Simon Taylor was one of his most talented protégés. George Edwards dedicated one volume of a work on birds to God and another to Bute—'as if,' wrote Walpole, 'he was determined to make his fortune in one world or the other'. Bute later built a 'marine villa' at Christchurch, in Hampshire, with a conservatory nearly three hundred feet long in which the plants were grown in the ground 'like an Indian grove', rather than in pots. About 1785 he published, in an edition of only twelve copies, his nine-volume *Botanical Tables*, 'composed solely for the amusement of the fair sex' and dedicated to Queen Charlotte. His death in 1792 was largely the result of a fall sustained two years earlier when reaching for a rare plant on the cliffs at Highcliffe. The sale of his library occupied ten days.

Another work dedicated to Bute and subsidized by him was the portentous *Vegetable System* of that strange figure—half genius, half charlatan—Sir John Hill. Linnaeus is said to have fainted at the sight of this seemingly endless succession of folios, adding, 'I could not but weep when I

---

[1] It is of interest to note that Bute's daughter-in-law, the 1st Marchioness of Bute, sent the first dahlia and several other important American plants to Kew from Madrid, where her husband was ambassador in the 1790s.

saw such a costly work without botanical science'. Hill had played some part in the planning of Augusta's gardens and was even referred to by Robert Thornton as their First Superintendant; he was, in fact, for a time in charge of the Gardens of Kensington Palace, with the enormous salary of £2,000 a year:

> Apprenticed as a youth to an apothecary, in due course [Hill] set up his own shop in London. But sighing uneasily after wealth and fame, he soon broke loose and embarked upon a series of enterprises which brought him neither the one nor the other. Garden-planning, botanizing, acting, play-writing, serious literature and the more scurrilous kinds of journalism proved equally unrewarding. . . . In 1759, he began his *magnum opus, The Vegetable System*, which was issued during the next sixteen years in twenty-six folio volumes containing 1,600 engravings of 26,000 different plants. Financially the enterprise was a total failure; but Hill's perseverance did not go wholly unrewarded: in 1774 he received from the King of Sweden the Order of Vasa.[1]

In an endeavour to recoup his losses Hill turned to quack medicine—but to little avail. After his death in 1775, his widow savagely attacked Bute in a pamphlet entitled 'An Address to the Public . . . setting forth the consequences of the late Sir John Hill's acquaintance with the Earl of Bute', in which she accused him of reducing her husband to penury and ruining his health; but she stormed in vain. The trouble with Hill, as Dr Johnson told the King, was simply this: he was 'an ingenious man, but had no veracity'. Hill did, however, produce the first catalogue of plants growing at Kew, his *Hortus Kewensis* (1768)—a work dedicated to Princess Augusta in which some 3,400 species were classed according to the Linnaean system. There followed in 1773 a slender folio entitled *Twenty-five New Plants, rais'd in the Royal Gardens at Kew*.

A second and far more valuable *Hortus Kewensis*—that by William Aiton— appeared in 1789 in three volumes, dedicated to the King.

Aiton—yet another Scot—came south and worked first for several years in the Chelsea Physic Garden under Philip Miller. He was soon considered the most competent man in England where tropical and sub-tropical plants were concerned, and Chelsea never recovered its importance after he abandoned it for Kew, where subsequently 'everything curious' was sent. He was in charge only of the Botanic Garden and Arboretum, Richmond Gardens and the Pleasure Grounds being under the supervision of John Haverfield. It seems probable that Aiton was at first Haverfield's assistant.

Aiton's *Hortus Kewensis*, the production of which had occupied his

[1] W. Blunt, *The Art of Botanical Illustration*, Collins, 1950.

William Aiton. Oil painting by George Engleheart, c.1768. He holds in his hand a spray of Aitonia capensis, *a South African evergreen shrub named in his honour by the younger Linnaeus.*

leisure hours for sixteen years, is described by Blanche Henrey as 'the most important of all eighteenth-century publications associated with Kew. It provided the botanist and the horticulturist with information which concerned not only the plants cultivated at Kew but also almost all the species then grown in England.'[1] No acknowledgement, however, is made of the great assistance Aiton received from two of Linnaeus's pupils—Daniel Solander, who was Banks's librarian until his death in 1782, and Jonas Dryander ('Old Dry') who succeeded him. The work is valuable both botanically and historically, giving as it does the date of the introduction of most of the 5,600 plants listed, together with the name of the collector, patron or nurseryman responsible. A second and enlarged edition by Aiton's son and successor, William Townsend Aiton, was published in 1810–3.[2] The elder Aiton died in 1793 and was buried in Kew Church, where a mural tablet extols the virtues of 'Flora's buried friend'.

Many of the tender exotics listed in these works were cultivated in the 'great stove' begun in Frederick's day but finished after his death by Chambers. Though in the event far smaller (only 114 feet long) than originally intended, it was at that time said to be still 'the largest in

[1] *British Botanical and Horticultural Literature before 1800*, O.U.P., 3 Vols, 1975—a work of immeasurable importance.
[2] See p. 78.

England'.[1] In its centre was a 60-foot-long 'bark stove', probably a bed of tan (bruised tree-bark) in which pots of plants were plunged to benefit by the moist heat generated by fermentation. The Stove, for the heating and ventilation of which the advice of the Rev. Stephen Hales[2] was taken, was demolished in 1861; but the site—in Augusta's Arboretum a little to the south of her late-lamented Temple of the Sun—is marked by an ancient wisteria[3] that once grew up its walls and is now trained over a kind of glorified bird-cage.

*   *   *

Among those birds of passage who alighted briefly at Kew but who were destined to win eventual fame in other fields was William Cobbett (1763–1835)—author of those *Rural Rides* that we all know so well by name but have never actually got round to reading. Cobbett worked for a short time at Kew in the 1770s as a gardener, and sixty years later he recalled the circumstances that took him there:

> At eleven years of age, my employment was clipping of box-edgings and weeding beds of flowers in the garden of the Bishop of Winchester, at the Castle of Farnham, my native town.
>
> I had always been fond of beautiful gardens; and a gardener, who had just come from the King's gardens at Kew, gave such a description of them as made me instantly resolve to work in these gardens. The next morning, without saying a word to any one, off I set, with no clothes except those upon my back, and with thirteen half-pence in my pocket. . . . A long day (it was in June) brought me to Richmond in the afternoon. Twopennyworth of bread and cheese and a pennyworth of small beer which I had on the road, and one half-penny which I had lost somehow or other, left three pence in my pocket.
>
> With this for my whole fortune, I was trudging through Richmond in my blue smock-frock and my red garters tied under my knees, when, staring about me, my eye fell upon a little book in a bookseller's window, on the outside of which was written: 'TALE OF A TUB; Price 3*d*.' The title was so odd that my curiosity was excited. I had the 3*d*., but, then, I could have *no supper*. In I went, and got the little book, which I was so impatient to read that I got over into a field, at the upper corner of Kew Gardens, where there stood a *hay-stack*. On the shady side of this I sat down to read. . . .

[1] This seems rather doubtful.

[2] Author of *Vegetable Staticks* and a pioneer of plant physiology.

[3] The Wisteria (*W. sinensis*) was not introduced (from China) until 1816, and this plant probably dates from about that time. Wisteria was named in honour of Caspar Wist*a*r, an American professor of anatomy; but since it was misspelt when first published, the error is retained.

I read on till it was dark, without any thought of supper or bed. When I could see no longer I put my little book in my pocket, and tumbled down by the side of the stack, where I slept till the birds in Kew Gardens awakened me in the morning; when off I started to Kew, reading my little book. The singularity of my dress, the simplicity of my manner, my confident and lively air, and, doubtless, his own compassion besides, induced the gardener, who was a Scotsman, I remember, to give me victuals, find me lodging, and set me to work. And it was during the period I was at Kew that the present King [William IV] and two of his brothers laughed at the oddness of my dress, while I was sweeping the grass plot round the foot of the Pagoda. . . .[1]

This amiable gardener—presumably Aiton—seeing the boy's passion for books, lent him some on gardening; but nothing could replace Swift's *Tale of a Tub* in his affection, and when later he lost it overboard on his way to Nova Scotia it gave him 'greater pain than I have ever felt at losing thousands of pounds. This circumstance, trifling as it was, and childish as it may seem to relate, has always endeared the recollection of Kew to me.'

[1] *Cobbett's Weekly Political Register*, 19 February 1820.

7

George III, Charlotte, and Joseph Banks

IN THE earlier years of his reign, George III and his rapidly-increasing family escaped as often as possible in the summer to the informality of life at Kew—first at Richmond Lodge, then, after Augusta's death, at the White House. There was also, exactly opposite the White House, the so-called 'Dutch House'—another of those royal establishments sometimes (and now usually) known as Kew Palace.

This little red-brick Dutch-style building had been erected in 1631, on the site of an earlier house, by a Dutch merchant named Samuel Fortrey. It was leased by Queen Caroline in 1728, and finally purchased by George III in 1781. At first it had chiefly served as a sort of occasional 'overflow' establishment—for example, a couple of princes with measles had been isolated there; but as, year after year, Charlotte added to the number of little princes and princesses,[1] the Dutch House soon became permanently occupied. In fact, the Crown was gradually obliged to acquire yet further houses on Kew Green and in Richmond to accommodate an ever-increasing flood of 'Court functionaries and officials of one sort or another: lords and ladies of the Bedchamber, wardrobe mistresses and pages and maids of honour, royal physicians and surgeons, governors and preceptors for the princes—the preceptors mostly bishops or bishops-to-be; governesses for the princesses, chaplains, musicians, gardeners, carpenters, riding-masters, and stable staff, a whole "class of assistants that increased in proportion as did the Royal Family".'[2]

The boys, as soon as they were old enough, were 'boarded out' in twos and threes to live in nearby houses in the charge of governors and preceptors. Though Gainsborough, commissioned in 1782 to paint thirteen of the Princes and Princesses, was 'all but raving mad with ecstasy in beholding such a constellation of youthful beauty', the boys were rowdy and undisciplined and those who had charge of them usually far too lenient. Lord Holdernesse, the Prince of Wales's governor, was ridiculed to his face by a pupil whom he found idle, deceitful and untruthful; he was soon replaced.

---

[1] There were eventually fifteen of them, and George Selwyn recalled once seeing a procession of coaches 'each stuffed with royal children, like a cornucopia with fruit and flowers'.

[1] S. Ayling, *George the Third*, Collins, 1972—one of three biographies of the King published in that year, all of them giving a more kindly portrait of him.

Kew Palace (The Dutch House). Etching by G. Shury after a drawing by W. G. Moss

So, too, was the Prince's preceptor, Dr Markham, Bishop of Chester, who was given 'a handsome copy of the *Odes of Pindar*' and 'kicked upstairs' to the Archbishopric of York. A nursery assistant, losing her temper with Prince William—described as wild and full of 'levity'—banged his head against a wall and was sacked by the Queen; yet it was by the Queen's orders that Prince Augustus was 'flogged for asthma'. Nor was the King, though a fond father and much loved by his daughters, more indulgent. Would it have been better for the Princes had they been sent to Eton? They would certainly also have been flogged there—but hardly for asthma.

The Queen saw her youngest children 'bathed at six every morning, attended the schoolroom of her daughters, was present at their dinner, and directed their attire when not publicly engaged'. Lessons began at seven o'clock, and at nine they all joined their parents for breakfast. Life was spartan, food simple; and some lived to regret the day when the Duke of Buccleuch introduced the King to porridge. George was almost a vegetarian; Charlotte, however, hankered after German sausages, which were supplied to her by the British Minister in Hanover.

In 1771 the nine-year-old Prince of Wales and his brother Frederick occupied when at Kew a suite of apartments in the Dutch House, where by the time the former was sixteen he had already (wrote Mrs Papendiek[1]) been

---

[1] C. Papendiek, *Court and Private Life of the Time of Queen Charlotte*, edit. by V. D. Broughton, 1886. Her recollections were not written down until the 1830s.

introduced by 'some of those about [him] to improper company when their Majesties supposed them to be at rest, and after the divines had closed the day with prayer'. Most famous of those whom his pages so obligingly smuggled into his private apartments was Mrs Robinson ('Perdita'), for whom he rashly signed a promissory note for £20,000, payable when he came of age.

Mrs Papendiek, who became Assistant Keeper of the Wardrobe and Reader to Her Majesty, has left us two little vignettes of the social life of the royal family when at Kew. The first refers to the summer of 1776:

> Kew now became quite gay, the public being admitted to the Richmond Gardens on Sundays, and to Kew Gardens on Thursdays. The Green on those days was covered with carriages, more than £300 being often taken at the bridge on Sundays. Their Majesties were to be seen at the windows speaking to their friends, and the royal children amusing themselves in their own gardens. Parties came up by water too, with bands of music, to the ait opposite the Prince of Wales's house. The whole was a scene of enchantment and delight; Royalty living amongst their subjects to give pleasure and to do good.

'The King never liked [the Richmond] Gardens on a Monday,' wrote Lady Mary Coke; 'they seem'd so dirty.' Incidentally, they had by this time been yet further landscaped by 'Capability' Brown, who had not only demolished Caroline's two follies, but had also eliminated any remaining straight walks and a rectangular pond, made what is now Rhododendron Dell, and generally 'improved'[1] the grounds. As a French wit wrote, to design an English garden 'on n'a qu'à enivrer son jardinier et à suivre ses pas'.[2]

Mrs Papendiek's second vignette dates from five years later:

> This spring, 1781, the whole of the Royal Family returned to Kew, to stay till after the prorogation of Parliament, which brought back for a time our former pleasures with increased gaieties. The nobility, on fine afternoons, came up in boats, other boats being filled with bands of music, to take the Prince to the promenade at Richmond. His Royal Highness was always accompanied by his governor and sub-governor, and returned for the Queen's party in the evening. Mr Zoffany had a decked sailing vessel, elegantly and conveniently fitted up, on board of which we frequently went, the Bachs[3] being of the party. He used to take his pupil [Miss

---

[1] Brown, for better or for worse, was quite ruthless: 'I wish I may die before you, Mr Brown,' said an acquaintance. 'Why so?' 'Because I should like to see heaven before you have improved it.'

[2] 'All you have to do is to make your gardener tight and then follow him.'

[3] Johann Christian Bach, known as 'The London Bach', and his wife. Bach gave music lessons to the Queen, who deeply mourned his death a year later.

Cantillo], as he wished to give her every opportunity of being heard. She sang with Madame Bach, whose voice was beautiful on the water.

Such was the brighter side of royal life at Kew before the King's mind had become permanently clouded; before his sons had become openly rebellious, before his daughters had flown the nest or declined into aimless spinsterhood. But how unspeakably dreary much of that court life must have been!

King George's household was a model of an English gentleman's household. It was early; it was kindly; it was charitable; it was frugal; it was orderly; it must have been stupid to a degree which I shudder now to contemplate. No wonder all the Princes ran away from the lap of that dreary domestic virtue. It always rose, rode, dined at stated intervals. Day after day was the same. At the same hour at night the king kissed his daughters' jolly cheeks; the Princesses kissed their mother's hand; and Madame Thielke brought the royal night-cap. At the same hour the equerries and women in waiting had their little dinner, and cackled over their tea. The king had his backgammon or his evening concert; the equerries yawned themselves to death in the anteroom. . . .[1]

*   *   *

'I wish the King had any taste in flowers or plants,' wrote Collinson sadly to William Bartram in February 1768; 'but as he has none, there are no hopes of encouragement from him, for his talent is in architecture.'

But the Queen, like the Empress Joséphine, loved flowers, and her enthusiasm was shared by several of her daughters, who joined with her to receive botanical instruction from (Sir) James Edward Smith, founder of the Linnean Society. The Queen and Princess Elizabeth also took drawing lessons from Franz Bauer,[2] one of the greatest of all botanical artists; but the Princess did not stay the course, for he proved 'a better philosopher than courtier, and his services, which were given gratuitously, were soon dispensed with'. The Queen, however, was an apter pupil, and tinted engravings of his drawings under the direction of the master. 'There is not a plant in the Gardens of Kew . . . ,' wrote Robert Thornton, of *Temple of Flora* fame and with flattering exaggeration, 'but has either been drawn by her gracious Majesty, or some of the Princesses,[3] with a grace and skill which reflect on these personages the highest honour'; and James Pye, worst of Poets Laureate, embroidered the theme:

[1] Thackeray, *The Four Georges*.
[2] See p. 120.
[3] A volume of flower paintings copied by Princess Charlotte (*c.* 1783), some architectural drawings made by George III when a boy, and further work by various members of the royal family, are in the Royal Library, Windsor.

Strelitzia reginae, *or Bird of Paradise Flower. Hand coloured lithograph from Franz Bauer's* Strelitzia Depicta, *1818. This spectacular member of the banana family, which was named after Queen Charlotte (a princess of Mecklenburg-Strelitz), is pollinated by sunbirds*

> While Royal NYMPHS, fair as the Oreade race
> Who trode Eurotas' brink, or Cynthus' brow,
> Snatch from the wreck of time each fleeting grace,
> And bid its leaves with bloom *perennial* glow.

Mrs Delany, an intimate friend of the royal family, had in her old age chanced upon a method of making flower pictures by pasting snippets of coloured paper upon a black background. In 1788, the year that Mrs Delany died, the Queen showed Lord Bute 'the beginning of an Herbal from Impressions on Black Paper' that she was compiling, no doubt in emulation of her friend's *collages* but using real plants. 'The Specimens of Plants being rather large,' she explained, 'it requires more Strength than my Arms will afford, but in the Smaller kinds I constantly assist. . .'[1]

Many botanical works, among them *The Temple of Flora*, were dedicated to the Queen, and when a spectacular new plant, the 'Bird-of-Paradise Flower', was introduced into England from the Cape in 1773, it was named *Strelitzia reginae* in her honour.[2] Four apples were also called after her, and

[1] See O. Hedley, *op. cit.*, p. 139, and W. Blunt, *op. cit.*, pp. 154–5.
[2] She came of the family of Mecklenburg-Strelitz.

she was probably the Charlotte of 'apple charlotte'.[1] A more debatably royal flower was the lovely *Streptocarpus rexii*, the Cape primrose. It was so named at the request of James Bowie,[2] who found it on the Knysna estate of George Rex—'a strange character who was in reality another of Queen Victoria's "wicked uncles". He was a natural son of George III and . . . had been sent to the Cape to be out of the way.'[3] Rex's mother was Hannah Lightfoot, known as 'the Fair Quakeress'; but whether or not George had sired him in his bachelor days remains uncertain.

After the death in 1788 of the Rev. John Lightfoot—author of the *Flora Scotica* (1777) but presumably unrelated to Hannah—the King bought his important herbarium as a gift for his wife:

> His Majesty purchased the whole for 100 guineas as a present to the Queen, the price having been fixed by an intelligent friend of the deceased. . . . The specimens, which had been generally gathered wild, were, after a while, discovered to be much infested with insects. The Queen, having a genuine and ardent taste for the study of botany, requested the advice and assistance of a gentleman well versed in the subject, and who, being consequently a constant visitor at the Queen's, gave a regular course of conversations rather than lectures, on botany and zoology, which her Majesty and the Princesses Augusta and Elizabeth honoured with their diligent attention; the Queen regularly taking notes of every lecture, which she read over aloud at the conclusion, to prevent any mistake. . . . This herbarium was not consigned to useless repose; it was allowed to be consulted frequently, on the subject of Scottish willows, and other useful matters. . . .[4]

In 1921, after many vicissitudes, the major part of it was presented to Kew by the Saffron Walden Museum.

The interest of the Queen and her daughters in flowers, though genuine enough, was of the kind soon to become fashionable, and largely as the result of this royal lead, with hundreds of young ladies throughout the land. For them, flower painting and mild botanizing were agreeable pastimes to while away those tedious hours that are now catered for by bingo or television. 'Farmer George' was, of course, more concerned with agriculture and live-stock, and a whole book[5] has been devoted to the subject of his Merino

---

[1]   The Charlotte brown, within whose crusty sides
         A belly soft the palpy apple hides.
                    J. Barlow, *Hasty-Pudding*, 1796.

[2] See p. 69.

[3] A. W. Anderson, *The Coming of the Flowers*, Williams & Norgate, 1950.

[4] W. C. Oulton, *Memoirs of Queen Charlotte*, 1819. The 'gentleman' was no doubt Smith.

[5] H. B. Carter, *His Majesty's Spanish Flock*, Angus & Robertson, 1964. Sir Joseph Banks also wrote a small work on the subject in 1809.

sheep, which were smuggled out of Spain in large quantities and bred in the royal farm on the east side of Kew Road, and at Windsor. The Queen also had her 'new menagerie' near the Queen's Cottage, in which, until its dispersal in 1806, kangaroos and other exotic animals were kept. These included a 'fine blue nylghau from India, Algiers cows, a "hog like a porcupine in skin, with navel on back" and a crown bird in the aviary'.[1]

As Augusta had her Bute, so Charlotte was to have her Joseph Banks— though here, of course, there was no question of a liaison other than botanical From her predecessors she also inherited William Aiton, and, for better or for worse, the extraordinary Sir John Hill.

> During the closing decades of the eighteenth century and the opening years of the nineteenth, [Sir Joseph Banks] occupied a unique position in the English scientific world. In his youth he had shown a pleasing impartiality in electing to be educated at Harrow and Eton successively; as a young man, his wealth and enthusiasm were ever at the disposal of any worthy cause; his house and collections in Soho were open to all who sought admission; and throughout his life he rendered incomparable service to the study of natural science by subsidising botanists, explorers and artists all the world over. . . .[2]

Banks when young was no 'closet' botanist: he was one of those who feel the irresistible urge to go to some remote, improbable, uncomfortable part of the world from where, unless they succumb to the climate or the assegai of an unsympathetic native, they ultimately return with a cornucopia of plants, seeds, and herbarium specimens. Today many of the novelties brought back are of interest to specialists only, among the last really sensational horticultural introductions being the regale lily (E. H. Wilson, 1904); two hundred years ago there was almost everything still to be discovered.

In 1766, at the age of twenty-three, Banks went to Newfoundland, and at a later date to Iceland; but his most adventurous journey was with Captain Cook in the *Endeavour* (1768–71)—the first of Cook's great voyages of circumnavigation in the southern hemisphere. Accompanying Banks, and engaged at his own expense, were five other men, among them Linnaeus's favourite pupil, Daniel Solander, who later became Banks's secretary and librarian, and the botanical artist Sydney Parkinson, who after making nearly a thousand drawings was to die on the homeward voyage.

It had been Banks's ambition to bring back from Polynesia a 'noble savage' to constitute the *pièce de résistance* of his collection: 'to keep as a curiosity as well as my neighbours do lions and tigers'; but his candidate

---

[1] Olwyn Hedley, *op. cit.*
[2] W. Blunt, *op. cit.*

Sir Joseph Banks.
Oil painting by Reynolds, c. 1773

died in Batavia on the homeward journey. However, Cook returned in 1775 from his second voyage with a great prize from the South Seas—a young native named Omai. Banks, who had not this time accompanied Cook, immediately took possession of Omai, and was no doubt present when Lord Sandwich presented him to the King at Kew. According to one account, Omai, though thoroughly rehearsed, panicked when the great moment came, believing that his Majesty intended to eat him. The bowing and the kneeling were forgotten. 'Extending his tattooed hand . . . and seizing the King's, he cried: "Howdo! King Tosh!" 'Tosh' being the best his Tahitian tongue could make of the royal name.'[1]

By the time Banks was thirty his *wanderlust* had been assuaged, and he settled down to his real life's work. In 1778 he became President of the Royal Society, a position he continued to occupy until his death more than forty years later, while from his country villa at Isleworth he watched over the destinies of Kew. But perhaps his greatest contribution to the Gardens resulted from his policy, sanctioned by the King—but often in part subsidised by himself—of sending a succession of collectors to all parts of the world.[2] During the reign of George III nearly seven thousand new

[1] Michael Alexander, *Omai, 'Noble Savage'*, Collins & Harvill, 1977.
[1] See chapter 9.

exotics were introduced into England, the large majority of them brought back by botanists despatched on the recommendation of Banks or of the Aitons.

Among those novelties secured by Banks for Kew through negotiation with merchants in the Far East were the garden hydrangea and the moutan (tree peony). Scheer wrote in 1840:

> We should like to see a pictorial representation of the scene of Sir Joseph Banks's introducing the first *Hydrangea hortensis* [*H. macrophylla*] to Kew about the beginning of 1789 for the inspection of the curious. It had begun to flower in the Custom House, and its green petals were a puzzle to the botanists of the day. The next day he exhibited it at his house in Soho Square, from whence it was removed, and lived in Kew, the parent of its numerous progeny now spread all over Europe, till within these few years. This year also saw the *Paeonia Moutan* [*P. suffruticosa*] introduced from China, and it is in the gardens to this day alive and well, a venerable monument of happier times. . . .[1]

[1] *Kew Gardens*, p. 20.

8

Brief Encounter

IN THE morning of 2 February 1789—a year memorable for the unfolding of a great drama across the waters which was soon to bring the King of France to the scaffold—there occurred in the remoter parts of Kew Gardens a tiny British royal drama which Fanny Burney (Madame d'Arblay),[1] who as second Keeper of the Robes to the Queen was very much involved in it, described later as 'the severest personal terror I ever experienced in my life'.

We must turn back for a moment to the previous June, when George III, who was then at Windsor, showed unmistakable signs of what was to prove the first really serious attack of the insanity which has only very recently been diagnosed as 'acute intermittent porphyria'.[2] A visit to Cheltenham temporarily restored him, but at Kew in October the symptoms, beginning with a 'spasmodic Byleous attack', returned in more severe form: cramps, rheumatic pains, giddiness, insomnia, ceaseless incoherent and sometimes indecent babblings, nervous tension, hoarseness of voice, and finally violence and delirium; his eyes, said the Queen, were like 'black currant jelly'. They carried him back to Windsor where the doctors—there was soon a whole horde of them—bled him and cupped him and purged him, and talked vaguely of 'bile', and bickered ceaselessly among themselves. On one thing only were they agreed: though the King had lucid intervals, his disease was incurable.

The Queen, kept apart from her husband, sobbed; the unfilial Prince of Wales had thoughts only of power seemingly almost within his grasp. It was with the arrival on the scene in November of a well-known alienist, Dr Anthony Addington, that hope was for the first time expressed of an eventual complete recovery. Addington recommended that the patient be removed to Kew, where he would be able to enjoy fresh air and take exercise in a privacy that was impossible at Windsor. The King refused to budge but was ultimately bullied and tricked into going. His discovery of the deceit practised on him—he had been told that he would be allowed to see the Queen there—only aggravated his condition.

[1] See *Diary and Letters of Madame d'Arblay*, 7 vols., London, 1854. Vol IV, part X, contains the account here used.
[2] See A. Macalpine and R. Hunter, *George III and the Mad-Business*, Allen Lane, 1969.

George III and Queen Charlotte walking in Kew Gardens. Hand-coloured engraving, 1787

The Prince of Wales had ridden on ahead to the White House where he had allotted the rooms, chalking the names on the doors as if it had been an inn. The King was given a large one on the ground floor with a 'new Water Closet' adjoining; the rooms above it were left empty and kept locked, so that he should not be disturbed by footsteps overhead. It was an exceptionally bad winter, and the 'state of cold and discomfort past all imagination', the appalling draughts which Colonel Digby tried in vain to prevent by the use of sandbags, have been graphically described by Fanny Burney, who suffered much from long hours of waiting in icy, uncarpeted anterooms. Many years earlier a page named Fortnum, unable to bear the misery, had resigned and set up a grocery business in Piccadilly.

The Queen now produced another alienist strongly recommended to her by Lady Harcourt—the Rev Dr Francis Willis, who was said to have effected almost miraculous cures in his private asylum in Lincolnshire. Willis examined the King and also predicted success; but his treatment involved the strait-waistcoat, obnoxious potions, and other brutalities and beastlinesses that were, however, considered at all events more humane than the customary flogging of lunatics into submission. The Queen, when told, was horrified; but Willis was unrepentent: 'When my gracious sovereign became violent,' he said later, 'I felt it my duty to subject him to the same system of restraint as I should have adopted with one of his gardeners at Kew.'

By the end of January so much progress had been made that the strait-waistcoat was replaced by a 'restraining chair'—'my coronation chair', the King used jocularly to call it when it was not in use. He was now allowed to see the Queen and the Princesses, and his walks in Richmond or Kew Gardens with Willis, his son (also a doctor) and two or three attendants became longer each day. But even when tolerably sane he could often be intolerably difficult: one day, being refused permission to ascend the Pagoda, he threw himself on the ground and had to be carried struggling back to the White House—a distance little short of a mile.

All the members of the royal household had the strictest orders to keep out of sight of the King; anyone, therefore, who felt like a walk inquired first which way his Majesty would be going. On that Monday morning in February, Fanny Burney, having been told that she would be safe in Kew Gardens since the King would be in the Richmond Gardens, set out in the direction of the Pagoda. She had nearly reached it when suddenly she saw several figures whom she took at first to be gardeners; then, to her dismay, she saw that one of them was the King:

Alarmed past all possible expression, I waited not to know more, but turning back, ran with all my might. But what was my terror to hear myself pursued!—to hear the voice of the King himself loudly and hoarsely calling after me, 'Miss Burney! Miss Burney!'

I protest I was ready to die. I knew not in what state he might be at the time; I only knew the orders to keep out of his way were universal; that the Queen would highly disapprove any unauthorised meeting, and that the very action of my running away might deeply, in his present irritable state, offend him. Nevertheless, on I ran, too terrified to stop. . . .

The steps still pursued, me, and still the poor hoarse voice rang in my ears:—more and more footsteps resounded frightfully behind me,—the attendants all running, to catch their eager master, and the voices of the two Doctor Willises loudly exhorting him not to heat himself so unmercifully.

Heavens, how I ran! I do not think I should have felt the hot lava from Vesuvius—at least not the hot cinders—had I so run during its eruption. My feet were not sensible that they even touched the ground.

Other voices than the King's were now calling her to stop. But not knowing to what danger she might be exposed 'should the malady be then high' she only increased her speed, which by now must almost have exceeded that of light; for even in her diaries Miss Burney, the author of *Evelina*, remained the novelist at heart. Then she heard one of the attendants crying, 'Dr Willis begs you to stop!'

' "I cannot! I cannot!" I answered, still flying on, when he called out "You must, ma'am; it hurts the King to run." '

So stop she did, and approached the King who, since he was now being held firmly by the two Willises while the three attendants were also 'hovering about', cannot have presented any great threat to her safety.

'Why did you run away?' asked the King, seizing her in his arms ('involuntarily, I concluded he meant to crush me') and kissing her on the cheek.

The King now ordered the Willises to leave him alone with Miss Burney, and this they thought it safe to do.

'What did he not say! He opened his whole heart to me. . . .' She describes in detail most of the conversation that ensued, which touched upon every conceivable subject; but what was spoken of his illness she preferred to leave unrecorded. Of Madame Schwellenberg, Queen Charlotte's domineering Keeper of the Robes and Miss Burney's 'coadjutrix' and *bête noire*, he said, 'Never mind her! . . . I am your friend! don't let her cast you down!—I know you have a hard time of it—but don't mind her!' At length the conversation turned to music and, inevitably, to Fanny's father, the celebrated musicologist, and to Handel, the King's favourite composer. It was only when the King began to sing, in a voice 'so dreadfully hoarse that it sounded terrible', excerpts from Handel's oratorios that the Willises attempted to break up their *tête-à-tête*.

At first the King flatly refused to be separated from his friend: 'No, no!' he cried, 'I want to ask her a few questions;—I have lived so long out of the world, I know nothing!' But eventually, and with a further assurance that he was her friend and that she was to take no notice of Madame Schwellenberg's hostility, he embraced her again and continued on his way. This chance encounter, doubtless over-dramatised by Fanny, seems to have marked the turning-point in the King's illness.

Fanny Burney had the highest opinion of Dr Willis senior—'a man of ten thousand; open, honest, dauntless, light-hearted, innocent, and high-minded'—and of his 'extremely handsome' son. The King thought otherwise, and he was soon sufficiently recovered to pull the Reverend

Doctor's clerical leg. Why, he asked Willis, did he abandon his religious duties to practise medicine?

'Our Saviour Himself,' replied Willis unctuously, 'went about healing the sick.'

'Yes,' agreed the King, 'but *He* had not £700 for it.'

On 12 February, while walking in the Exotic Garden, the King overheard his gardener, William Aiton, 'promise to make up a Basket of Exotic Plants for the Doctor [Willis] some of these days; & on hearing this, he added, "Get another Basket, Eaton [sic], at the same time, & pack up the Doctor in it, and send him off at the same time".'

Whether Willis's treatment had effected the cures or whether the attack had run its course, it is hard to say; but there could be no doubt that His Majesty was Himself again. Four days later Fanny was able to note in her Diary 'the joyful news that the King and Queen were just gone out, to walk in Richmond Gardens, arm in arm!' But the Prince of Wales found the news far from joyful, and at the thanksgiving service at St Paul's on St George's Day, he and his brother of York chatted to one another throughout and ate biscuits noisily during the sermon.

Banksian Collectors[1]

THE FIRST of the botanical collectors to be sent out from Kew under the aegis of Sir Joseph Banks was Francis Masson (1741–1805), a young Scot trained there under William Aiton. Captain Cook, sailing in 1772 on his second voyage of discovery, dropped Masson off at the Cape, which was to be the base of his activities for the next three years and again from 1786 to 1795. The journeys he made into the hinterland, two of them in the company of Linnaeus's brilliant but conceited pupil Thunberg, were richly rewarding, adding (Banks told Linnaeus) 'upwards of 500 new species to His Majesty's collection of living plants'. In short, Masson's appointment was 'among the few Royal bounties which have not been in any degree misapplied'. Eighty-eight heaths, fifty pelargoniums (geraniums) and nearly seventy mesembryanthemums were among the novelties introduced by him from South Africa, and his forty stapelias provided the material for his *Stapeliae Novae* (1796–97). The cineraria (*Senecio cruentus*) that he brought back from the Canaries on the way home from his first expedition was to provide the world with one of its most popular house-plants (see p. 119).

Less rewarding was Masson's expedition in 1778 to the West Indies, in the course of which he was taken prisoner by the French on Grenada and subsequently lost all his collections and most of his possessions in a hurricane. His final journey—he had no pension to enable him to retire—was to North America and Canada, where the King was 'graciously pleased' to send him in 1797. He was now fifty-six, his health none too good, and the climate in winter intolerable to a man who had spent nearly half his life in hot countries; it was hardly surprising, therefore, that his collecting suffered. He died in Montreal in the bitter winter of 1806.

David Nelson, a young Kew gardener, sailed in 1776 as assistant to the surgeon-botanist, Dr William Anderson, on Captain Cook's last and tragic voyage. Nelson was 'the first to send home specimens of the acacias [mimosa, or wattle] and eucalypts that are so widespread in Australia and Tasmania',[2] and among the earliest collectors in the Aleutian Islands, whose buttercup (*Ranunculus nelsonii*) honours his name.

[1] For the adventures of most of these collectors see Alice Coats's invaluable *The Quest for Plants*, Studio Vista, 1969.
[2] Anderson, *op. cit.* pp. 144–5. The index to Miss Coats's book mentions one Nelson only: 'Nelson, H.'—who turns out to be a well-known sailor of that name.

Captain Bligh ('Breadfruit Bligh' or 'Bligh of the *Bounty*'), who had been sailing-master in Cook's *Resolution*, took Nelson with him when he sailed in 1787 in the *Bounty* to collect breadfruit trees (*Artocarpus communis*) in Tahiti and carry them to the West Indies. In the spring of 1789 the *Bounty* left Tahiti with a thousand young breadfruit trees, and seven hundred other plants destined for Kew. Then came the famous mutiny. Nelson was among those cast away in an open boat with Bligh, who recorded that he was 'assisted only by Mr Nelson'. The unlucky collector just survived those awful eleven weeks at sea, but only to die a day after reaching Kupang (Timor).

Captain Bligh and his party cast adrift by the mutineers from HMS Bounty, *28 April 1789. Two Breadfruit Trees can be seen on the deck.*
Coloured print by Robert Dodd, c. 1790

On his second, and successful, mission in 1791 Bligh was accompanied by two more Kew gardeners, Christopher Smith and James Wiles. Wiles stayed on in Jamaica, but Smith returned to England with a large consignment of Jamaican plants for Kew.[1] Smith later collected with much success in India and the East Indies. Meanwhile the breadfruit trees flourished exceedingly in Jamaica, but the natives much preferred bananas

[1] Ronald King (*The World of Kew*, p. 14) reproduces two pages from the Kew Records Book listing some of these.

and ignored them; so far as we know, they did not even use the fruit (as Tahitian girls did) for a kind of football.[1]

William Kerr, described by Banks as a 'considerate and well-behaved man', travelled with David Lance, a factor of the East India Company, to Canton in 1803, Kew paying his salary. He was the first resident, professional collector in China, where he remained for eight years though he got no further than Canton and Macao. He also, however, collected extensively in Cochin China and Manila, and though many of his plants were lost at sea, many more survived. Among his introductions (which were tactfully credited to Lance or the E.I.C.) were the tiger lily, the Banksian rose, and the kerria. Kerr was subsequently appointed superintendent of a new Botanic Garden in Ceylon; but in November 1814, little more than fifteen months later, he died. There is some reason to believe that he became an opium addict.

Banks's fame, generosity and influence must have been widely known, for in 1795 a Yorkshire stable-lad named George Caley, a youth with a taste for botany, sent him a moss he believed to be unrecorded, together with a request for help in finding a job in a botanic garden.

Caley was brought south and given employment in the Chelsea Physic Garden. A year later Banks offered him work at Kew, but it is uncertain whether or not he accepted; he did, however, soon afterwards agree to go at Banks's expense to Australia as a collector. His benefactor must have thought very highly of his ability, for the young Yorkshireman, though he had the sterling qualities of a northerner, was obstinate, truculent, and quarrelsome, creating trouble wherever he went; 'Had he been born a gentleman,' Banks was later to say, 'he would long ago have been shot in a duel.'

Caley spent ten years in Australasia, sometimes exploring regions so remote that on one excursion he encountered no living animals beyond two crows, whose presence in that desert seemed explainable only on the supposition that they had lost their way. In 1802 he met Robert Brown, later to become perhaps the greatest of all British botanists, who had arrived in Sydney with Captain Flinders in the *Investigator*, there being also on board the botanical draughtsman Ferdinand Bauer and a Kew gardener named Peter Good. Caley resented what he considered intrusion into his private preserve, and brusquely rejected an invitation, sanctioned by Banks, to join forces with Flinders's party. But Brown was big enough to overlook Caley's shortcomings as a man because of his merits as a plantsman; and Allan Cunningham, Kew's next collector in Australia, was justified in calling him

---

[1] '. . . and she who comes off victorious has the Liberty of exposing her nakedness to the Croud about them & this right they are always sure of asserting' (David Samwell).

'a most accurate, intelligent and diligent botanist'. Caley was his own worst enemy.

In 1811, accompanied by an aboriginal slave whom he called 'Dan', Caley returned to England, and five years later was posted to take charge of the Botanic Garden in St Vincent, in the West Indies. Having remained there long enough to quarrel with everyone on the Island he once more came back to England, where he died in 1829, bequeathing enough money to the faithful Dan to enable him to return to Australia.

Caleana—'a small genus of botanically interesting orchids, remarkable for their irritability'—appropriately honours his memory.

The Napoleonic wars delayed the departure of fresh expeditions, but they were resumed in 1814 when Allan Cunningham and James Bowie were despatched by Banks to Brazil.

Allan Cunningham (1791–1839), soon to become Australia's greatest botanist-explorer, possessed all Caley's good qualities and none of his bad. His connection with Kew began when he and his younger brother Richard went there in 1808 to help the younger Aiton in the preparation of an enlarged edition (1810–13) of his father's *Hortus Kewensis*.[1] In 1816, Bowie, who had been a gardener at Kew, was sent from Brazil to South Africa, and Allan Cunningham to Australia, which was to be his base for the next seventeen years.

Cunningham also visited Tasmania and the remote Norfolk Island (where he was nearly murdered by convicts), and was the first botanist to explore the interior of New Zealand (1826–7). He returned to England in 1831 and bought a 'pretty cottage' at Strand-on-the-Green, near Kew. However, after all those years abroad he could not adjust to suburban life; in 1836 he therefore accepted the post of Colonial Botanist at Sydney in succession to his brother Richard, who had recently been murdered by aborigines. But the job—it consisted largely of growing vegetables for Government House—proved unrewarding. He was also already a sick man, and within eighteen months he had died of consumption.

Soon after the death of Banks in 1820 the annual Government grant for botanical collectors was halved, and in 1823 Bowie was recalled from the Cape. He brought home a fine batch of plants and herbarium specimens, and was for a time employed at Kew in arranging the latter; but according to John Smith he developed 'loose habits, spending his evenings in the public-house telling stories of his encounters with buffaloes, etc.'. He returned in 1827 to the Cape, where he died in poverty twenty-six years later. Since he was about eighty at the time of his death, it would seem that his habits had not been as loose as Smith would have us believe.

* * *

[1] See p. 78.

These men were probably the most important of the collectors sent out by Banks, but Kew also received material from other sources or by exchange. William Roxburgh (1751–1815), for example, a botanist in the service of the East India Company, began in 1789 to send home

> that flood of botanical drawings by native artists (amounting finally to more than 2000) a selection from which was published by Banks as *Plants of the Coast of Coromandel* (1795–1819). From Calcutta Roxburgh sent to Kew great quantities of material—specimens, drawings, seeds and living plants. . . . They were not all Indian species, for Calcutta had long been a repository for plants from China and other parts of the East. . . .[1]

Then there was Archibald Menzies, who accompanied the famous navigator Vancouver as botanist and surgeon on his voyage of discovery in 1791. It is related that while dining with the Viceroy of Chile Menzies was offered for dessert some unfamiliar nuts, several of which he pocketed and planted when he returned to the ship. They germinated well in 'a glazed frame erected on the quarter-deck' which (wrote Vancouver) Menzies had made 'for the purpose of preserving such plants as he might deem worthy of a place amongst his Majesty's collection at Kew'.

Five of the seedlings were duly delivered to Kew, where they proved to be the extraordinary and previously unrecorded 'Chile Pine' or 'Monkey Puzzle'[2] (*Araucaria imbricata*, now *A. araucana*). About 1817, the sturdiest of the young trees was sent to Carlton House to impress the guests at one of the Regent's gala parties; but servants 'very imprudently attached lamps to the branches' and destroyed it. The others, however, flourished, and in spite of the smoke and fog which are inimical to araucarias, one survived at Kew until 1892. In 1833 William IV presented an araucaria to Lady Granville for her collection at Dropmore. By 1880 it had grown to some sixty feet, but it was still 'much inferior' to another raised from a cutting 'stolen by a lady from the original plant at Kew'. Really fine specimens are a magnificent sight; but so often they look mangy and miserable in towns, or are wantonly cut down because they are considered to stick out like a sore thumb in an English garden.[3]

Vancouver was a harsh disciplinarian; but he was apparently kind to Menzies, nor can one blame him for having one of the crew—the odious and truculent young Lord Camelford—flogged thrice, put in the bilboes and finally deposited in Hawaii and left to make his own way home.

*   *   *

[1] Alice Coats, *The Quest for Plants*, p. 149.
[2] The puzzle is that there are no monkeys in Chile.
[3] Sixty years ago a friend of mine regrettably felled a handsome specimen and converted the stump into a sun-dial which he inscribed: ARAUCARIA; HORA CARIOR (Araucaria, but Time is more precious).

Banks wanted Kew to be the finest botanic garden in the world — which was, of course, very proper. He was, however, accused of meanness because of his consequent reluctance to distribute duplicates, cuttings, or seeds of rare plants to other horticulturists. The most savage attack on him on this score came from the pen of a distinguished clerical botanist — the Hon. the Rev. William Herbert, son of the first Earl of Carnarvon, and later Dean of Manchester:

> The illiberal system established at Kew Gardens by Sir Joseph Banks, whereby the rare plants collected there were hoarded with the most niggard jealousy, and kept as much as possible out of the sight of any inquirer, led, in the first instance, to a feeling of satisfaction whenever it was known that the garden had been plundered, and some of its hidden treasures brought into circulation; and the indifference with which such thefts were regarded, if they were not actually winked at, by cultivators, led to such great laxity of conduct that, until the practice was stopped by a prosecution, every private collection became exposed to like depredations; and the falsehoods that were told to cover the theft occasioned a great deal of confusion concerning the native habitation of plants introduced at that period.
>
> It was the narrow-minded doctrine of Sir J. Banks that he could only render the king's collection superior to others by monopolising its contents. By so doing he rendered it hateful and contemptible; whereas, if he had freely given and freely received, and made its contents easily accessible to those who were interested in them, it would have been a pleasure and a pride to the nation. It is now near twenty years since I have visited that odious and useless establishment. Formerly, I went there often, but always in vain; for if I inquired for any rare plants which I had reason to believe were in the collection . . . my conductor always denied any knowledge of them; and if I asked whether I could speak to a person better acquainted with the plants, I was told that I could obtain no further information. The multitude of rare plants that have flourished and perished there unobserved, I believe to be very great. . . .[1]

In fairness to Herbert it must be mentioned that in a 'supplemental observation' at the end of his book he confessed that he had 'incautiously admitted a stronger expression concerning the unpopularity of the principle on which that garden has been conducted, than I should wish to have used'; and he added that he did not, of course, condone theft in any circumstance. But in fairness to Banks it must surely also be asked whether the Dean's somewhat un-Christian attack may not have been in part motivated by spite. Moreover Scheer,[2] writing three years later, states that 'it was, we believe,

[1] *Amaryllidaceae*, 1837.   [2] *op. cit.*, p. 60.

The New Palace from the river, by C. Hullmandel after Richard Westall, 1823

the practice of Sir Joseph Banks to retain rare plants at Kew for one year after they had flowered, and then they were liberally distributed to learned societies and eminent men'.

During the last fifteen years of his life, Banks suffered so severely from gout that at times he completely lost the use of his legs; but his mind remained active and his enthusiasm undimmed almost until the time of his death, at his house in Isleworth, on 19 June 1820. He bequeathed his extensive herbarium, his library and his splendid collection of botanical drawings, together with his London house, to his librarian, Robert Brown, for his life, with a reversion to the British Museum—of whose botanical department Brown was to become the first Keeper.

For Kew, 1820 was the end of an epoch, and difficult days lay ahead.

*   *   *

In 1802 the White House had been demolished, and the following year James Wyatt began to erect, on the banks of the Thames opposite 'the smoky and dusky town of Brentford, one of the most detestable places in the vicinity of London,' the 'very unkingly as well as incommodious' New Palace. So Wraxall,[1] while another contemporary compared it to the Bastille, adding that its walls could never contain more than 'a series of large closets, boudoirs, and rooms like oratories'. In the event it was never to be more than a shell; for in 1804 the King had his third serious attack of insanity, and two years later work on it was discontinued. The King never returned to Kew after this, but the Queen came from time to time to the Dutch House. In 1827, when George IV had this castellated folly with its

[1] Sir Nathaniel Wraxall, *Memoirs*, Vol. V, pp. 378–9.

cast-iron beams demolished, eight workmen[1] lost their lives by the premature collapse of one of its towers. The site of the Castle was beside what is now the Brentford Ferry Car Park.

On 5 November 1817 Princess Charlotte, the 21-year-old daughter of the Regent, died in childbirth, the infant (a boy) being still-born. She had been the heiress-presumptive, next in succession after her father, and her death created a near panic; for of the seven sons of George III who had survived infancy, three were at that time bachelors and the four who were married were either childless or without lawful issue. The bachelor Dukes were therefore rushed into matrimony,[2] the marriages of the Duke of Clarence (afterwards William IV) and the Duke of Kent taking place on 11 July 1818[3] in the Queen's Drawing-room on the first floor of the Dutch House at Kew. For the Duke of Kent this was the second ceremony, the first having been solemnised at Coburg six weeks earlier; and the following year was born the child who was to become Queen Victoria.

The King had been permanently insane since 1810, and the Queen, after so much misery, had long been a very sick woman with now only four more months to live. She had never been pretty—'Yes, I do think that the *bloom* of her ugliness is going off,' her Chamberlain, Colonel Disbrowe, had said rather unkindly of her in middle age; and in 1816 Baron von Stockmar, the future confidant of Queen Victoria, had described her as small and deformed. Olwen Hedley comments that Stockmar was a doctor and 'should have known a dying woman when he saw one'.

The Queen, heroic in long suffering, died peacefully at the Dutch House on 17 November 1818, of '*Hydrothoraxy* or Dropsy of the Chest'. The chair in which she died—for it had been considered best for her to remain upright—may still be seen in the Queen's Bedroom on the first floor.

> At ten o'clock on the morning of Wednesday, 2 December, Queen Charlotte's body was taken from Kew in a hearse drawn by eight horses with black velvet coverings and ostrich plumes.... Mrs Barrett's husband went to see it pass and found himself obliged, by the vastness of the throng on Kew Green, to climb on a wall. His wife learned from him that 'fine ladies pushed into the mud and splashed up to their eyes' to follow the simple procession as it turned towards Kew Bridge....[4]

---

[1] Some accounts say only one.

[2]   Agog are all, both old and young.
              Warm'd with desire to be prolific
          And prompt with resolution strong
              To fight in Hymen's war terrific.
                          (Peter Pindar on the bachelor Dukes.)

[3] J. Pope-Hennessy, *Queen Mary*, p. 28, gives 11 June as the date of this double marriage, the *D.N.B.* 18 July; but both are mistaken.

[4] O. Hedley, *op. cit.*, p. 300.

Night was falling when they reached Frogmore, the Queen's house in Windsor Great Park where she had done much of her botanizing. Here the royal mourners joined the procession, which continued by torchlight to the Castle. To deaden the sound, the inner court had been covered with straw; but in any case the eighty-year-old King, blind and almost deaf, all reason gone, heard nothing, understood nothing of what was happening. It was the Archbishop of Canterbury, he believed, who was keeping him confined. If only they would let him have his favourite cherry tart more often. . . .

After the death of the Queen, the Regent, considering the Dutch House 'unworthy of repair', gave orders for its demolition—orders that, fortunately, were countermanded. But 'Kew Palace'—as it was often called after the absurd castellated Palace had been swept away—was shut down, to remain unoccupied and unused for nearly eighty years. Then in 1897, on the occasion of her Diamond Jubilee, Queen Victoria had the building renovated, and soon afterwards it was opened to the public. The ground and first floor rooms of the Palace have now been sparsely furnished, two of them constituting a museum with miscellaneous 'royal bygones, family playthings, etc.', among them being George IV's fishing tackle; a hand-out directs attention to what is of especial interest. Perhaps the most unexpected portrait is that of Madame de Pompadour; what the devil is she doing in this galley?

Decline and Reprieve

AFTER THE death of Banks in 1820, Kew entered upon the two darkest decades of its history. Indeed it sank so low that at one time what Augusta and Bute had so lovingly created, what Banks had so skilfully nurtured, seemed about the decline into kitchen gardens to provide cabbages for Kings.

George IV had taken a momentary, though quite unbotanical, interest in Kew, and had even thought of building a new palace there. With this in view, he obtained the permission of Parliament to add to the royal estate a tapering piece of Kew Green that extended as far as the Dutch House, together with a further portion of it which his successor restored to the parish.[1] However, in the event his architectural activities locally were limited to the demolition of his father's ludicrous gingerbread castle.

William IV was also alleged to have retained an affection for the scene of much of his childhood; but, like his brother, he really regarded Kew principally as a convenient free source of flowers, fruit and vegetables for his various establishments elsewhere. All that came of it, so far as the Gardens were concerned, was the then unrealised project of a Palm House, the gift of a superfluous greenhouse—one of a trio—from Buckingham Palace, and the erection of yet another neat little temple in the Chambers tradition.

The greenhouse, a 'simple heathen temple', stands just inside the main entrance to the Gardens; it now serves as the Aroid House. King William's Temple, which crowns a mound planted with dwarf rhododendrons between the Temperate House and the Palm House, contained busts of members of the royal family which were later transferred to Windsor, and a series of iron tablets bearing the names and dates of battles fought by British soldiers during the reign of George III. Further, from 1891 until quite recently the two niches under the eastern portico boasted a pair of very interesting sculptures that had long been regarded as no more than commonplace garden ornaments. The story of the peregrinations of these and their eleven equally distinguished companions over two centuries is so curious that it deserves to be summarised here.[2]

* * *

[1] The demarcation line is marked today by the railings that cross the Green near the Herbarium. There was at that time a central road with an entrance gate surmounted by a lion and a unicorn; these may still be seen over the Lion and Unicorn Gates in Kew Road.

[2] See the *Burlington Magazine*, XCVIII, 1956, pp. 77–84, for a full account.

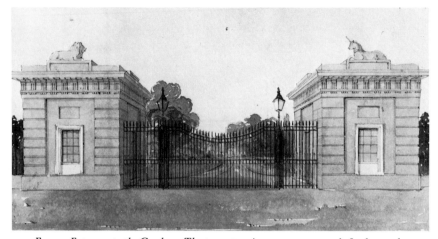

Former Entrance to the Gardens. The present main gates were erected, further to the west, in 1845

In 1752, thirteen remarkable life-sized marble sculptures of gods and goddesses by the sixteenth-century Franco-Italian artist, Pierre de Francheville (Pietro Francavilla), were despatched by sea from Italy to Kew, where they long languished in their unopened cases 'under a shed'. They had been purchased on behalf of Frederick, Prince of Wales, shortly before his death, and presumably his widow or Chambers had either forgotten about them or rejected them.

Some time between 1816 and 1819 the cases were opened, and Diana, Flora, Pomona and Syrinx sent to Hampton Court. From there they were transferred a decade later to the East Terrace Garden at Windsor, but have now just been moved again to Wren's Orangery at Kensington Palace. The fate of the remainder was less fortunate. They, too, passed in due course to Windsor and into the hands of Wyatville, who seems to have intended making use of them in the 'ruins' at Virginia Water or at Royal Lodge, on which he was working at the time. In the event, however, they were abandoned and unceremoniously buried in 'a secluded part' of Windsor Great Park, some of them being destroyed or irreparably damaged in the process.

Possibly a head remained in part visible after this hasty and amateur interment, for in 1852 three of the figures—Venus, Apollo and Zephyr— were exhumed and, after restoration by Thornycroft, presented by Queen Victoria to the Horticultural Society.[1] Apollo and Zephyr were life-sized, but Venus, at 8 feet 7 inches, was very much the odd woman out; the Society

---

[1] The R.H.S. did not become Royal until 1861.

*'Apollo' by Pietro Francavilla
(1548–1618) one of two of his
statues now in the Orangery*

therefore installed the two gentlemen in the Conservatory of its temporary Gardens in Kensington. What it did with the giant goddess will probably never be known, for we next hear of her being dug up 'near Croydon' in 1919 and sold to America. She is now in the Wadsworth Atheneum, Hartford, Connecticut.

Apollo and Zephyr accompanied the Royal Horticultural Society when it moved to Chiswick and were placed in the Vinery, then in 1891 transferred to King William's Temple at Kew. Eventually their importance was recognised. In 1961, after a short sojourn in the Victoria and Albert Museum, they were returned to Kew and displayed in the Orangery after its rehabilitation at the time of the bicentenary. And here, let us hope, they may be allowed to remain.[1]

[1] They were visible in 1976, but on a visit in April 1977 I found them completely boxed in by a fresh crop of those screens mentioned on p. 40!

An ardent archaeologist, could he locate that secluded spot in Windsor Great Park, might, I suppose, recover at least a limb or two of the six missing deities.

*   *   *

The younger Aiton was in his middle fifties when Banks died, and had already worked for nearly forty years in the King's service—first as his father's assistant, then since 1793 as head gardener at Kew. He was also responsible for various other royal gardens, 'in consequence of which, it is said, not one of the whole is planted or kept in order as it might be'.[1] Obviously his task was an impossible one, and it was probably good that William IV, on his accession in 1830, deprived him of the control of all but Kew Gardens; in Ray Desmond's opinion, however, the King's action may have been a spiteful retaliation for an offence Aiton had committed when William IV was Duke of Clarence, rather than the result of any desire for improved efficiency. But the editor of the *Gardener's Magazine*, who was soon to start a full-scale attack on the administration of the Gardens, was delighted: 'The monopoly which Mr W. T. Aiton enjoyed of Kew, Kensington, Buckingham Palace, Hampton Court, Cumberland Lodge, the Royal Lodge, Virginia Water, and we are not sure we have included all, has been very properly broken down.'

Aiton was a botanist of some distinction; if only he had retired gracefully some twenty years earlier, he would have been remembered with greater respect. He produced, though without making any acknowledgment of the considerable help received from Dryander and Robert Brown, a valuable five-volume extended edition of his father's *Hortus Kewensis* (1810–13); he also knew more about the cultivation of the cucumber than any other living man, and was very properly awarded the Horticultural Society's silver medal for a paper on the subject. But probably the best service he ever rendered Kew was his appointment in 1822 of a young Scot, John Smith,[2] to work in the Gardens.

'Old Jock', as this able but intractable man was habitually called in later years, was soon put in charge of the hothouses and propagating department, and it must have been almost entirely due to his skill and devoted attention that many valuable plants received from Brazil, South Africa, New South Wales, India and Trinidad survived in their overcrowded houses. William Hooker was later to write that 'but for the truly parental affection cherished towards [Kew Gardens] by Mr Aiton, and the able exertions of his foreman . . . Mr Smith', their fate would have been worse. His praise of Aiton may have been over-generous.

[1] *Gardener's Magazine*, 1830.
[2] For Smith see Ray Desmond's article in the *Kew Guild Journal* 1965, pp. 576–87, and his own unpublished MS at Kew.

Two particular complaints about Kew were common in the early years of the nineteenth century: that visitors to the Botanic Garden were treated as potential criminals, and that the Crown continued to be mean about the distribution of plants and seeds; in the thirties came the further charge of neglect. John Lindley, writing in 1847, referred to the bad old times under the younger Aiton:

> Look at the state of things in former days. You rang at a bell by the side of a wooden gate, which of itself was perfectly emblematic of the secrecy, the unnatural privacy, of the working principle within. You were let in as if by stealth, as if the gate-keepers were ashamed to see you come, or you yourself were ashamed to be seen there. And when you were there, you were dogged by an official as if you were likely to carry off the St Helena willow-tree[1] in your button-hole, or one of the smaller hot-houses in your waistcoat-pocket. You entered unwelcome, you rambled about suspected, and you were let out with manifest gladness at your departure.

Where meanness was concerned, Aiton was eventually shamed into a token gesture of generosity by the gibes of the *Gardener's Magazine*.

In October 1837 a vicious attack by George Glenny appeared in the *Gardeners' Gazette*, a paper of which he was the founder and editor; it was he who was principally responsible for the action that was eventually taken:

> We have had our eye some time upon the state of the gardens and plants at Kew . . . We begin by roundly asserting that the plan of keeping up these gardens, and refusing the public the benefit of the collections under any circumstances, is both foolish and unnational. The state of the place is slovenly and discreditable, and that of the plants disgracefully dirty . . .
>
> The Kew Gardens are a sort of Government receptacle for everything new, good, or rare; and there is a kind of national pride, which, if the meanness of the Government willed it otherwise, would force upon them the necessity of keeping up, at any fair expense, the value of the collections. But, did the public, or did the founder of the establishment, ever contemplate that Kew Gardens were to be the *last* receptacle for everything?

He re-affirmed Herbert's complaint of the dog-in-the-manger attitude of the authorities except towards foreigners, who, he alleged, received preferential treatment:

> When her excellent Majesty reads the *Gardeners' Gazette*, which we hope is a favourite paper at the Palace, we trust some of our present and future remarks may fall under the royal notice; and we are quite sure that the

---

[1] Raised from a cutting of the tree growing over Napoleon's grave. It may still be seen near the pond in front of the Palm House.

Queen will insist that gardens, kept up at no small expense, shall answer some good purpose. To the slovenly state of the place we advert, only to let our friend Mr Acton [sic] see that we have noticed it. . . . Any man who has been taught the art and mystery of sweeping a crossing could suggest many useful hints, and keep the place in better order. And, as to the state of the plants, it would serve our worthy friend right to make him tuck up his shirt sleeves and wash every inch of plant with a proper brush and soap and water, until the myriads of bugs . . . with which they are infested are banished altogether. A new set of men, or a new master over them, has become indispensible, and we give Mr Acton notice to reform—or quit.

'A Lover of Botany, and of Truth' replied, defending Aiton and alleging that Glenny had written 'Acton' (which was merely a printer's error) to avoid a libel action. Glenny immediately responded with a withering attack on this 'dolt', this 'creature', this 'blundering scribbler', this 'contemptible shuffling thing', this 'trimmer between a knave and a fool'. On 31 October 1837, *The Times* weighed in with a more reasoned assessment. While admitting that lack of money was in part to blame, the writer made no attempt to deny the truth of Glenny's allegations:

There does not appear to have been the slightest progress in improvement for many years; the old conservatories and hot-houses seemed crammed with plants, in a state of decay or stagnation; every thing looks dingy and dirty. . . . A little repair would not hurt one or two of the temples in the pleasure-grounds; and it would also be quite well if the piece of water, once called the lake, but now an unseemly pond, were emptied of its mud and filth, or quite filled up.

Glenny was a conceited and unattractive man,[1] but he did a useful job in ventilating the matter.

Another grievance, one which was voiced with mounting indignation throughout the thirties, was that England, almost alone among the great nations of Europe, had no national botanic garden attached to her capital city. In 1831, 'R.S.' had written in the *Gardener's Magazine*: 'We have heard botanists regret and express their astonishment at the non-existence of a public botanic garden in the neighbourhood of London, in which the most perfect collection that the scientific connections and resources of the empire could furnish should be preserved and cultivated. Such an institution, they represent . . . would, did it exist, give a prodigious impulse to the progress of botany.'

In December 1837, 'C.C.' came forward in the same periodical with a specific and practical plan which foretold, with almost uncanny accuracy, what was in fact to be realised a decade or so later:

[1] See W. Blunt, *Of Flowers and a Village*, Hamish Hamilton, 1963, p. 212.

What we beg to suggest is, that Kew Gardens be ceded to the public, of course under the usual reservation of the crown property, and converted into a regular botanic garden; lecture rooms built; professors appointed; and the series of plants now in the Botanic Garden gradually increased, so as to make it completely adapted to the purposes, of utility and scientific research; for which, the foundation being laid, and houses already built, a comparatively small outlay would be required.

In addition to the smaller plants, it will be indispensible to add an arboretum.[1] As the extent of the grounds at Kew may not be quite sufficient for this purpose, I should propose that 100 or 200 acres be taken from Richmond Park, where they can be perfectly well spared . . . Preparations should also be made for the gradual construction of houses, on a larger scale, for the principal tropical and tender trees of known utility in our dominions. . . . The cost of all this would be comparatively moderate, if properly managed. A twentieth, or even fiftieth, part of the money wasted by one of the follies of George IV at Brighton, Windsor Cottage, or Buckingham House,[2] would suffice to raise a monument worthy of the sovereign and a liberal government. . . .

I now earnestly call on the government, and on the patriotic and independent members now taking their seats in the first parliament of Victoria, not to lose this favourable moment. . . . Sooner or later it must be done; and if properly done, we shall be as far above, as we are now below, other nations in this grand department of human knowledge.

But something was, in fact, just about to be done. Only a month later a committee was set up to inquire into the management of the Gardens and report on what their future should be. It was headed by Dr John Lindley, one of the leading younger botanists of the day, who was joined by two practising gardeners: Joseph Paxton, head gardener to the Duke of Devonshire at Chatsworth, and John Wilson, gardener to the Earl of Surrey, Lord Steward of the Royal Household; Glenny had been invited to participate, but he felt he had already had his say in print. In the bitter February of 1838 the committee inspected Kew.

Anyone who has been slowly dragged round a large garden in mid-winter will readily appreciate how difficult it is, in such circumstances, to make a fair assessment of its true merits. The committee's findings, published a month later, were far from flattering. It was accepted that, considering the crowded state of the houses and the inadequate funds available, the gardeners deserved credit for 'the mere cultivation of this place'. But

---

[1] Augusta's Arboretum was tiny.
[2] For a time, the building, in Queen Charlotte's day called the Queen's House, was indifferently referred to as 'Buckingham House' or 'Buckingham Palace'.

it is impossible to speak of the general management in similar terms . . . No communication is maintained with the Colonies. It is admitted that there is no classification observed in the Garden. What names are to be found have been furnished by Mr Smith, the foreman, and the Director[1] does not hold himself answerable for them . . . This most important duty is thrust upon a foreman, paid small weekly wages for cultivating plants, who, whatever his zeal and assiduity may be (and in this case they have been such as to deserve the greatest praise), has no sufficient means of executing such an office.

Smith, though he himself had come through with flying colours, felt that some of this criticism was unfair, and in particular the charge that Kew had not kept in touch with the Colonies. Furthermore:

The examination of the Garden took place in the month of February, 1838, just after one of the severest winters on record, and heaps of melted snow still lying on the ground, and all evergreen shrubs presenting a sorrowful aspect, and, as the time occupied in examining the Garden, hothouses, collections, and books was only a few hours . . . it could not otherwise be expected [than] that some inaccuracies were the result, and unfavourable impressions formed. For instance, as regards the herbaceous ground, if it had been examined in summer, and time taken, it would have been found to consist of about 2,500 species of perennial plants, arranged according to the Linnaean system . . . each genus having its name printed on a large iron label. Besides the grass collection being named as stated in the Report, it would also have been found that the large collection of succulents and other conspicuous plants had their names printed on iron labels.[2]

The committee's conclusion was that if the control of the Garden were relinquished by the Lord Steward's Department, then 'it should either be at once taken for public purposes, gradually made worthy of the country, and converted into a powerful means of promoting national science, or it should be abandoned. It is little better than a waste of money to maintain it in its present state, if it fulfills no intelligible purpose, except that of sheltering a large quantity of rare and valuable plants.'[3] In other words—either spend a lot more money on it, or scrap it altogether.

The Queen was in no doubt: she wanted to be rid of the incubus. In her diaries (28 February and 12 April 1839) she refers to discussions on the subject with Lord Melbourne:

[1] W. T. Aiton was 'Gardener to His Majesty'. Sir William Hooker was to become the first *Director* of Kew.
[2] Smith, J., MS at Kew quoted by Ray Desmond, *Kew Guild Journal*, 1965, p. 579.
[3] For the Report, see the *Gardener's Magazine, 16* (1840).

Talked of . . . the Botanical Garden which Lord Duncannon[1] purposes to take off the Lord Steward's department and to have a grant for. Lord M. was for giving it quite up, which I am for, but the Duke of Bedford and others say, that wouldn't do.

Talked of that Botanical Garden at Kew being a great expence, and my not caring for it; and Lord M. said the only thing was, that if the Public gave a grant for it, it became in fact, public property; but that he would speak to Rice[2] about it.

The Lord Steward informed the Treasury that he was only too willing to hand this tiresome baby over to the Commissioners of Woods and Forests; but money was very tight at that moment—there had been a succession of deficits in the budget—and Spring-Rice, notorious in any case for dilatoriness, did nothing. When, in September 1839, he was created Baron Monteagle and virtually disappeared from public life, the *Gardener's Magazine* openly rejoiced:

We very much fear that this most discreditable apathy and pro-crastination must be charged on my Lord Monteagle, who had it in his power to leave a noble monument of his administration. . . . but, preferring the honours of the stock exchange to the promotion of science, chose to vanish amid a shower of exchequer bills, leaving the amateurs of natural history anything but cause to lament his exit.

But worse was to follow. In February 1840 it was learned that Mr R. Gordon, Secretary to the Treasury, had offered large consignments of plants from Kew to the Horticultural Society of London and the Royal Botanical Society in Regent's Park, both of which bodies honourably, instantly, and indignantly refused them.[3] On 18 February the kitchen gardener told Smith that he had been ordered by Lord Surrey to empty the Botany Bay House, destroy the rare Australian plants it contained and convert it into a vinery. The news created great public anger, and a fortnight later Lord Aberdeen raised the matter in the House of Lords; he was assured by Lord Duncannon that the Government did not have, and had never had, the slightest intention of destroying Kew! A scapegoat had to be found to cover up this lie, and inevitably it was Gordon who was accused of acting 'on his own responsibility, without consulting the Government'. The scientific world was not deceived.

What probably really saved Kew was a sudden change of heart by the Queen. On 9 March 1840 Aylmer Bourke Lambert, who had to some extent

[1] Chief Commissioner of Woods and Forests, and also Lord Privy Seal.
[2] Thomas Spring-Rice, Chancellor of the Exchequer.
[3] See the introduction to Frederick Scheer; *Kew and its gardens*, 1840.

succeeded Banks as unofficial Director of the Gardens, wrote to John Smith:

> You will not be a little surprised, and I think not less grateful, when I tell you your letter that you wrote me giving particulars of the origin of Kew Gardens, and the interest taken by the Princess of Saxe Gotha, that said letter went to the throne, and [was] read by Her Majesty and Prince Albert; they were much interested in it. There is no doubt that was the reason Lord Ilchester came to Kew, as he is one of Her Majesty's household.

In May, more than two years after the committee's Report had been drawn up and published, it was finally laid before Parliament. The outcome was that the little Botanic Garden and Arboretum, the Pleasure Grounds and the Old Deer Park—some six hundred and fifty acres in all—were transferred, as the committee had originally proposed, from the Lord Steward's Department to the Commissioners of Woods and Forests.

In a very odd little book, *Adam and Evelyn at Kew* by Robert Herring,[1] there is the synopsis of an imaginary film about the history of Kew Gardens. This critical moment, when the future of Kew hung in the balance, was to be treated as follows:

> There's all kinds of other stuff to be done—Queen Victoria deciding to keep Albert's memory green by turning Kew into a kitchen-garden; and crowds besieging the Palace with outstretched arms, just like a Russian film, with banners saying, 'Keep Kew Clean', 'Save our Sanctuary', and 'Roses, not Rhubarb'. That is so that the film will sell in India.

Nonsense, of course. But if the subject were treated wittily, might not a very entertaining series of television programmes be made of the history of the Gardens?

[1] Illustrated by Edward Bawden, Elkin Matthews, 1930.

William Hooker

So KEW had been saved: but who was to be given charge of it?

No one had watched the progress of the battle of Kew Gardens with greater concern, or learnt of its outcome in the spring of 1840 with more excitement, than had Sir William Jackson Hooker, for the past twenty years Regius Professor of Botany at Glasgow.

Hooker, born in Norwich in 1785, was the son of a merchant who had established there 'a bombazine business in connection with the East India Company's trade'. At the age of ten, the boy inherited the reversion of the considerable estate in Kent of his godfather, a rich brewer named William Jackson. But botany, rather than brewing, called him, and it was his discovery in 1805 of *Buxbaumia aphylla*, a moss never before recorded in England, that first brought him to the notice of Dawson Turner,[1] Sir Joseph Banks, and other leading botanists of the day. *B. aphylla*, it must be confessed, is to the layman a plant of considerable dullness: an inch-high thread with a blob on the end, looking like an outsize crotchet; yet young Hooker, who was also a talented draughtsman, would certainly rather have found this humble vegetable than a dozen splendid drawings by Rembrandt in a local junk shop. And certainly his 'remarkable little moss', as he called it, was to stand him in good stead, for within a year it had led to his becoming a Fellow of the Linnean Society.

During the fifteen years that followed, Hooker had worked ceaselessly. He had botanized in Scotland and on the Continent. He had visited Iceland, but only to lose his entire collection (and almost his life) by fire on the homeward voyage. He had married Dawson Turner's daughter, fathered his first four children and more than his first four books. He had briefly, but unhappily, become partner in a brewery. But by ill-advised investment he had also lost much of the money he had inherited; in 1820, therefore, he was glad enough to accept the offer, made on Banks's recommendation, of the Regius Professorship at Glasgow which, though poorly paid, did at least enable him to keep half a dozen hungry mouths tolerably fed.

In a way Hooker could have counted himself lucky to have been offered the job, for he had no paper qualifications whatever: 'he had never taught, lectured, or even heard a course of lectures'. But the wisdom of the

[1] Dawson Turner (1775–1858)—banker, botanist and antiquary.

Sir William Hooker. Oil painting by S. Gambardella, c. 1843. Linnean Society of London

appointment—from Glasgow's point of view, at all events—was soon to become apparent, for he revolutionised the teaching of botany in the University. His success as a lecturer was phenomenal. People spoke of his 'tall figure, commanding presence, flexible features, good voice, eloquent delivery and urbane manners'. He thought nothing of working eighteen hours or walking sixty miles a day, and his periodic botanical forays in the Western Highlands, which lasted for the best part of a week, left his students as delighted and as instructed as they were footsore and weary.

His salary rose as his merits became recognised, and in 1836 he was made a Knight of Hanover. But though many distinguished botanists of the day were Scottish, they mostly headed for England at the first opportunity. So Hooker, finding himself increasingly cut off, and suffering also from jealousies aroused by the success of a mere Sassenach, developed before long 'a perfect longing to return to the south'. He followed attentively the constant rumours throughout the thirties of Aiton's imminent retirement from Kew, and campaigned energetically to assure himself of the support of influential backers when the time came.

There were several potential contenders for the post. In the opinion of 'J.W.' writing in the *Gardener's Magazine*, 'If Mr Aiton should resign, and any other person be appointed to fill his place except Mr Smith, an act of injustice, and still more of impolicy, will be performed, which it is revolting to the mind to think of'; but Smith, a working gardener though admittedly a very able one, was never really in the running. Nor, any longer, was Robert Brown—probably the most brilliant botanist of his day, but now too old—who some years earlier had told Hooker he 'expected to have the appointment'. The obvious candidates were Hooker and John Lindley, Hooker's junior by thirteen years.

Hooker, though obliged to carry on most of his campaign from distant Glasgow, had succeeded in winning powerful allies. In particular, he had hitched his waggon to a couple of very influential Dukes. 'The Duke of Argyll,' he informed a friend in April 1838, 'promised me this situation 5 years ago when there sh^d be a vacancy'. But above all, he gained the support of John Russell, sixth Duke of Bedford—an enthusiastic naturalist. Though over seventy, the Duke was tireless in his efforts to see Kew made worthy of the nation, and to frustrate the establishment of the cheap little alternative of a national botanic garden in Regent's Park; his death on 20 October 1839 was a serious setback to the cause he had espoused.

The Duke believed Hooker and Lindley equally qualified to become Director of Kew Gardens, and even at one time suggested a duumvirate. But Hooker cunningly persuaded his rival that the post would not suit him. 'My dear Friend,' he wrote to Lindley on 3 March 1838:

> I must still beg that if you see a prospect of some appointment at Kew suited to your views, you will not overlook it;—for assuredly you ought to act as if you did not know I was a Candidate for anything of this kind. I can however see that a more moderate income at that place would satisfy *my* wishes [better] than *yours*,[1] in the first place, because though I have nothing to complain of here, yet I have reason to believe that my income is much less than yours, & because I am willing to make some sacrifice to be enabled to return & spend the rest of my days among my friends & connections in England . . .,

Bedford, when assured that Lindley (though urged by the Duke of Devonshire to stand) did not wish to be considered, adopted Hooker as his candidate.

In March 1841 Hooker heard that the Botanic Garden at Kew was to be his, the Pleasure Grounds and Vegetable Gardens remaining for the time being in the charge of the 75-year-old Aiton. His salary was fixed at £300 a year, with an allowance of £200 for the rent of a house. The one he found—'plain, but perfectly gentlemanly, ample for all of us (54 windows)'—was called Brick-farm, soon to be renamed West Park, only ten minutes' walk (for so sturdy a walker) from the Gardens.

Packing up was a mammoth operation, the books and herbarium alone—

---

[1] Lindley was trying to pay off his father's debts.

the latter the largest in Europe—requiring '60 great packages' and the whole being transported in five different ships to London, from where it was taken by lighters almost to his door. It was May, 'the Laburnam [sic] so full of blossom' in his garden that he fell in love with his new home at sight. He was fifty-six; but to his father-in-law, Dawson Turner, he wrote, 'I feel as if I were going to begin life over again'.

He was. His greatest achievement still lay in the future.

12

Kew Redivivus

THE GROUNDS of West Park, so Mea Allan informs us, have now been swallowed up by the Kew and Richmond Sewage Works; I take her word for it. But the house itself, though much modified and in part incorporated in the factory buildings of Bush Television, still stands. It was as large as its fifty-four windows suggest, for it proved possible to set aside no less than thirteen rooms for Sir William's library and unique herbarium. He described it all in a letter to his son Joseph, then on a four-year voyage in the southern seas.

Hardly had he moved in when he began to consider what most urgently needed doing at Kew. 'Having no instructions for my guidance,' he wrote, 'I determined to follow the suggestions of Dr Lindley's report.' There was great need for more and better glasshouses, and as further acres fell under his control there came also the question of the lay-out of the grounds. He immediately opened the Botanic Garden and Houses every weekday afternoon, allowing the public to wander freely in them, unharassed by over-vigilant officials. In 1841 there were 9,174 visitors; when he died, in harness, in 1865, by which time the pleasure-gardens were also open daily, the number exceeded half a million annually. Within two years of his taking office, the editor of the *Gardener's Magazine* saw fit to write:

> Kew Gardens, since they have been under the direction of Sir William Hooker, have undergone very great improvements, which fully justify the government in having employed that enthusiastic and active-minded accomplished man. The wall which separated the botanic garden from the pleasure-ground has been thrown down,[1] so as to admit views to glades among the trees and shrubs; some new houses have been built, and others have been altered and greatly improved. . . . We were much gratified to observe a very complete collection of British plants arranged according to the natural system, and correctly named; but we cannot altogether approve of an avenue of standard roses carried through the middle of the botanic garden. . . .
>
> We were also glad to see the heaps of rubbish commonly designated rockwork done away with, conceiving them, unless constructed in a very

---

[1] But replaced by a fence. It was a long-standing grievance of Kew gardeners that they had to make many unnecessary detours.

The Palm House, looking unfamiliarly leaden as seen from the air. A certain amount of formal bedding may be appropriate here, but there is still too much of it in the Gardens as a whole. The Pond is seen at the bottom right-hand corner of the photograph

different manner from what they have ever been at Kew, as totally unsuitable for botanic gardens. . . . The next thing that we should like to see done at Kew would be an extension of the arboretum, or rather the planting of a new one, to extend along the whole of the circumferential plantation of the pleasure-ground. . . .

This was in fact begun in 1848, and by 1850 it could boast 2,325 reputed species of trees and shrubs and 1,156 hybrids which Sir William believed to constitute 'perhaps the most complete collection in any single arboretum' in the world.

The great Palm House, erected between 1844 and 1848, and the later Temperate House shall have a chapter to themselves. In 1845, Decimus Burton, designer of the latter and part designer of the former, was also responsible for the impressive main entrance, whose wrought-iron gates led directly to the new Broad Walk. William Andrews Nesfield (1793–1881), an artist turned garden-architect, had been called in by Sir William to plan the

Victorian carpet bedding, *Royal Botanic Gardens, Kew*

lay-out of the Gardens. He made the Palm House the focal point of two wide grassed avenues, Pagoda Vista and Syon Vista, while his Broad Walk changed direction sharply near the Orangery to lead to a formal pond opposite the Palm House, created out of what remained of the shapeless stretch of water known as George III's Lake; the present lake in the southern part of the Gardens was Sir William's own idea, formed in the late eighteen-fifties from marsh and from old gravel pits which provided the foundations for the Temperate House. Nesfield's plans had to be modified when the latter was erected.

The immediate surroundings of the Palm House called for some kind of formal treatment, but here Nesfield proved himself less successful. As Bean says, 'His numerous intricate "geometric" flower-beds, with the box-edging and gravel paths, were in keeping with the puerile fashion of the day, but they have long since given way to an ample though still formal arrangement.' Sir William disliked formal bedding[1] because it was both botanically boring and wasteful of gardeners' time that could have been better employed, but he had orders from on high to provide it; artists

[1] And so did his son—see footnote p. 166.

Kew Gardens in the time of Sir William Hooker. Photograph taken in 1864

deplore it on aesthetic grounds. Today there is still far too much of it, and in particular the horrendous display in recent summers of grinning, screaming bedding-out plants (tagetes, erigeron, salvia, etc.) near the Dutch House ought never to be seen, or heard, again.

But in general there was unstinted praise for what Sir William and his fellow-workers had achieved. In 1847, Lindley, after writing that acid paragraph about Kew in Aiton's day that we quoted earlier,[1] continued:

How gratifying is the contrast now! You go in by one of the most beautiful entrances that have been erected in modern times. . . . There is no unlocking of a dark door—you walk in freely. Turn to the left, you wander amid the more secluded scenery of the old gardens until you reach the hothouses and the adjacent beds. Or walk straight forward along the bold, broad promenade immediately after you enter—visit the conservatory on your right, and at the end of this promenade turn to the left and ramble along the far finer promenade, adorned on either side by flower beds, lawns, and shrubberies, and terminated by the new conservatory [the Palm House], now in course of erection; its terrace and sheet of water; all bounded by the views in the pleasure grounds beyond. It is scarcely conceivable that in so short a time the change from the old close, crabbed, cramped, suspicious, dark system could have been so complete. . . .

[1] See p. 79.

This was generous of Lindley, who had himself once rather wanted the directorship of Kew.

But twenty years later there was some sharp criticism from young William Robinson, soon to become the champion of the 'wild' garden:

> Kew . . . in some respects superior to any botanic garden or botanical establishment in the world, is in point of design no higher than a chess-board. That breadth—i.e., an open spread of lawn here and there—is the most essential principle in garden-design one would think known to anybody arranging or planting a public garden or park. Without this we cannot get anything but a confused effect—we cannot see the beauty and dignity of our now rich arboreal flora; without this we may have a thousand kinds of noble trees, and get little better effect than in an unthinned plantation. It is, in fact, as impossible to make a really beautiful garden or park without open turfy lawns as it is to make a lake without water. At Kew, both in general design and in the arrangement of details, this principle is completely ignored, and the good old one adopted of putting in a tree wherever there is room for it. The result is that the largest botanic garden in the world is devoid of any picturesque beauty.[1]

This seems to me unfair. The broad vistas were there; the hinterland was, very sensibly, used to grow as many different species as possible, planted as close together as their ultimate growth allowed.

During his years in Glasgow Sir William had accumulated a large collection of 'raw and manufactured objects of vegetable origin' for use in his lectures on economic botany. One day in 1846, his son tells us, he set these out on a long trestle table in the old apple store and invited the Commissioners of Woods and Forests to see them. His 'eloquent discourse' gained him permission to convert the store into Kew's first museum and the first museum of economic botany in the world. News soon spread that here was the perfect repository for miscellaneous vegetable bric-à-brac which had served its immediate purpose elsewhere, and after the closure of the Great Exhibition of 1851 the apple store was bursting at the seams. As will be described in a later chapter, this led to the building in 1857 of Museum I, opposite the Palm House.

In 1852 Hooker moved into Methold House, a relatively small house on the south side of Kew Green which remains to this day the Director's official residence. It was naturally more convenient—he could pass through is own little garden directly into the Gardens; but he missed the spaciousness of the grounds of West Park, and there was of course no possibility of his now

---

[1] *The Parks and Gardens of Paris*, 1869, p. 72, quoted by G. F. Chadwick, *The Park and the Town*, 1966, p. 148.

having room for his library and herbarium. Fortunately arrangements were able to be made for them to be kept in Hanover House.[1]

Hooker's powers of work were prodigious, and it is impossible here to do more than hint at the magnitude and variety of his achievements in addition to his reformation of the Gardens and Houses and the constant and arduous labours of administration. He edited and contributed to various scientific periodicals such as the *Botanical Magazine*, and his own *Icones Plantarum* and *Journal of Botany*. He planned and initiated innumerable floras of countries over which Britain then ruled, and 'produced either as author or editor about one hundred volumes devoted to systematic and economic botany', not a few of which were illustrated by himself; his *magnum opus* was his five-volume *Species Filicum*, a standard work on ferns which occupied him on and off for eighteen years. He sent Kew gardeners to establish or revitalise botanic gardens all over the world, arranged for the receipt and despatch of thousands of plants, and corresponded regularly with every notable botanist of his day.

Indeed, the two Hookers: William, and his son Joseph—for ten years his assistant and subsequently his successor—were giants of the kind that the Victorian age alone seemed able to mass-produce in this country. They came to Kew in the right order: first William, the able administrator; then Joseph, the more distinguished man of science. But it must never be forgotten that William rose, as it were, from the ranks, while Joseph was born into the botanical purple. They seem to have been devoted to one another, and Joseph's tribute to his father, published in the *Kew Report* at the time of his death in 1865, is more than the polite eulogy expected in those days of a dutiful son.[2] 'This is not the place,' he begins, 'nor would it be fitting in me to dwell on the merits of my father . . .'—and then proceeds to do precisely that:

> Whether as the restorer of these gardens, who by his sagacity and energy raised them above all others in excellence, beauty and utility—or as the originator and founder of museums of economic botany—or as the projector and able assistant of those efforts on the part of our Home and Colonial Governments that have led to the formation of botanical and horticultural establishments in so many of our colonies, in India and in our foreign possessions,—or as the liberal and distinterested patron of private scientific enterprise everywhere, and especially among the officers of the army, navy and civil services, the late Director of Kew has won the esteem and gratitude of his countrymen, and left a name that will ever

[1] See chapter 15.
[2] Joseph (says Mea Allan) 'deplored the fact that *The Times* did not even notice his father's death, though it gave half a column to that of a pugilist who died at the same time'.

occupy one of the most prominent positions in the history of botanical science.

Sir William was something of a courtier, and Joseph often regretted the many valuable hours his father wasted dressing up and showing round the Gardens royalty and other distinguished visitors from whom the institution would receive no benefit. Indeed, his last visit there, only the day before the onset of his brief final illness, was an exhausting perambulation of it in the company of the indefatigable Queen Emma of the Sandwich Islands.

Certainly, the father was a very much nicer person than the son. 'Sir Joseph,' wrote Ray Desmond, 'was a proud man, autocratic and somewhat intolerant. He did not have his father's charm and amiability': what Darwin called his 'remarkably cordial, courteous, and frank bearing'.

13

Palm and Temperate

THERE ARE two buildings at Kew that no visitor is likely to forget: the Pagoda, and the Palm House.

All agree that the Palm House (or 'Great Stove') is magnificent; and as all who describe it unfailingly observe, it appears, when seen from the far side of the Pond, like a stupendous swan poised on the surface of the water. But include its reflection and it becomes a dirigible. Completed in 1848 it was in its day, and long remained, the largest Palm House in the world, though soon to shrink into a mere cygnet by comparison with Paxton's Crystal Palace.[1] See it when the late afternoon sun streams through its panes, silhouetting the palm-tops; see it (from that Athenian bus-stop shelter[2]) in driving rain: it is always surprisingly and freshly beautiful.

There had been talk, ever since Bute's time, of building a Palm House, and in 1834 plans for one had actually been drawn up by Wyatville; but those were doldrum days at Kew, and nothing was done. Ten years later, however, Hooker resurrected them and submitted them to the Commissioners, who sought the advice of Decimus Burton. Meanwhile Wyatville had died, and it was hardly surprising that Burton preferred to produce something of his own, which was duly approved by the Commissioners.

Hooker had received orders that the new Palm House was to be erected where it could not be seen from Kew Palace; but when the Queen visited the Gardens in October 1843 and was shown a preliminary model of the proposed building, she delighted Hooker by expressing the hope that 'so handsome a structure' would be placed in a conspicuous position. There were, however, also technical problems to be considered; and John Smith, who had recently been appointed Curator, has an interesting account[3] of the visit made by Burton to the Gardens to choose a site:

> On his coming to Kew, he had not been more than half an hour in the Grounds when he fixed upon the site where it now stands. Being present,

---

[1] The vital statistics of the Palm House (approximate, for even Turrill gives different figures on different pages of his book) are: length, 362 feet; maximum height 66 feet, transept 100 feet wide. The Crystal Palace was 1608 feet long.

[2] See p. 43.

[3] MS at Kew quoted by Ray Desmond, *Kew Guild Journal*, 1969, p. 581ff.

The Palm House

I thought it my duty to say it would never do here, for where we now stand is a bog the greater part of the year, and water was always to be found within a few feet of the surface. He said, 'Oh, we will make that all right'. . . . My objection to this site was that it . . . consisted originally of lagoons and swamps connected with the Thames. George III took advantage of these lagoons and converted them into a lake which, after the King's illness and removal to Windsor, was neglected, and in 1812 filled up, the only part left being now ornamental water lying between the Palm House and Museum. . . .

On 4th April 1844 Mr Burton sent his assistant to mark the exact site, as regards length and width of the house; this being my last opportunity, I strongly protested against its position. . . .

Smith was, of course, worried about the possible flooding of the furnaces which were to be placed under the Palm House, and his worst fears were to be realised; but Hooker told him sharply to mind his own business. However, soon after this the Director made amends by taking Smith with him to Burton's London office to examine the designs in detail:

The plan consisted of a curvilinear structure similar to the Duke of Devonshire's house at Chatsworth, the profile having an imposing appearance, with which Sir W. Hooker was much pleased. I, however, was more concerned about the interior, and, on examination, I found that there were so many pillars and they were so close together that there would not be room for the full expansion of the leaves of the large palms. On my calling attention to this, Sir W. Hooker was of the same opinion, and on calling Mr Burton's attention to it he said he would try another way. With this our interview ended.

About this time Mr Richard Turner of the Hammersmith Iron Works, Dublin, having heard of the intended erection of a large hothouse at Kew, came over to see about it, and having obtained an introduction to the Commissioners of Works they requested him to furnish a plan and estimate for an iron structure in conjunction with Mr Burton, which he obligingly did. On his informing me of this, I said, 'I hope you will not have so many pillars in the centre as in Mr Burton's plan.' 'Oh, no,' he said, and took a piece of paper, and drew a pen and ink profile of the Palm House as it was to be erected, being quite different from Mr Burton's plan, having no pillars in the centre.

Hooker approved Turner's proposals; but the Board of Works rejected them and, in Turner's words, 'a most absurd set of plans was produced by Burton with the help of an engineer'. However, Turner persuaded the Duke of Newcastle to intervene. The Board of Works changed its mind; Burton's revised plans were rejected, and Turner was back again in the picture.

So who, in fact, must take the principal credit for the Palm House? It was certainly not Burton alone, as we had long been led to believe. According to Joseph Hooker, it was 'from the designs of Decimus Burton, F.R.S., and the Director'; he does not even mention Turner. Mea Allan says that William Hooker and Burton visited Syon and Chatsworth together, and no doubt they learned from what they saw there. John Smith too, who knew at least as much as (in his own opinion, far more than) Hooker about what hothouse plants needed, perhaps also played a part.

But if we are to attribute the design of the Palm House at Kew to any one man, then it should probably be to Turner, its parentage being Paxton's Conservatory at Chatsworth and the 'iron train halls' of London's first railway stations. We know that Turner made at his own risk and expense a full-sized portion of the structure, which was duly tested and approved. Further, Smith himself stated[1] that 'Mr Turner was the sole designer', and Turner agreed that 'the palm-house was not only erected by him, but was solely his design, although carried out under the supervision of Mr Decimus Burton'. As Ray Desmond points out, 'The Palm House has the functional

[1] *Building News*, 20 March 1880.

simplicity one would expect from an engineer. Decimus Burton's conception of a glasshouse is demonstrated in the heavy and ornate Temperate House' that was his, and his alone.[1]

Now step inside.

A Palm House probably suggests a very lush version of a hotel 'palm court' filled to bursting-point with those great fronded plants, native only of the tiny Lord Howe's Island in the southern Pacific, called 'palms' by the vulgar and formerly Kentias by the botanists. But Kentias no longer, I find, for the genus has now been redistributed into the eight genera *Chambeyronia*, *Gulubia*, *Hedyscepe*, *Howea*, *Hydriastele*, *Kentiopsis*, *Lepidorrhachis* and *Ptychosperma*; the Palm Court palm has become *Howea fosterana*.

But if by 'palms' we mean 'members of the family Palmaceae, or Palmae', then the Palm House at Kew contains a large majority of plants—screwpines, bamboos and cycads, for example—that really ought not to be there, while other Palmae are to be found in the Aroid House; it is just a matter of practical convenience. Nor let thoughts of hotel Palm Courts mislead the visitor into imagining that there is any longer (though there used to be) even the humblest bench in the Palm House, where on cold or wet days he can snatch a moment's rest. Yet it is at all events warm there, and it was for this reason, Burne-Jones tells us, that he often chose it for assignations with one of his girl-friends.

It must frankly be admitted that 'palms'—if I may use the word loosely to cover all the inmates of the Palm House—are, like ferns and mosses, something of an acquired taste for most of us. People while in glass-houses should not, I know, throw stones; but everything here is so very green, and there is little that produces what the non-botanist would call a flower. Yet this crystal palace comes as near to a tropical forest as many of us will ever get, and no one can fail to be impressed by the towering trees that in its centre have room to grow to sixty feet. These were formerly best seen from the gallery, but this is now closed to the public—for fear (I gather) of Irish bombs. A handy little leaflet tells one all about cycads—sole survivors of a group of plants diverse and widespread a hundred and fifty or so million years ago; and in particular it directs our attention to a specimen of a lanky, leaning tree: *Encephalartos longifolius*—'sent from South Africa by Francis Masson in 1775, and probably the oldest glasshouse plant at Kew, being much older than the Palm House itself'.[2] I hope the bicentenary of its arrival was fittingly commemorated. Incidentally, *Cycas revoluta* produces the

---

[1] See also an article by Peter Ferriday in the *Architectural Review*, February 1957.
[2] 'In 1819 it produced a male cone, which, being considered remarkable, led Sir Joseph Banks to come and see it, such being his last visit to the garden' (Smith, *Records*, p. 132).

The Palm House, interior. Illustrated London News, *7 August 1852*

leaves seen in Roman Catholic churches on Palm Sunday. Holman Hunt mentions that he carried off (with the Director's permission, one hopes) a palm leaf to use in his 'Christ and the two Marys', adding that when he got home he found a dead bat in it.

There are also a number of 'economic' (i.e., utilitarian) plants such as coffee, cocoa, coconut, pawpaw and banana—the last-named a great attraction when bearing a gigantic truss of fruit from which hangs a wonderful kind of velvety Victorian bell-pull, always removed before the fruit reaches the greengrocer. And here I am reminded of the sad story of how Thomas Meehan, a young gardener at Kew from 1846 to 1848, irrevocably blotted his copybook with Sir William on an occasion when the Queen visited the Gardens in 1848:

> A very fine bunch of bananas had been cut that morning, and Sir William thought to present it to her. I was working near, in my shirt-sleeves, when he asked me to go as hastily as possible and get the bunch before the Queen left. Without waiting to get my coat, I tore away and came up with the bananas near the entrance gate. It was a very heavy bunch; I held it in one hand and my hat in the other, while Sir William explained to Her Majesty facts in its history. I found it impossible to keep it up with one hand, so put my hat on my head and used both. Subsequently Sir William sent for me, and asked how I dared to appear before Her Majesty without my coat and to wear my hat in her presence. . . . Sir William was right, though I did not think so then.[1]

Poor Meehan was not forgiven for letting the team down, and very possibly he was sent to work in the Cactus House—at that time a regular form of punishment. In any case, soon afterwards Hooker found an excuse to sack him (actually he was 'ordered to resign') when he loyally refused to reveal the names of some of his fellow gardeners who had been taking home leaves of rare plants for their own herbaria. Meehan next got a job at Alton Towers (so he still had a pagoda!), only to lose it because his religion was 'not considered to be of the right kind'. So he went to America where he got on famously, wrote a book on the American flora, corresponded with Darwin, and was finally commemorated by an obscure plant called *Meehania*. He died in Philadelphia in 1901.

It had been considered unsightly for the elegant Palm House to have chimneys. There had therefore been constructed, about a hundred and fifty yards to the south-east of it, a tower more than a hundred feet tall to dispose of the smoke from the furnaces and to provide a reservoir with sufficient pressure to water the tallest palms from above.[2] The pipes leading to the tower were placed in a tunnel with a two-track railway to bring fuel to the Palm House and remove the ashes.

Chambers would no doubt have disguised his tower as a minaret or a Trajan's Column; Burton opted for an Italianate campanile in stock brick

---

[1] *Kew Guild Journal*, 1894, p. 42.
[2] Automatic watering 'simulating rainfall' was introduced in 1960.

with red trimmings, commonplace but not displeasing. The only trouble with this ingenious contrivance was, as Smith must have predicted and as his diary was to confirm, flooding:

> October 1st [1848]. Water rising fast in the furnace rooms.
> November 1st. Two men constantly pumping assisting stokers.
> November 2nd. Water nearly up to fire bars. Stokers working nearly up to their knees in water and the coke to feed the furnaces soaked.
> February 24 [1849]. Constant pumping from last date. Two fire-engines constantly going.
> March 1st. Tunnel full of water. More men required.
> March 2nd. Water in tunnel like a running stream.
> May 3rd. Springs becoming stronger. Water nearly up to furnace bars. Two fire-engines continual [sic] at work day and night.
> May 5th. Water rising faster. Men quite exhausted with pumping. . . .

And so on, throughout the summer; and the following summer also, for we read, 'June 16th 1850. Pumping all night.'

Every possible remedy was tried—but in vain. A well was sunk, but the flooding continued; when the furnaces and boilers were raised, the fires sulked; when the flues were rebuilt to counteract this, the heat in the furnace rooms became almost unbearable; and when convectors were installed, the joints of the coils soon gave way. So, in the end, the Palm House had to have its own little chimneys after all.

Smith, when writing about the Palm House, has some interesting things to say about Sir William, and more particularly about his son Joseph, whose practical knowledge of horticulture Smith despised and whose interference he resented; we must allow for some possible prejudice. Initially, Sir William had favoured conservation; but in 1855, after Joseph's appointment as Assistant Director, 'this policy began to waver, and in time changed to a destructive policy the first act of which was to cut down the climbers which occupied the whole of the staircase pillars and gallery rails, thus leaving the iron work as bare as it was left by the Architects'.

Perhaps the Hookers had a point here, for the spiral staircases are very attractive; but this was only the beginning of his butchery, for

> Sir William and Dr Hooker took it into their heads to destroy many old specimen plants, which since their accommodation in the Palm House, had become the pride of the house, for which no reason was given, and it appeared to me nothing but wanton mischief. . . . The mode of proceeding was, Sir W. Hooker would fix his eye on a plant, ask its history, then say 'Away with it!' And in a moment the foreman's big knife made the bark hang in ribbons. This was the signal for the men to break it

up, and convey it, and the box in which it was grown, to the rubbish yard. Plant after plant followed in the same way with apparently as much indifference as if they had been common laurels . . . and when I said, 'What a pity!' I was only laughed at.

Though Sir William is here described as ordering the massacre, Smith makes it plain that Joseph, who had his doting father completely under his thumb, was really the villain of the piece. There is evidence that Joseph, after he had become Director, could on occasions treat even his Curator, John Smith II,[1] like a naughty schoolboy. In 1869 Kew had acquired a specimen of an exceptionally difficult west African plant, the narras (*Acanthosicyos horrida*)—a kind of melon much favoured by Hottentot women eager to put on that extra weight their menfolk so greatly admired. In a letter of such enormous length that we can only quote a fragment of it here, Joseph gives the Curator a 'dressing down' for his alleged neglect of this awkward customer:

> Of course I here refer to the critical state of the Narras Plant—which was not repotted under your supervision; and I do not know which surprises me most,—that you should be supposed to care so little about it, or that it should be potted without your cognizance, or that any one in a Foreman's or any other place should have the unparalleled vanity and presumption to wish to pot a unique plant, known to be the most difficult in the world of cultivation, *on his own sole judgment and responsibility*. A plant in which every scientific Botanist in Europe is interested, and in the success of which the credit of this whole establishment is at stake. . .

The narras died; but, more surprisingly, Smith II survived.

The Palm House celebrated its centenary safely; but soon afterwards 'certain movement of the main structural girders' and other troubles became apparent, and in November 1952 the building was closed for seven years for extensive repairs. It was at first feared that it would have to be completely rebuilt, and there was talk of taking over and adapting the arches at that moment straddling the Mall for the coronation; but damage proved to be less than anticipated, and by piecemeal restoration the work was carried out with the loss of fewer plants than the Hookers might have axed in the course of a single morning.

The Chatsworth Conservatory and the Crystal Palace—the masterpieces of that genius whom Queen Victoria had once scornfully dismissed as 'a common gardener's boy'—are no more. But the Palm House at Kew still

---

[1] John Smith was succeeded in 1864 by his unrelated namesake. John Smith II always wore frock coat, top hat and kid gloves when on duty.

stands, rebuilt but glorious as ever, and likely to continue to delight us until the first atom bomb falls on London.

*   *   *

Kew now had a splendid hothouse but the important collection of 'tender' (i.e., not quite hardy) trees and shrubs were still battling for survival in houses that were too small and too low; as soon, therefore, as trees began to 'put on weight', or height, they had to be mutilated or destroyed. Then in 1848 one of these houses—in point of size the least inadequate—was condemned as beyond salvation and demolished. It was therefore Sir William's next major task to build a Temperate House worthy of Kew. In 1859, after a year of campaigning, Parliament sanctioned a grant and Decimus Burton was again put to his drawing-board.

People have been unnecessarily rude about Burton's Temperate House. Certainly it is no swan: you could never imagine it taking off into the empyrean. But it is a vast and impressive if earthbound building, covering an area not far short of two acres. The centre block, sometimes known as the Winter Garden, and the two octagons were built between 1860 and 1862 at a cost of about £29,000. And then, I suppose, the money ran out, for it was not until the closing years of the century, and largely through the good offices of Joseph Chamberlain, then Secretary of State for the Colonies, that the building was completed, as originally designed, by attaching the Mexican and Himalayan Houses to the Octagons. An inelegant but useful annexe, intended for non-hardy rhododendrons, dates from 1925.

It is impossible to particularize the contents of the Temperate House because, at the time of writing, it has long been closed for eventual extensive repairs; in January 1977, however, came the welcome announcement that the Department of the Environment had agreed to restorations being carried out at an estimated cost of £1.22 million, and now the work has actually begun. Through grimy windows can be glimpsed some forlorn and lonely giants, mounting guard over a wilderness of rubbish. Its only other living inhabitants are the birds that flutter in through the broken panes and—for all I know—an occasional gardener comforting the remnants that remain . . . Ichabod indeed!

But Kenneth Lemmon,[1] writing in the early 1960s, has nicely described it as housing 'the sub-tropic splendours':

> The tree-ferns from New Zealand and Australia and the new wealth from the Himalayas, China, Chile and Japan, the lapagerias, the lily of the valley tree (*Clethra arborea*), the luxurious camellias, oranges and lemons, tender graceful conifers, and the rhododendrons from the Himalayan

[1] *The Covered Garden*, Museum Press, 1962.

The Temperate House. Illustrated London News, *11 May 1867*

slopes. From the gallery surrounding the central house there was a bird's-eye view over the tops of noble tree-ferns, palms, araucarias, the bunya-bunya, the Norfolk Island pines, the bananas, the wattles and all their associated flora, representing a then strange and almost unknown world.

At the north end of the Palm House is the little Water-lily House in which the giant *Victoria amazonica*, the subject of the chapter that follows, was first grown at Kew. All summer long it is a riot of exciting things: tropical water-lilies of various colours, the handsome papyrus — the predecessor of paper — from Upper Egypt,[1] and the upstanding *Nelumbo* (sacred lotus) of India and the Far East with its pink or white flowers and sugar-castor seed-pods, fill the pool, while gourds and calabashes and loofahs (*Luffa*) bump against your head as you circle it in the agreeable company of a lavender-flowered convolvulus (*Ipomoea digitata*) that runs round the railings. This House may be rather small, but in other respects it could hardly be bettered: all it really needs is a crocodile or two . . .

[1] *Cyperus papyrus* is also found wild in Sicily.

14

A Vegetable Wonder

IN THE very heart of House 10 of the T-range there may be seen in late summer one of the most spectacular of all flowering plants: the giant water-lily, *Victoria amazonica*. And the visitor may well find it hard to believe that a seed no bigger than a pea, sown in a pot in January and planted out in May, can by the end of July have produced sufficient growth to fill a pool half the size of a tennis-court.[1]

The first flowering in England in 1849 of this tear-away created a sensation comparable to that caused by the arrival a century later of our first giant panda. But the story begins (or appeared, at that time, to begin) on the evening of 7 September 1837, when the members of a society known as 'The Practical Botanists' met at the Anchor Tavern in the Strand to hear the report and study the accompanying drawings of a young Silesian explorer, (Sir) Robert Schomburgk, who had been sent by the Royal Geographical Society to British Guiana. Schomburgk wrote:

> It was on the 1st of January 1837 . . . that we reached a spot where the river [Berbice] expanded and formed a currentless basin. Something on the other side of this basin attracted my attention: I could form no idea what it might be; but, urging the crew to increase the speed of their paddling, we presently neared the object which had aroused my curiosity—and lo! a vegetable wonder! . . . . There were gigantic leaves, five to six feet across, flat, with a deep rim, light green above and vivid crimson below, floating upon the water; while in keeping with this astonishing foliage, I beheld luxuriant flowers, each composed of numerous petals, which passed in alternate tints from pure white to rose and pink . . .

And he goes on to describe in detail the flower, and the extraordinary ribbed structure of the leaves, criss-crossed by lesser veinings 'which give the whole the appearance of a spider's web, and are beset with prickles'.

Schomburgk had asked for the plant to be named *Nymphaea Victoria* after the young Queen, and she had graciously granted permission; examination soon showed, however, that the water-lily was *not* a *Nymphaea*, but apparently a species of a new genus. John Gray, President of the

[1] Though a perennial, in England *Victoria amazonica* is usually treated as an annual.

Society, therefore moved a resolution that it be named *Victoria Regina*. Unluckily for the peace of the botanical world, Schomburgk had at the same time sent a duplicate set of the drawings and description of the plant to the Royal Geographical Society, his sponsors, at whose request John Lindley had named it *Victoria regia*. The first published account, in the *Athenaeum*, referred to it (with unintentional impartiality) in the text as *V. regina* and in the index as *V. regia*. Here were the makings of a glorious botanical storm-in-a-teacup, and since such storms are part of the taxonomist's way of life, it may be of interest to describe this one in some detail.

Gray, a cantankerous man, maintained that the form used in the index was a slip; Lindley, on the other hand, took the line that the editor, a sound classical scholar, found *V. regina* bad Latin (it should, of course, be *reginae* if the noun is used) and had therefore changed it in the index. Two months later, the *Edinburgh Magazine of Zoology and Botany* further confused the issue by publishing a picture of the plant captioned *Victoria regalis* though referred to in the text as *V. regina*.

Lindley was too much of a gentleman to call Gray a liar, but he did go so far as to dismiss his defence as a 'tissue of mistakes'; Gray, for his part, had no such inhibitions. It was now that the dreadful discovery was made that the plant had already been found by several earlier botanists—Haencke (1801), Bonpland (1820), D'Orbigny (*c.* 1827) and Poeppig (1832)—the last of whom had described it fully and named it *Euryale amazonica*; this, therefore, by the rigid Rules of Nomenclature, appeared to be its correct scientific name. Nobody, of course, dared to tell the Queen that the plant was no longer hers at all!

But was the plant a *Euryale*? *Euryale ferox*, a native of the East Indies, is another enormous tropical water-lily, second in size only to the newcomer and superficially very similar. But careful examination confirmed that the latter was *not* of the same genus; so, by those inflexible Rules, the generic and specific epithets first applied to it had to be retained: the plant was therefore *Victoria amazonica*. Poor Sir William found himself in a dilemma: *botanically* the problem had been solved, and the Queen put back in the picture; but, as he wrote in 1851, the specific *amazonica*, though referring to the river and not to a masculine female, was 'totally unsuited to be in connection with the name of Her Most Gracious Majesty and must therefore forthwith be rejected'. Thus, so long as Her Majesty lived, a conspiracy of silence surrounded the true name of the great water-lily, and only relatively recently have the plants at Kew been openly labelled *Victoria amazonica*.

But to return to the water-lily itself. The excitement caused by its discovery naturally led to a desire to attempt its cultivation in England, but this was not to prove easy. The first batch of seeds sent by Schomburgk to Kew germinated, but did not survive. In 1849, however, a further consignment, despatched this time on Hooker's advice in phials of pure water, produced three plants; one of these was given to the Duke of Northumberland at Syon, another to the Duke of Devonshire, whose gardener—the famous Joseph Paxton, of course—collected it himself and nursed it like a child all the way to Chatsworth, where he planted it in a specially-constructed twelve-foot tank with the water kept at 85°F.

Then the race began: a race as exciting in its day as Scott's and Amundsen's to the South Pole or the Americans' and the Russians' to the moon. While the plants at Kew and Syon sulked, that at Chatsworth grew so vigorously that its tank had more than once to be enlarged, and finally replaced by a new, specially built, conservatory. But would it produce a flower? On 2 November, Paxton wrote excitedly to the Duke, who was in Ireland: 'Victoria has shown flower!! An enormous bud like a poppy head made its appearance yesterday. It looks like a large peach placed in a cup. No words can describe the grandeur and the beauty of the plant.' He wrote also, triumphantly, to poor, defeated Hooker, 'The sight is worth a journey of a thousand miles.' It was only a hundred and sixty miles to Chatsworth, but Hooker preferred to remain at Kew.

Having made up its mind to flower, nothing would stop *Victoria amazonica*. Almost ceaselessly for a whole year it continued to produce blooms at the rate of some two a week. The Duke had hurried home from Ireland; a flower and a leaf were carried to the Queen at Windsor; and when, the following year, the plant at Kew flowered also, tens of thousands of people made the journey from London to see it. Hooker had been beaten to the post; but the Queen tactfully summoned him to Osborne so that she might see a specimen from royal Kew. 'Pray tell Sir William,' she said to Lady Jocelyn, 'that I am delighted with the flower he was so good as to bring for me. It was in the most beautiful state possible.'

The flowers are of a punctual disposition. About 2 p.m. the white bud begins to emit a strong smell, variously compared to that of pineapple or melon, and two or three hours later the petals expand and gradually colour. But towards ten o'clock the same night they begin to close, never to reopen—this slow death continuing all the following day as they assume a 'drapery of Tyrian splendour' till finally the flower collapses and sinks beneath the water.

But it is the leaves, almost more than the flowers, that astonish those who come to see the mammoth water-lily: leaves like 'green tea-trays floating, with here and there a bouquet protruding between them', wrote a botanist who had seen plants in the wild. They are often more than six feet in diameter, and so prodigious is the speed of their growth that an increase of between four and five square feet has been recorded in a single leaf in the course of twenty-four hours.

It was, however, the under-surface of the leaf, which suggested 'some

*The Giant Water-lily (*Victoria amazonica*) in flower at Chatsworth.* Illustrated
London News, *17 November 1849*

strange fabric of cast iron, just taken from the furnace', that most impressed
scientific minds. The pockets thus produced retained air, so creating
buoyancy; and it had been noticed in South America that the natives, when
collecting seed from which they made a kind of bread, often deposited their
children on goatskins on the leaves. Many experiments were now made to
find out what weight a leaf could bear. In November 1849 the Duke of
Devonshire and Lady Newburgh placed Paxton's seven-year-old daughter,
dressed as a fairy, on one:

> On unbent leaf in fairy guise,
> Reflected in the water,
> Beloved, admired by hearts and eyes,
> Stands Annie, Paxton's daughter.

But Annie Paxton was a mere featherweight: though faked photographs are
all too easy to make, there is reliable evidence of a man of eleven stone
remaining afloat for more than two minutes, and even this record is said to
have been broken at a later date. (It is, of course, necessary to use a flat board
to distribute the weight.)

The leaf afforded, indeed, a practical lesson in natural engineering. So
delicate is the surface that a straw dropped vertically from a height of five
feet will pierce it; yet the ribs, set as they are at right angles to the surface,
give it immense overall strength. Paxton himself took nature's hint when

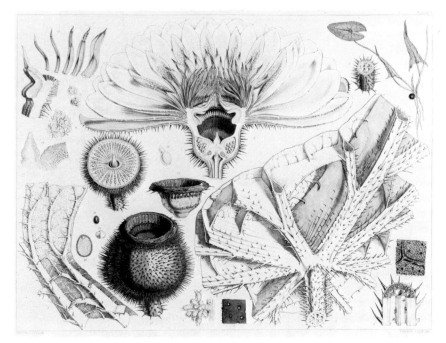

Victoria amazonica. *Lithograph by Walter Fitch, 1851, showing the structure of the leaf which inspired Paxton when designing the Crystal Palace*

designing the Crystal Palace. 'Nature,' he said, 'has provided the leaf with longitudinal and transverse girders and supports that I, borrowing from it, have adopted in this building.'

Hooker may have lost the race; but it was *he* who had germinated the seed of the first plant to flower in captivity, and he was determined that his name should for ever be associated with it. So in 1851 he produced a vast, slim folio, *Victoria Regia*, illustrated with splendid hand-coloured lithographs by Walter Fitch, which made the giant water-lily known throughout the world.[1] Botanic gardens everywhere, unmindful of the huge expense involved in the cultivation of this demanding but status-giving monster, clamoured for seed, which Hooker was soon able to provide. And almost everywhere the royal water-lily flourished.

Victoria amazonica did two botanists a good turn: it gained Paxton his knighthood and, as will be told later, it earned Fitch a pension.

---

[1] Another vast folio—*Victoria Regia* by J. F. Allen, with six plates by William Sharp—was published in Boston, Mass., in 1854. The water-lily had been flowered near Philadelphia in 1851.

The Temple of Bellona and *Cotinus obovatus* 'Chittam'.
Photograph by Jane Stubbs, late October 1975

The North Gallery. Photograph by Prudence Cuming

The Chokushi Mon and Japanese azaleas.
Photograph by F. N. Hepper, May 1975

Victoria amazonica: the expanded flower.
Hand-coloured lithograph by W. H. Fitch, 1851

The Orangery

The Palm House. Colour linocut by Edward Bawden

15

The Herbarium

THE VISITOR who approaches the main entrance to the Gardens by the road that runs along the north side of the Green will observe, just before he reaches the gates, a handsome red-brick eighteenth-century house standing a little back from the road; this, together with its innumerable modifications and extensions over the years, now constitutes the Herbarium, the Library and the residence of the Keeper of the Herbarium.[1]

The original building, known as Hunter House, was purchased in 1818 by the Crown at Sir Joseph Banks's suggestion for use as a herbarium; but at the time of Banks's death in 1820 nothing had been done, and three years later George IV secretly disposed of it to pay off some of his debts. As will be told in a moment, this transaction remained unknown to everyone until 1876, and William IV, with apparent generosity, allowed his unpopular younger brother Ernest, Duke of Cumberland, who had spent his childhood at Kew and was fond of the place, to live there. Ernest became King of Hanover in 1837, Victoria being debarred by Salic law from succeeding to the Hanoverian throne;[2] he returned once only—for three months in 1843—to what had become known as 'Hanover House'.[3] He died in 1851, and a year later the Crown, though not in fact its owner, allowed it to be converted, as originally intended, into a herbarium.

The royal dukedom of Cumberland, though it had started auspiciously enough with Prince Rupert, was in Hanoverian days borne in turn by three of the most hated of all royal princes: William, Henry and Ernest—uncle, brother and son respectively of George III. There is, indeed, a tendency to merge all three in the memory into one unspeakably black prince; but were they really all as ink-black as they were painted? I must confess that I prefer to forget, when smelling a sweet William, that the flower was named after the first of them, the Butcher of Culloden;[4] and Henry, not without some musical taste, was 'coarse and brutal in his everyday life' (*D.N.B.*). Few people in England had a good word for Ernest, who 'even as a youth had

---

[1] The Herbarium and Library are normally accessible only to *bona fide* students, but almost every spring the public is given a chance to see 'behind the scenes' on an 'open day'.

[2] Ernest 'was (to the nation's horror) Queen Victoria's heir-presumptive until the birth [in 1840] of her first child, Victoria Princess Royal' (*Queen Mary*, by James Pope-Hennessy).

[3] The name has been retained by the house next door, which was originally included in Ernest's establishment.

[4] 'Stinking Willie' (ragwort) more appropriately commemorates him in parts of Scotland.

shamed the family by trying to kiss the Mother Superior of a French Convent'; but though accused in his lifetime of such peccadillos as murder, rape, adultery, sodomy, and incest, he had a better side to his nature. He was brave in battle, charitably-minded, and—for a Hanoverian prince—quite intelligent. He ruled Hanover well. As his brother William once said, he was 'not a bad fellow'; he added, however, 'but if anyone has a corn he is sure to tread on it'.[1]

Thirty years ago, when I was writing my *Art of Botanical Illustration*, I spent a good deal of time in the Library, which was then housed in the old building. The main room was a charming place to work, fragrant with the aroma of ancient books and loud with the hum and the scurry of modern botanists whose conversation, being largely in Latin, hardly disturbed my reading. These amiable and dedicated men (today they carry walkie-talkies, like the police) were very kind to me—to one who from their point of view was concerned mainly with the frivolity of 'pretty pictures of coloured simples, those gazing-traps of simpletons'[2]—and even the busiest of them would not hesitate to interrupt his serious scientific labours to find me a book or to answer a question that revealed my shameful ignorance of things botanical. They lived in a world that was utterly remote from mine, which was that of the artist and the schoolmaster; and when from time to time they broke into English—let us say, to dispute what was the most suitable kind of watercress to introduce into Trinidad—I, eavesdropping, would marvel at the heat so humble a vegetable could generate. Two schoolmasters in disagreement over an umpire's decision in a house-match, two art historians wrangling over the attribution of a *quattrocento* painting, could not have reacted more passionately.

I suspect that I, almost alone of the users of the Library, ever spared a thought for those who had once lived in it: for unloved Ernest; for his plump, twice-widowed wife, Frederika of Mecklenburg-Strelitz, who had earlier jilted the Duke of Cambridge, and for their pathetic little son George, afterwards King George V of Hanover. Ernest lost an eye at the first battle of Tournai; his son lost both—the left probably after a childhood illness, the other when, at the age of fourteen, he was playing at Kew with the boy across the road—his young cousin George (later the second Duke of Cambridge)—and in spite of a warning struck it with a heavy purse he was joyfully swinging after being given a 'tip'.[3] In later life the blind King, who

---

[1] I can't devote more space to him here, but see Roger Fulford, *Royal Dukes*, 1933, and Anthony Bird, *The Damnable Duke of Cumberland*, 1966.

[2] Said about Bute by one of his detractors.

[3] The circumstances in which he lost his right eye were disclosed only after his death in 1878. They must have deeply impressed my grandmother, who had just come to live at Petersham, because as a child I was always warned by her, when swinging anything, to 'remember the blind King of Hanover'.

by then had lost his throne as well as his sight, revisited the house in which he had spent 'the happiest days of a long and turbulent life', and was still able to describe the rooms exactly and to grope his sightless way round them. I often felt that their ghosts were still very present.

But valuable though the Library is—and it contains more than a hundred thousand volumes—the Herbarium is of even greater scientific importance. Its nucleus was the loaned private collection of Sir William Hooker, which after his death was purchased by the Government for £5,000. By then it was believed to contain 'a million ticketed specimens, and was considered in extent, arrangement and nomenclature certainly the finest in existence; it had been upwards of sixty years in formation; there was evidence of upwards of £9,000 having been expended upon its formation by its possessor, exclusive of rent for its accommodation; and it must have cost a much larger sum'. At the same time the Government acquired for £2,000 Sir William's library and his collection of about 29,000 letters from over 4,000 individuals; this correspondence has been bound in 76 quarto volumes.

The collection of pressed plants has now been augmented by purchases and bequests until today it contains more than six million specimens, several hundred thousand of which are 'type' specimens.[1] All these are housed in three prisons—I can find no better word for these cavernous, echoing halls, known as Wings C, B and A—which stretch, seemingly for ever, to the westwards of Hanover House; any reader who has watched *Porridge* on television will seem to recognise them.

It was in 1876 that Sir Joseph Hooker sought permission to build the first of these ('Wing C'). He met with fierce opposition from the Duchess of Cambridge, who objected to an intrusion into what was then believed to be land still the property of the Crown, and little sympathy from his Chief, Lord Lennox—the First Commissioner of Works. Then, suddenly, the surprising and glorious discovery was made that Hanover House and its grounds did not after all belong to the Crown! Sir Joseph wrote exultantly to his friend the American botanist, Asa Gray:

> The Cambridge family who had an eye to the ground and house, were bitterly opposed to it, and got over that false, weak, vain, half idiot, my present chief, who, after the Queen had given the site, continued throwing obstacles in the way. When lo! by a stroke of luck, it turned out, when preparing for a legal transfer of the site, that the present Herbarium House and grounds all belong to us!—that old scamp, George IV, having sold it for £18,250 to pay his debts, in 1823! There was no legal conveyance, but the receipt of the money is to the fore! Thus both

[1] A type specimen is—to put it simply—the actual specimen from which a plant was originally named.

William IV and Victoria have for half a century been giving to others . . . a house which is not their own. . .

The strange design of Wing C, which was pointlessly repeated in Wing B and even in Wing A (1931–32), was intended to provide optimum daylight in the time before Kew had got round to gas. There is some elegant Victorian cast-ironwork in the spiral staircases, but some of the best, in the panels of the gallery railings, was subsequently removed on the grounds that it harboured dust; it can be seen in an early photograph. I cannot feel that loganberries-and-cream was the most suitable choice of colour to paint what remains.

Fifteen years ago I described the Herbarium—rather uncharitably, perhaps—in a work of fiction:

> To a mere flower-lover it's one of the most depressing places imaginable—a sort of botanical cemetery with a million vegetable dead awaiting Judgment Day in their brown paper shrouds. It reeks of decay and dissolution.[1] As I looked at its hundreds of little cells, each with its imprisoned botanist and his sheaf of plant folders, the whole place seemed to have so little to do with *flowers* that I found it almost possible to believe the old story of the botanist who failed to recognise in the common daisy the familiar *Bellis perennis* of his *hortus siccus*. There was Benjamin Robinson, the American botanist, who when asked to identify a wild flower always replied, 'Press it, dry it, bring it back, and I'll name it for you'. I do so agree with Professor Dawson, who said: 'I hate Theology and Botany, but I love religion and flowers.'[2]

This rarefied, highly-specialised ivory-tower aspect of the Herbarium was also observed by Beatrix Potter[3] when she visited Kew with her uncle, the distinguished chemist Sir Henry Roscoe. The year was 1896, the Director (Sir) William Thiselton-Dyer,[4] and the writer a spinster of thirty with the first of those little books which were to make her famous still unpublished. Miss Potter had been making a study of fungi and lichens, and wanted to propound some heretical views on the subject.

They called first on the Assistant Director, Mr Morris, 'who disclaimed all knowledge of fungi—"I am exclusively tropical", he was sorting crumply papers containing very spiky, thorny gums from Arabia, fastened down by

---

[1] This odour comes, I imagine, principally from the fumigation necessary to discourage the activities of the wicked drug-store beetle (*Stegobium paniceum*)—a pest that is as voracious as it is 'choosy', greedily gobbling up members of (for example) the daisy family yet with never even a nibble at grasses or ferns.

[2] *Of Flowers and a Village*, Hamish Hamilton, 1963.

[3] *The Journal of Beatrix Potter* transcribed from her code writing by Leslie Linder, Frederick Warne, 1966.

[4] For Thiselton-Dyer, see chapter 25.

Wing C of the Herbarium, erected in 1876

multitudinous slips'. Then came Mr Baker, the Librarian and Keeper of the Herbarium—'a slim, timid looking old gentleman with a large, thin book under his arm, and an appearance of having been dried in blotting paper under a press', and finally the Director himself—'a thin, elderly gentleman in summery attire, with a dry, cynical manner, puffing a cigarette, but wide awake and boastful, [who] discoursed vaingloriously upon his Establishment and arrangements, and his hyacinths, better than the Dutch. . .'

There are thumb-nail portraits of other members of Kew's behind-the-scenes staff, whom for the most part she found kind but concerned only with their tiny corners of knowledge: 'They are almost too much specialists,' she wrote; 'they really seem less well informed than an ordinary person on any subject outside their own, and occasionally regard it with petulance.' There was the mycologist Mr Massee ('I opine that he has passed several stages of development into a fungus himself'); Mr Kirby 'who stutters a little', and 'Mr Waterhouse (beetles),—two ladybirds rotating in a glass pill-box—is so like a frog we had once, it quite puts me out. I should like to know what is Sir W. Flower's subject besides ladies' bonnets'.

Further visits were not much more productive, the authorities being disinclined at first to take her theories seriously. Once she panicked and bolted without even exchanging a word with Thiselton-Dyer, whom she had come to see:

> I saw Mr Thiselton-Dyer through the window. I sat for about ¼ hour in a small room watching a large, slow clerk cut snippets from a pink newspaper and paste them carefully on a sheet of foolscap with the Royal arms. I felt all over the patterns on the legs of a cane-bottom chair, and read an advertisement of foreign steamers.
>
> An old gentleman Mr Baker, put his head in at the door with an unintelligible message, regarding me with curiosity. Then I incontinently fled. . . .

On another occasion Miss Potter was kept waiting even longer with the clerk and his glue-pots before the Director was ready to see her:

> I was beginning to think the delay uncivil when Mr Thiselton-Dyer bounced in, very dree he was, and in a great hurry. I was not shy, not at all. I had it up and down with him. His line was on the outside edge of civil. . . . He indicated that the subject was profound, that my opinions, etc., "mares nests" etc., that he hadn't time to look at my drawings. . . . I informed him that it would all be in the books in ten years, whether or no, and departed giggling. . . .
>
> I went to the Herbarium and found Mr Massee had come round altogether and was prepared to believe my new-thing, including Lichens. He was making efforts to grow *Bulgaria inquinans* quite ineffectually. I gave him a slice of *Velutipes*, highly poisoned.
>
> I don't think he has a completely clear head, it is a conceited way of talking, but it is extraordinary how botanists have niggled at a few isolated species and not in the least seen the broad bearings of it. He would never have found out the bearings of the lichen. . .

It appeared that Thiselton-Dyer, whose sense of humour was limited though that of his self-importance was not, had been far from amused by Miss Potter's gentle leg-pulling. Next morning Sir Henry received from the Director a letter so '*rude* and *stupid*' that he would not even let his niece read it. 'I was much surprised,' wrote Miss Potter. 'I had thought the Director took it as a joke.' She knew a lot about botany—but not much, it would seem, about botanists.

However, Mr Massee did eventually accept that this strange young woman had discovered something of interest; for in the *Proceedings of the Linnean Society of London* it is recorded that on 1 April 1897 'the following paper was read: "On the Germination of the Spores of *Agaricineae*" by Miss Helen B. Potter (Communicated by Mr George Massee, F.L.S.)'

*   *   *

Let us be fair. The work done in the Herbarium is often of enormous botanical and economic importance, though admittedly it also (among other things) adds to the misery of gardeners by constantly changing the scientific names of familiar plants. It must not be forgotten that the labours of dedicated men and women there and in the Gardens made it possible for Joseph Chamberlain, when Secretary of State for the Colonies, to say in the House of Commons on 2 August 1898, 'At the present time there are several of our important colonies which owe whatever prosperity they possess to the knowledge and experience of, and the assistance given by, the authorities at Kew Gardens'.

Kew also publishes a large number of floras, monographs and periodicals—for example, the *Flora of Tropical East Africa*, the *Flora of Iraq* and the *Flora of Cyprus*; monographs of the *Camellia* and the *Fritillaria*; the *Kew Bulletin, Icones Plantarum, Index Kewensis* and, above all, the celebrated and still flourishing *Botanical Magazine*[1]—the oldest and most revered of such periodicals, whose first number appeared in 1787. The staff reply to thousands of inquiries every year, many of which involve a good deal of research to answer[2] and not a few of which hardly deserve the courteous attention that all receive. For an example of the latter, which I have no doubt was answered kindly, there is a card addressed in May 1957 to 'The Scientists of the Backroom, Kew Gardens,' deploring (among other things) that the authorities fed live babies to the giant water-lily and kept 'men-eating trees, who live only on human flesh'. Also mentioned was something known to few botanists: that 'at the estate of the Earl of Jersey there was and probably still is a member of their family changed in a tree. . . . We have known a man who did suicide, because he heard him talk'.

Charming, and less sinister, is the following letter, enclosing two dried specimens:

1st Floor, Staff quarters in hostels,
opp. Narendra Chhatralaya
Ahmedadabad 9, India

7 February 1953

Respected Sir,

In consequence of my study on the development of male and female gametophyte, mode of embryo development of the two plants enclosed herewith, an intricating crux as to the correct nomenclature of the genera and species arose. I pursued with advancing zeal to name them, and more difference appeared and finally a stage has been reached leading to the ultimate chaos.

---

[1] In 1922 the publication of the *Botanical Magazine* passed into the hands of the Royal Horticultural Society; but the editing and illustration remained at Kew, which has now also taken over the publication.

[2] Such as, 'Is there any kind of acacia thorn that might be suitable for gramophone needles?'

To guide me in the spur of the moments, I approach our world's foremost herbarium to finally stamp the generic and specific names and resolve the deadlock in my mind.

This letter is from a bubble gazing at the vast ocean of Botanical treasure. My joy shall know no bounds, the moment—the eventful moment, when I shall read a letter from Herbarium Kew.

Yours sincerely
C. K. Shah

Letters addressed to 'The Hibernatium' and 'Queue Gardens' are not unknown; and the Herbarium staff must have read with alarm an article in the *Field* (29 May 1969) congratulating Kew on its 'decimation' of plant material throughout the world.

A small team of highly skilled botanical artists is always at work in the Herbarium, and it may surprise the mere amateur painter of flowers to learn that, so accustomed have some of them become to drawing from pressed specimens that—like the American botanist mentioned earlier—they sometimes find them more acceptable material than the living plant. A large collection of botanical prints and drawings is also preserved in the Herbarium, where they are classified and boxed according to genera and species. This is of course convenient for the botanist, but the system has had sad consequences: an artist like John Moggeridge, for example, who was rash enough to portray different species on a single sheet, has had his lovely drawings snipped into little pieces so that each can be filed in its appropriate box.

In 1969 a further extension was made to the Herbarium complex to rehouse the ever-growing Library. This is—internally, at all events—an admirable building perfectly suited to its purpose, and its construction was undoubtedly necessary; but there are no ghosts here, and I for one mourn the relegation of that handsome eighteenth-century room to a kind of botanical dump.

Closely associated with the Herbarium, but situated within the Gardens, is the Jodrell Laboratory, built and equipped in 1876 at the expense of a friend of Sir Joseph Hooker for the study of plant anatomy, morphology, and so on. The original laboratory was an unassuming little bungaloid affair, to which a studio and photographic dark-room were added in 1934; but it has recently been replaced by a larger two-storey building, no doubt more commodious but certainly more aggressive than its predecessor. In conjunction with it there is a big transparent lecture-room, best viewed from the top of a 27 or 65 bus.

16

Botanical Artists

IN MY book *The Art of Botanical Illustration* I dealt fairly fully with the work of botanical artists associated with Kew; I shall therefore treat the subject here with more brevity than it deserves.

Georg Dionysius Ehret (1708–70), the greatest botanical artist of his day, is represented at Kew only by paintings made in the closing years of his life, when his eyesight was failing. Redouté, on the other hand, when he came to Kew in 1786 to make drawings for some of the plates in Charles l'Héritier de Brutelle's *Sertum Anglicum* or 'English Garland' (1789–92), was still in his twenties. The engravings are uncoloured, and though of

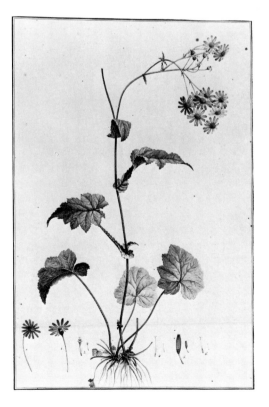

Cineraria cruenta. *Engraving by Maloeuvre after P. J. Redouté. This humble Cineraria, from the Canary Islands, is the parent of our flamboyant house-plants*

'*The late Mr Worthington G.
Smith sketching under difficulties*'.
From the Gardeners'
Chronicle, *1917*

plants exciting to the botanists of the day they are of little interest to the
mere lover of 'pretty pictures of flowers'. Possibly that is why no book on
Kew Gardens until Ronald King's (1976) even mentions Redouté's visit,
but more probably it is due to the artist's relatively recent meteoric rise to
popularity.

In 1790 a young Austrian named Franz (Francis) Bauer arrived in
England, where his botanical drawings immediately attracted the attention
of Sir Joseph Banks, who had long been wanting to attach a resident artist of
high ability to the Gardens. With the King's approval and his own
characteristic generosity he engaged Bauer and agreed to pay his salary.
Bauer settled at Kew where he made magnificent paintings of plants
introduced by collectors from all over the world and, as has already been
mentioned, gave lessons to the Queen and Princess Elizabeth.

Bauer had not remained content to draw the mere outward appearance of plants; he had become a highly skilled botanist, famous also for his microscopic work which he was still able to pursue even when over eighty. Asa Gray, who visited him at Kew in 1839, found him 'much broken down, but still hard at work, and making as beautiful drawings as ever (beyond comparison excellent), and as delicate microscopical observations'. Bauer died the following year (the same year as Redouté) at the age of eighty-two, and was buried in the churchyard at Kew by the side of Gainsborough and Zoffany. It is hard to decide whether the sedentary Francis or his restless brother Ferdinand is the greatest of all botanical artists; certainly they have no rivals.

Two amateur artists—simple working gardeners with a taste for drawing—were employed by the younger Aiton to record new introductions. The first, a Scot named Thomas Duncannon, worked from 1822 until he became insane four years later. He was succeeded by George Bond, who continued until he left the Gardens in 1835. Between them they produced some two thousand drawings, the very large majority of them by Bond, which after various vicissitudes found their way back to Kew. They are of considerable botanical importance but of little artistic merit.

Both the Hookers were fairly competent botanical draughtsmen, William, for example, taking upon himself in 1826 the whole burden of the illustration of the *Botanical Magazine* for nearly ten years, and Joseph making the field sketches of Himalayan rhododendrons that were redrawn and lithographed by that most prolific of all Victorian botanical illustrators—Walter Hood Fitch (1817–92). A comparison with Joseph's original rhododendron drawings shows how much the published plates owe to Fitch.

William Hooker had discovered young Fitch in Glasgow, where he was apprenticed to a firm of calico designers, and, recognising his talent, repaid his apprenticeship fee and so secured his services. Then in 1841, when Hooker was appointed to Kew, he carried his protégé south with him. Fitch's industry was prodigious. He was the sole artist of the *Botanical Magazine* for more than forty years, and the total of his published lithographs reached the almost unbelievable figure of 9,960. Joseph Hooker paid many tributes to the 'incomparable artist' with his 'unrivalled skill in seizing the natural character of a plant'. 'I don't think that Fitch *could* make a mistake in his perspective and outline,' he once said, 'not even if he tried.'

But Fitch's very facility had its dangers; and as one surveys the faultless acres of his lithographs one cannot help wishing that somewhere he had betrayed a moment of hesitation or perplexity. Moreover, though his draughtsmanship is impeccable, most of his work lacks sensibility. His contours, often drawn with a pen and lithographic ink, are too rigid to blend with the texture of the chalk shading; and when towards the end of his life, in making his lily drawings for Elwes, he worked with chalk only, his line became altogether too swift and too loose. But, all things considered, Fitch probably remains the most outstanding botanical artist of his generation in Europe.

William Hooker almost lost the services of Fitch in 1847 when the latter resigned because he felt he was being underpaid, and later there were also misunderstandings between the artist and Joseph Hooker. But that Joseph bore him no permanent ill-will is proved by the trouble that he took in 1879 to persuade Disraeli to grant Fitch a pension. The Prime Minister hesitated; but Hooker 'played upon his imperialist feelings' by showing him the big lithographs which the artist had made of the *Victoria amazonica* water-lily at Kew, and the following year Fitch was granted a Civil List pension of £100 per annum. After Fitch's retirement, various artists—including Joseph Hooker's daughter, Lady Thiselton-Dyer—held the fort until Matilda Smith, another member of the Hooker clan, came to the rescue; their work was lithographed by John Nugent Fitch, Walter Fitch's nephew.

Of more recent Kew artists I will mention three only—not because there is any lack of splendid talent, but rather because there is such a plethora of it that space would permit of no more than a tedious catalogue of names. Lilian Snelling (1879–1972) worked for the *Botanical Magazine* for thirty years and made fine plates for the *Supplement to Elwes' Monograph of the Genus Lilium* (1934–40) and F. C. Stern's *Study of the Genus Paeonia* (1946). I would like to digress for a moment about a delightful visit I paid her, more than twenty years ago, which I have described fictionally elsewhere.[1]

Lilian Snelling (as far as I can remember) lived with her two equally ancient sisters in an old farmhouse near Orpington which had been in the family for generations. Within its doors one was immediately back in the world of *Cranford*—but alas! a Cranford now utterly desecrated by the sprawling tentacles of suburbia. Traffic roared by the house, factory hooters hooted, other people's wirelesses were turned on full blast. One sister ran the house, another weeded incessantly a seemingly weedless garden full of old-fashioned flowers—and Lilian painted. I bought from her a picture of a Madonna lily which had been used in her King Penguin, *A Book of Lilies*; I paid her nearly twice the sum she proposed, and still feel ashamed that I acquired so much beauty for so little. It hangs beside a Ruskin orchis in my spacious loo—a room which contains my choicest flower paintings so that I can enjoy them every morning.

It is an even more invidious task to make a choice among the living. Miss Mary Grierson (b. 1912) came to Kew in 1960, and besides her work for the *Botanical Magazine* and other periodicals and books she has been responsible for the design of a number of floral stamps for special issues of

---

[1] *Of Flowers and a Village*, pp. 187–89.

*Madonna Lily (*Lilium candidum*). Watercolour drawing by Lilian Snelling*

the G.P.O.; she has recently been painting specie tulips for Dr Michael Hoog. Miss Margaret Stones (b. 1920) arrived in England from her native Australia in 1951 and since 1958 has been the principal artist of the *Botanical Magazine*. She has also illustrated many books, and will perhaps be best remembered for her contributions to the *Supplement to Elwes' Monograph of the Genus Lilium* (1960, 1962) and the five volumes of *The Endemic Flora of Tasmania* of which she is co-author. The work of both of these highly gifted botanical artists is seen at its best in watercolour.

So much for scientific illustration; but the Gardens, too, attract artists, though in the nineteenth and twentieth centuries their appeal seems to have been chiefly to the amateur. The great English landscape painters of the day were apparently either unaware of or impervious to the charms of Kew. Van Gogh, who in 1876 spent six months at Isleworth, never so much as mentions the Gardens in a copious correspondence; nor, so far as I know, did Monet, who at various times spent many months painting in London, visit Kew, where he might so easily have added *Victoria amazonica* to his bag of water-lilies. An exception was Camille Pissarro, whom we find writing in June 1892 to his friend Octave Mirbeau: 'I am at Kew, profiting by the exceptional summer to throw myself wholeheartedly into *plein air* studies in this wonderful garden of Kew. Oh! my dear friend, what trees! what lawns! what pretty, imperceptible undulations of the ground!' Three of these pictures (which might really have been painted almost anywhere) were exhibited at the Hayward Gallery, London, in 1973.

More recent artists do not seem to have found much inspiration at Kew, though mention should be made of two striking linocuts—of the Pagoda and the Palm House—by Edward Bawden. The latter is reproduced in colour in this book.

17

A Sudden Shower

SOME FIFTEEN years ago, the following passage, attributed to a certain Wilfrid Sharp, appeared in a frivolous little book of mine that I have already mentioned more than once:

I went to Kew again yesterday, and having half-an-hour to spare I looked into the Gardens . . . But it was so hideously cold that I soon took refuge in Museum 2 — 'Economic Products derived from Monocotyledons and Cryptogams'. It really is a *horrifying* place; even the meanest Oxford Street window-dresser could effect an improvement in ten minutes. The cases are stuffed to bursting-point with vegetables and nightmare objects of vegetable origin. Gewgaws that the most magpie of Anglo-Orientals would hardly dare to bring back to the Motherland struggle for breathing-space with oddities from nearer home: a temple modelled in ivory nut, a Formosan fan, a tablet of vegetable carbolic soap, 'a pair of Parisian anti-rheumatic shoe-pads', and 'a needle-case made by Bavarian convicts'. (One longs to know more about the Miss Hipkins who

One of the Kew museums as it was formerly, showing a slight tendency to overcrowding

presented the Kaffir snuff-spoons.) There are things in bottles that would turn a man's stomach against pickles for a fortnight. The labels are printed in the sort of fount that one associates with parish magazines; the photographs look wan and tired; an odour of putrefaction is every-where . . .

This is, of course, unkind; but at the time when Wilfrid Sharp wrote it, it was not wholly untrue. Sir Sydney Cockerell, formerly Director of the Fitzwilliam Museum at Cambridge but living in retirement at Kew, felt the same, complaining to Sir Edward Salisbury of the 'lamentable arrangement' of the exhibits in the Museums, then in the charge of Dr John Hutchinson. 'I criticised very frankly and severely,' he wrote after one of a number of talks with Dr Hutchinson; 'but I am not sure that much sunk in.' There has since been some improvement; but the fact remains that Kew's Museums are still not worthy of its glorious Gardens.

For the art of display has made gigantic strides of recent years, as anyone who visits most of London's major museums will know. But it would appear that the botanists have not yet realised that showmanship is an art, and that they need the advice of experts if they are to make their museums attractive to the general public. That all but the Orangery (which sells guidebooks and souvenirs) appear to be largely deserted except when serving as shelter from a sudden shower, surely speaks for itself.

If we exclude Kew Palace and the Orangery, both of which have already been discussed, there remain three other museums at Kew: the North Gallery, the Wood Museum (Cambridge Cottage), and the General Museum; Museum 2, so savagely attacked above, has since been turned into a reference collection and is not open to the public, but to judge from what one can glimpse through the windows it is not often referred to. The North Gallery and the Wood Museum each requires a chapter to itself; I will therefore now deal with the General Museum.

This unpretentious three-storied ochre-coloured building facing the pond and the Palm House, designed by Decimus Burton and erected in 1856, was immediately severely criticised in the *Gardeners' Chronicle* (6 December 1856):

> As to the new Museum, for which so much of the beautiful piece of water, so many noble trees, and so picturesque a part of the garden have been needlessly sacrificed, it is difficult to conceive what head could have planned such a monstrosity. Seen from the road . . . it is frightful, seen from the garden it is mean as well as misplaced.

Paxton was even more savage, comparing it to 'a third-rate lodging house.' It is not really so awful as that: not externally, anyway.

On the ground floor (the rest is at present closed) the objects are still displayed in the original ponderous mahogany cases, so fashionable in Victorian days but now replaced in almost all museums elsewhere by something more elegant and practical; and the floors are covered with that chocolate-coloured linoleum often to be seen in the corridors of antiquated hospitals. Even electric light is referred to (almost apologetically) in a hand-out in the Museum as a 'comparatively recent addition'.

Some old friends formerly in Museum 2 have been transferred here, and though I have failed to find the Parisian anti-rheumatic shoe-pads and the needle-case made by Bavarian convicts, there are still Miss Hipkins's snuff-spoons from Zululand, and kindred objects such as a rice-drainer from Afghanistan and the basket made in 1886, from the leaves of *Chamaerops*, by a prisoner in Tangier gaol. 1886 was a fruitful year for acquisitions, and it was then that the museum also received the model of an indigo factory at Nuddea, made for the Colonial and Indian Exhibition and presumably dumped on Kew when it closed.

But let us be fair. There are also interesting and sensibly devised cases dealing with the story of rubber, of tobacco (no government warning), and of sugar; the origin of plant cultivation; vegetable dyes and arrow poisons; the history of the potato, and so on. Some wax models of flowers are also astonishing. It is simply imaginative display that is lacking; the whole presentation is not just twenty years behind the times, it is Victorian.

There are a number of 'quiz sheets' available which deal with the museums as a whole and with particular exhibits such as those mentioned above. Here are some of the questions, none of which I can answer:

What did the Peruvians use for cleaning their teeth?
What is $C_{12}H_{22}O_{11}$?
What is a bagasse?
Give the latin names for Bish, Opas and Sassy.
What did the Natufians take with them when they moved?
Name the glucosides in Acokanthera venenata.

And while answering—or failing to answer—these, one may rest upon a seat made of the wood of one's choice: padauk (*Pterocarpus indicus*), Indian laurel (*Terminalis tomentosa*), Borneo camphorwood (*Dryobalanops aromatica*), kerung (*Dipterocarpus*) and so on.

Undoubtedly there is plenty in this building to interest the student of economic botany; but today the contents of a museum, if they are to win the attention of an *uninformed* visitor, must look as if they were tended with affection, not merely tolerated with reluctance. So it comes as a sudden pleasure to stumble, in a far corner of this rather depressing place, upon a number of little glass receptacles containing English wild flowers freshly gathered and attractively arranged by someone who obviously loves them.

There is a question that I should like to add to one of those 'quiz sheets': 'Who is responsible for this charming exhibit?'

But it has stopped raining. I and the only other visitor, an elderly schoolmistress (I would guess) who had been making copious notes about the origin of crop plants, emerge gratefully into the fresh air. . .

Footnote, April 1977. The above was written in the late autumn of 1976, and I must in all fairness add that some mild improvement was effected during the following winter. Moreover, though it was not raining I found more than a dozen people there besides myself.

An exhibit that seemed to me to be new (though I may have overlooked it on previous visits) was a fragment of the famous piece of tapa cloth made for King Josiah Tubo of Tongabatu; impossible in any case to have shown all of it, for the whole cloth was two miles long and 120 feet wide! Is it listed in the *Guinness Book of Records?*

18

Quinine and Rubber

AMONG THE most important functions of Kew over the years have been the export of trained gardeners and the distribution of plants — especially economic plants — to all parts of the globe. Here are one or two examples of the latter in the time of the Hookers.

Ascension Island possessed but a single tree: Kew clothed its nakedness. Cork oaks were sent to Australia, cacti to the Canary Islands to rear the cochineal insect, and tussock grass brought home by Joseph Hooker from the Falkland Islands proved a suitable fodder-plant in the Shetland Islands. The nutmeg was introduced into Jamaica, tobacco into Natal, and Liberian coffee into India and other parts of the Empire. A single plant of the Brazilian ipecacuanha (a native word meaning 'roadside sick-making plant'), sent to the Calcutta Botanic Gardens in 1866, led to the extensive though not always successful cultivation of it in India. In 1869 enormous quantities of economic plants were despatched to Australia, New Zealand, South Africa and the United States. In addition, hundreds of thousands of trees and shrubs have been reared at Kew for planting in public parks and gardens throughout the British Isles.

Moreover, some of those mysterious happenings behind closed doors in the Jodrell Laboratory and the Herbarium have led to the breeding of disease-resistant or more productive strains of crop plants. Indeed, it is hardly too much to say that if our descendants do not starve to death, Kew will have played a large part in their survival. There is space here to consider in any detail only two of the plants in whose triumphal progress Kew has played a prominent part: quinine and rubber.

In Westminster Abbey there is, as everyone knows, a monument to the Unknown Soldier; surely there ought also somewhere to be one to the Unknown Peruvian Indian who made a chance discovery destined over the years to save millions of lives and relieve immeasurable misery: that the bark of certain trees, the cinchonas, could be used to produce a preventative and palliative of malaria. Though the *cause* of malaria — a parasite of the anopheles mosquito — was not identified until the close of the nineteenth century, the discovery of quinine is said to have played as important a role in the history of medicine as did that of gunpowder in the history of war.

The cinchonas (there are a number of species, all evergreen trees of the

Cinchona *sp. (right) and* Cassia *sp.*
Engraving from Diderot's
Encyclopédie

Andes) are members of the Rubiaceae,[1] of which only the gardenia is
generally familiar to horticulturists. When the Indians first found out the
use to which the cinchonas could be put is not known; perhaps they were in
no great hurry to pass on their secret to their unloved Spanish conquerors,
but they themselves may hardly have appreciated its true importance.

The following story was current in the seventeenth century and believed
for three hundred years. It alleged that in 1630 the Corregidor (magistrate)
of Loxa,[2] who had perhaps ingratiated himself with the natives, was
provided with a bitter-tasting febrifuge, made from the bark of a cinchona,
which miraculously cured his intermittent fever; and that eight years later,
hearing that the Condesa of Chinchón, wife of the Viceroy of Peru, was
suffering from a severe ague, he sent her a parcel of the powdered bark,
which saved her life. In 1941, however, it was revealed that much of this

[1] Nothing to do with *Rubus* (blackberry, etc.), which is a rose. Ipecacuanha (*Cephaelis
ipecacuanha*) and coffee (*Coffea* spp.) are also members of the Rubiaceae.
[2] Or Loja, now in Ecuador near the Peruvian border—the source of *C. officinalis*.

account, written by a seventeenth-century Spanish doctor named Sebastian Bado, could not be substantiated.[1] The Condesa vanishes from the story, and we are left with the Conde, who undoubtedly did introduce the bark into Spain. Later, Linnaeus, getting the name wrong, created the genus *Cinchona*—and this, in spite of many remonstrances, it has remained.

In Europe, quinine was known as 'Peruvian bark', as 'the Countess's powder' (thanks to Bado), and as 'the Jesuits' bark' or 'the Cardinal's bark' (because the Jesuits, and Cardinal de Lugo in particular, disseminated it widely). There is space only to hint at what followed.[2] In Rome, the medical profession scorned it while the Church promoted it; when, therefore, it reached England it was condemned as popish, and Cromwell was left to die because it was denied to him. Charles II, treated with a secret elixir (later found to be quinine and wine) by a fashionable quack named Robert Talbor (later Talbot), so benefited from its use that, to the fury of the medical profession, the latter was made a royal physician and knighted. In France Talbot saved the life of the Dauphin and in 1681 sold his secret to Louis XIV for 3000 louis d'or, a substantial pension, and the promise that it would not be made public in his lifetime. He died the following year, aged only forty-two, and might surely have been included in the *D.N.B.*

A century later, the French botanists La Condamine and Joseph de Jussieu studied the genus scientifically and made the first, but unsuccessful, attempt to introduce living plants into Europe. Meanwhile the bark continued to be so extensively exported that there seemed a serious risk of the genus being exterminated in the wild. In the first half of the nineteenth century the Dutch did succeed in cultivating a few plants in Java; but it was left to the British to make the real break-through, with (Sir) Clements Markham, a young clerk at the India Office who knew Peru, the principal actor in this drama, and the two Hookers at Kew in perpetual, beneficent attendance in the wings. Markham's ambition was to establish the cinchona in India and Ceylon, where malaria killed more than a million people annually.

In 1859 he was authorised to organise an expedition to collect seeds and plants of every known species of *Cinchona* in Peru, Ecuador and Bolivia. With him went a gardener named John Weir; and on William Hooker's recommendation a Kew gardener, Robert Cross, joined forces in Ecuador with Dr Richard Spruce, a brilliant botanist and traveller who had been living for many years in South America, and Dr James Taylor, lecturer in anatomy at Quito University.

The local authorities guarded their cinchonas jealously, and all these

---

[1] See A. W. Haggis, 'Fundamental Errors in the Early History of Cinchona', *Bulletin of the History of Medicine*, 1941.
[2] See M. L. Duran-Reynals, *The Fever Bark Tree*, W. H. Allen, 1947—an admirable little book.

collectors were destined to run into trouble. A self-important local official gave orders for the arrest of Markham and the confiscation of his plants. He managed to evade his pursuers and reach the Peruvian port of Islay; but his troubles were not yet over, for while he was at Lima getting clearance, an attempt was made to pour boiling water over his Wardian cases.[1] Cross, establishing himself in a remote hut on the western slopes of Chimborazo put at his disposal by a friendly native, had succeeded in getting plants of *C. succirubra*, and later a hundred thousand seeds of *C. officinalis*, down to the coast. Much of all this material, and much more in the years that followed, reached Kew, and in due course continued on its way to Ceylon, southern India and other places where the climate was considered to be suitable. So successful were these various ventures that by 1893 — incidentally the year in which poor Spruce died miserably — the cost in Bengal of a dose of quinine, formerly beyond the means of all but the rich, had fallen to a farthing.

Markham, who later became very distinguished, was awarded the K.C.B. by the Queen, and by the botanists the *Markhamia* — a tropical tree with 'flowers yellowish with chocolate or red stripes or greenish-yellow with purple spots and brownish-purple lobes, rarely lilac'; it sounds exciting. Richard Spruce, who has no connection with the tree that bears his name, was given a moss (*Sprucea*) and a liverwort (*Sprucella*) — a sort of botanical M.B.E. for a man who really deserved the equivalent of a V.C. Cross, of course, got nothing, though his were the first cinchona plants to reach India in a healthy condition and though later he also helped considerably with the importation of rubber from Brazil: he was just 'the gardener'.

What was scandalous was that, in spite of Markham's repeated efforts, for an achievement that was to save hundreds of thousands of pounds and millions of lives his splendid team received either little or nothing tangible beyond their stipulated pay. The health of both Spruce and Weir was ruined for life; yet the former was eventually awarded by a reluctant Government a pension hardly visible to the naked eye, while the latter was left dependent upon an income of £27 a year subscribed by sympathetic Fellows of the Royal Horticultural Society. Markham wrote bitterly:

> It is unnecessary that I should give further expression to the indignation I feel at the injustice with which those have been treated who have done an inestimable service to mankind. If the people of England, and still more, the people of India, are contented that this should be the requital for such service, there is nothing more to be said.[2]

---

[1] The Wardian case — a kind of miniature portable greenhouse, almost hermetically sealed — was invented by Nathaniel Ward in the 1830s and immediately proved invaluable for the transport of plants over long distances.

[2] Clements Markham, *Peruvian Bark*, John Murray, 1880; p. 281.

Quinine was first produced synthetically in 1944—a considerable technical achievement but one of no great commercial value. Drugs largely replaced quinine during the Second World War; but in the 1960s certain strains of malarial parasites became resistent to synthetic quinine and there has been some return to the natural article.

*   *   *

In the year 1755, José Manuel, King of Portugal, sent several pairs of his boots to Brazil to be waterproofed by the application of a remarkable material called 'caoutchouc' (rubber),[1] and four years later he was presented by the government of Pará with a suit of rubber clothes. A whole century was to pass before Kew began to play its important role in the dissemination of rubber trees in India and Malaysia.

Though trees yielding latex of a sort are found in tropical Asia (for example, the ubiquitous house plant, *Ficus elastica*) and Africa, as well as in Central America and Brazil, it would appear that Columbus was the first to mention the 'white milk' oozing from the bark of certain trees as they were being felled by his men in Haiti in 1493. Thirty years later some Spaniards observed natives playing with a ball made of a black substance derived from this latex, and in 1615 a Spanish chronicler of the New World noted that such balls, 'though hard and heavy to the hand, bounded and flew like footballs without there being any need to inflate them. . . . The ball could be struck every time it bounced—which it would do several times, so that it looked as if it were alive. . .' Thus humbly begins the story of a substance that was one day to transform all our lives.

It was La Condamine, mentioned already in connection with quinine, who brought the first specimens of caoutchouc to Europe, and Joseph Priestley[2] who first observed its use as an eraser of pencil-marks. As such it scored a commercial success, with the result that artists dubbed it '(India)-rubber'[3] — *West* Indies, of course—thus giving it for all time a name derived from the most trivial of its innumerable services to mankind.

In 1791 an Englishman named Samuel Peal was granted a patent for his method of rendering 'perfectly waterproof all kinds of leather, cotton, linen, and woollen clothes, etc.' by means of an infusion of rubber. Charles Macintosh (1766–1843) followed—but he had problems: the first macintoshes[4] became stiff as iron in winter and melted in summer, while

---

[1] *cao o'chu*, 'weeping tree'. The natives had a simpler way of going dry-shod: they poured the latex over their feet.
[2] *Familiar Introduction to the Theory and Practice of Perspective*, 1770.
[3] 'Caoutchouc . . . popularly called rubber, and lead-eater.' (Howard, *New Royal Encyclopaedia*, 1788–89.)
[4] I prefer this spelling, which is allowed by the *O.E.D.*

*Tapping a Rubber Tree,
British Malaya, 1925*

ladies wearing the new elastic suspenders were recommended to keep well away from fires. Then the American, Charles Goodyear, discovered 'vulcanisation' (heating rubber with sulphur), and all was set for the great rubber boom to begin.

Meanwhile the survival in relatively accessible parts of the Amazon forests of *Hevea brasiliensis*, source of the best rubber, was being threatened; in any case, rubber was soon destined to join tea, coffee, tobacco, cotton, wheat, and wool as an essential 'universal product' that could not be produced in sufficient quantities without cultivation on a large scale. As with cinchona, it was once again the English who came to the rescue.

The first attempts to germinate seeds at Kew for the despatch of young rubber plants to India were far from successful; for little was as yet understood about the way of packing them for long journeys, and of a consignment of two thousand sent to Joseph Hooker in 1873 by a man named Farris only twelve germinated. Hooker next thought of (Sir) Henry Wickham, a young botanist and explorer who had already published a lively travelogue on his experiences in Brazil, where he had been trading in rubber and studying the trees in the wild. Wickham's first consignment also failed, but in 1876 his luck changed dramatically.

He was on the Tapajos Plateau, miles from anywhere, when news reached him that the *Amazonas*, the very first steamship of Inman's 'Liverpool to the Alto-Amazon direct' service, had arrived at Santarem, a small trading station some five hundred miles from the coastal port of Pará (now Belém). Almost immediately came further news: the *Amazonas* had been abandoned by the supercargoes, and her unhappy Captain left with an empty ship on his hands for the return voyage to Liverpool. Wickham now did a very brave thing—some people might have called it foolhardy: though without authority and without money, he chartered the ship on behalf of the Government of India and hurried to an arranged rendezvous with the Captain at the junction of the Amazon and the Tapajos, near Santarem.

Here he was in the jungle, with an impatient captain waiting at port on an empty steamship. Jumping into an Indian canoe, he paddled up the Tapajos, a dangerous trip, particularly in that season, and struck back into the woods where he knew the full-grown *Hevea* trees to be. . . . Accompanied by Indians he daily went through the forests and packed pannier baskets with loads of seed. It was a delicate operation, for the seed is rich in a heavy oil that quickly becomes rancid, a condition that destroys the power of germination. With remarkable astuteness he did what no other had done—packed the seed to avoid decay.[1]

But the most critical moment of all was still to come: clearance of the Customs at Pará. 'It was perfectly certain in my mind,' wrote Wickham, 'that if the authorities guessed the purpose of what I had on board, we should be detained under the plea of instructions from the Central Government at Rio, if not interdicted altogether'—and even delay would have been disastrous. However, his luck still held. The British Consul at Pará was an old friend, with whose aid he was able to persuade the Customs officials that he was the bearer of 'exceedingly delicate botanical specimens specially designed for delivery to Her Britannic Majesty's own Royal Gardens at Kew', and clearance was immediately accorded.

[1] William C. Geer, *The Reign of Rubber*, Allen & Unwin, 1922 —*q.v.* for his treatment of the seed.

In June the *Amazonas* berthed at Liverpool, where a special train bore the traveller and his precious cargo to London. The 70,000 seeds were immediately sown at Kew, and within a fortnight 2,397 of them had germinated—disappointingly few, but in the event adequate for the despatch of enough young plants in Wardian cases to Ceylon to start an industry which was soon to spread throughout a large part of the East Indies. Wickham did not accompany his plants to Ceylon, and according to H. N. Ridley[1] took no further interest in rubber; his knighthood, not conferred until 1920, seems a somewhat belated recognition of his great services.

Soon after Wickham's return to England, Robert Cross, who had been sent to collect plants of another rubber-bearing tree, *Castilloa*, also came home with seedlings. Geer alleges that these 'never thrived'; but Markham mentions 134 of Cross's plants 'in a flourishing condition at Kew Gardens' which were subsequently forwarded to India. There may have been some rivalry involved, and—as so often—it is hard now to discover the truth.

Synthetic rubber, which dates from the beginning of the present century, was used in Germany in the 1930s and in America in the Second World War because of Japanese aggression in the Pacific. Today the use of synthetic rubber exceeds that of the natural product.

---

[1] 'Evolution of the Rubber Industry', *Proceedings of the Institution of the Rubber Industry*, vol. 2, No. 4, 1955. Ridley, whose active life was cut short in 1956 at the age of 101, played an important part in the establishment of rubber in Malaysia.

19

Cambridge Cottage

THE WOOD Museum is now housed in Cambridge Cottage, the last addition made to the Gardens. This homely Georgian building—one longs to live in it—originally comprised several small houses, two of which had been in their day the *pied-à-terre* of Lord Bute when at Kew. The entrance to the Cottage was formerly under the *porte-cochère* on the south side of Kew Green, almost opposite Kew Church; but today the museum is entered from the Gardens, through two gates[1] in the boundary wall of what was originally the private garden of the Cottage.

For the last ten years of his long life, Cambridge Cottage was the home of Adolphus, Duke of Cambridge, Queen Victoria's uncle and Queen Mary's grandfather. In old age Adolphus, eccentric and by then very deaf, made things difficult for the curate of Kew Church, the front pew of which the Duke occupied regularly on Sunday mornings. 'Let us pray!' said the curate; 'By all means,' replied Adolphus, amiably and all too audibly. When the sixth commandment, 'Thou shalt do no murder' was read, the Duke observed with evident self-satisfaction, 'I don't. I leave that to my brother Ernest'; and when, one very dry summer, the curate prayed for rain, the voice of the familiar commentator rang out, 'Amen!—but you won't get it till the wind changes.' The curate, no longer able to bear the strain, eventually resigned.

After the Duke's death in 1850, Cambridge Cottage continued to be occupied by his widow and their family, and in later life Queen Mary recalled the penance of compulsory visits made as a child to the formidable and ailing old Duchess, her 'stingy' teas of buns and rusks, and her insistence on her grandchildren singing *Les Trois Anges* and *God Save the Queen* to relieve her boredom.

The Dowager Duchess and her younger daughter, Princess Mary Adelaide—'the stout parties from Kew', as Lord Clarendon irreverently dubbed them—were a considerable nuisance to William Hooker in the middle years of the last century.

In 1842, Hooker had obtained the Queen's permission to extend the

---

[1] If gossip is to be believed, Bute must have passed through one of these to keep his trysts with Augusta (see p. 24).

Cambridge Cottage. Watercolour drawing by Henry Walter, c. 1850. Kew Church in the background on the right of the drawing

Gardens; but there was a 'nice piece of water', described by the Duchess as her 'fishing ground', that he wanted to include, and she raised every possible objection. 'I am sure it is a happy thing for the Garden,' Hooker wrote to his father-in-law, Dawson Turner, 'that the *Queen* does not take an interest in Kew, like the Duchess of Cambridge!' Unluckily for Hooker, the following year the King of Hanover spent several months at Kew and joined energetically in the fray. He 'swore with horrid imprecations,' Hooker told Dawson Turner, 'that I should *not* carry the contemplated alterations into effect', and rushed off to London to enlist the support of Lord Lincoln, the Commissioner of Woods and Forests.

These were dangerous adversaries, well placed to wreck Hooker's schemes. But the King returned to Hanover, and the Duchess presumably found other and more important battles to fight. By comparison, Princess Mary was no more than a perpetual pest: a gadfly (if one can apply the word to a girl so monumentally built). One of the Kew gardeners, Thomas Meehan, described her in 1879 as 'a rollicking, good-natured girl of fourteen, to whom the spirit of mischievous fun came as a second nature'. He enjoyed seeing her around; but for at least a decade she made the life of poor 'Hookey', as she called him, a misery. At first, and perhaps not inappropriately, the Princess had been infatuated with the royal cows, among which she had her 'special pets'; but, unfortunately, when she was about twenty she transferred her attentions to horticulture. Since there was no enthusiasm on the part of any suitable prince to propose to her (she was to be thirty-three before the miracle happened), she had all the time in the world to indulge her new hobby, and all the material for it on her very doorstep.

*Sir William Hooker, Princess Mary Adelaide, Miss Ella Taylor and George Craig in
Kew Gardens. Pencil drawing by Ella Taylor, the Princess's lady-in-waiting,
October 1858*

'The Gardens at Kew were a source of endless pleasure to Princess
Mary,' wrote C. K. Cooke[1], 'and she made *great friends* with the Director,
Sir William Hooker, who taught her the first principles of gardening' (the
italics are mine). But Cooke, though discreet always, allows his readers a
glimpse of the truth. Hooker hated his flowers being picked, but the Princess
generally managed to wheedle some out of him:

> On one occasion, some rare calceolarias, of which Sir William was
> specially proud, had attracted her attention. She obtained permission to
> gather some, and ran off by herself to the hot-house. Presently she
> reappeared with her arms full of the beautiful blossoms, and with much
> pride showed her spoils to Sir William, whose consternation was great
> when he realised that instead of the few calceolarias he had intended her
> to take, she had picked nearly all his precious flowers!

No doubt Hooker sometimes gave her flowers simply to get rid of her. She
noted in her diary for 21 April 1853: 'After my music lesson . . . I took a walk
in the Gardens, Hookey raining camellias upon me!' But the Princess
became an even greater nuisance when she took up garden planning, her

[1] *A Memoir of Her Royal Highness Princess Mary Adelaide, Duchess of Teck* . . . 2 vols., John
Murray, 1900.

chief pleasure being the designing of innumerable formal beds of hideous and complicated shapes—something that Hooker particularly disliked. On 29 September 1860, she wrote:

> Sir William has in a measure made over the arrangement and colouring of the flower-beds to me, so that I have plenty to do—and the Scotch flower-gardener,[1] a nice, intelligent man, and I, work together in grand style. I *invent* and he draws out the plans and carries them out. I cannot tell you the amusement it is to me!... I have just now a good many improvements on hand for next year...

It is never easy to snub a Princess. But patience has its limits, and it is with pleasure that we read on 1 March 1861 of Hookey putting his foot down: 'After [Major Dormer's] visit we drove down to Kew, where I worked away in the Gardens, and was getting on capitally till Hookey came and spoilt all my arrangements'. A last quotation from the diaries must suffice:

> *3 October 1862.* Gave my attention to the locket and necklace bed, and to a chain of beds to be introduced at the back of the palm-house . . . Hunted out old Hookey from his den, and dragged him round the shrubberies, but all to no purpose. Home in a rage with the old piece of obstinacy!

One day little Charley Hooker, having climbed a tree in the Gardens, succeeded in hitting the Princess with his pea-shooter, thus reminding his grandfather of one of the uses to which a humble vegetable could be put. If the tree can still be identified, surely it deserves a commemorative plaque!

On 6 March 1866, the handsome but penniless young Prince Teck arrived in England from Vienna. He met the Princess the next day at St James's Palace, and exactly a month later, to the astonishment of everyone, he proposed to her in the Rhododendron Walk at Kew and was accepted. She was thirty-three, he four years younger, and the Dowager Duchess must have breathed a royal sigh of relief at having at long last succeeded in marrying off her amiable but elephantine daughter. No doubt Sir William, receiving the news in his 'den' at Kew, was hardly less delighted.

After the marriage service in Kew Church, the royal party and their more distinguished guests breakfasted in the library at Cambridge Cottage. Among the former was the Queen, so rarely to be seen by her people since her widowhood; among the latter the Bishop of Winchester, who had assisted the Archbishop of Canterbury at the service. And the visitor to the Wood Museum, as he wanders among those acres of timber stacked in that very room, may perhaps care to speculate just what social solecism or disaster it was that caused the Queen subsequently to write to one of her

---

[1] Craig, who later went off his head.

relations in Germany, 'The Fracas with the China caused by the Bp. of Winchester was *considerable. Such* an absurd thing to happen!' The Queen, it may be remembered, once said, 'We do not like bishops'.

Princess Mary's elder brother George, second Duke of Cambridge,[1] was also to become a nuisance in the Gardens. It had always been accepted that members of the royal family technically retained the privilege of riding and driving sensibly in the Pleasure Grounds; but after these had been landscaped and planted, the more reasonable Princes took great care to avoid causing any damage. Not George, however, who persisted in driving wildly everywhere, smoking in the Houses and ignoring all the regulations clearly posted at every entrance. The circumstances were reported to Thiselton-Dyer, who wrote the Duke a letter so long, so grovelling and so full of circumlocutions that it is surprising that he grasped its meaning. But grasp it he did, and commanded that Dyer be informed of his 'amazement' at the suggestion that damage might have been done, adding that neither Sir William nor Sir Joseph would have written him so impertinent a letter.

For a time he seems to have behaved himself; but five years later there was a fresh crop of outrages, duly reported in a paper called *Modern Society*[2] which must have been the *Private Eye* of its day. The Duke, said the writer, 'is one of those happy personages who are a law unto themselves'. On a recent visit to the Gardens

> George and his party 'did' the plant houses. Thinking, probably, that 'weeds' were the natural companions of plants, he smoked away like a chimney on fire. Up comes a keeper. 'Beg pardon, gentlemen, but I can't allow smoking here; it's against the rules.' Our fierce turkey-cock gobbled and spluttered out, 'I am the Duke of Cambridge'. 'Cambridge or Oxford, out you go, and your pipe first', should have been the answer of the keeper. But in this case, we regret to say that 'the keepers of the house trembled', and let the party pollute the plant house at their pleasure.
>
> It seems that this was not old George's only attempt at hectoring and breaking the law. For we are informed that two or three days ago he drove a carriage and pair through the same gardens. . . . Yet he had previously been reported for a similar offence, and had promised not to do it again. . .

The Duke, after further lengthy correspondence with Dyer, eventually came to heel. 'Almost every crowned head in Europe,' we are informed, 'has at some time or another visited the Gardens, and in every case on foot.' Alone the Sultan of Turkey 'tried it on' but was outmanoeuvred. Even lame old Queen Isabella of Spain, when invited by Dyer to remain in her carriage, insisted on alighting at the entrance and hiring a common bath-chair.

---

[1] Second and last: he had made a morganatic marriage with an actress, Louisa Fairbrother (Mrs FitzGeorge).
[2] 11 July 1891.

After the death of the Duke in 1904, King Edward VII, to the great annoyance of his daughter-in-law, the Princess of Wales, presented the Cottage and its grounds to the nation. The Duke, who once announced that 'all change is for the worse', would have been horrified could he have known that his old home would one day be converted into a public museum; he might, however, have found some consolation in the fact that since its opening in 1910 no attempt has been made to modernise the manner in which its contents are displayed.

The first room as you enter contains one or two objects calculated to stir the imagination. I can remember from my childhood the great slice of a giant redwood (though then, I think, housed in the Orangery) showing the 1,335 annual or growth rings which establish that it started life about the same time as the Prophet Mahomet. But the contents of the principal room of the Museum, however stimulating they may be to the expert, fail to excite the general public. They may well be, as the 1951 guidebook assures us, 'a rare feast to the eyes of a timber enthusiast', who can here 'study the colour and texture of the wood, the ripple and curl of the grain, and compare one kind with another to his heart's content'; but to many people they appear no more than a kind of palisade of all-too-similar planks.

The garden is very pleasant: the sort of garden that one would like to have. But the remarkable sundial in it which the 1975 *Souvenir Guide* still urges us to admire was, I gather, removed many years ago. Where is it now?

20

The Conservatory Range

CLOSE TO the immense ginkgo planted about 1760[1] in Augusta's Botanic Garden is a cluster of glasshouses comprising the Conservatory, the two principal Ferneries, and the Succulent House; since Kew does not appear to have given it a name I will refer to it as the Conservatory Range. These Houses have a large number of doors, not a few of which are labelled PLEASE USE OTHER ENTRANCE; but perseverance will ultimately be rewarded by admission. The two Ferneries—the Tropical and the Temperate—are in the north-west part of the complex; both have been recently, and very successfully, 'landscaped' so as to reduce to a minimum the battery of potted plants.

The great fern craze in this country—the pteridomania, as Charles Kingsley called it[2]—was a Victorian phenomenon, though by comparison with the tulipomania in Holland in the seventeenth century it was a very sober affair indeed. The invention of the Wardian Case, and the discovery of the uses to which it could be put in the living-room, started the craze, to which the enthusiasm of pteridologists such as Sir William Hooker and the first John Smith gave momentum and added respectability. The Kew collection of ferns has therefore always been an important one.

Ferns are ancient plants—dating from an age of such innocence that they never learned how to flower—and for many people they seem as monochrome and unexciting today as do those black-and-white engravings also much admired a century ago. But if ferns have no flowers or seeds, then how do they reproduce themselves? The botanists are eager to tell us:

> The fern prothallus [or gametophyte] is a small parenchymatous mass of photosynthetic cells ... It lacks stomata, lignification, vascular bundles, and any differentiation into stem, leaf, or root. On the underside it bears microscopic male and female sex organs, similar to the gametangia of seaweeds but provided with a sterile, protective layer of cells. The male organs, called antheridia, produce larger numbers of sperms (antherozoids of botany) set with many flagella by which they swim in films of

[1] The R.H.S. *Dictionary of Gardening* is much mistaken in saying that the ginkgo was not introduced into this country until 1874.
[2] *Glaucus*, 1855, and see *The Victorian Fern Craze* by David Elliston Allen, Hutchinson, 1969.

Elk's Horn Fern
*(*Platycerium grande*)*

water between the prothallus and the soil to the female organs, which are
called archegonia. . . .[1]

And so on. I now understand why I did not become a botanist.

On entering the Tropical Fern House—hot and sweaty as Colombo, so
that spectacles instantly cloud over—the visitor may be tempted to echo the
lament (was it Wilde's?), 'Nature is badly lighted and too green'. But he
soon begins to have green thoughts in this lush green shade, and to
appreciate that Nature was rarely so daedal as when she was fern-making.
But she could also be grandiose. A spectacular fern here is the *Angiopteris*—
a member of a genus which some botanists believe to have a hundred and
twenty species, others only one. It rather suggests a mammoth version of the
'Palm Court' palm, fully-spread fronds resembling the branches of a tree.
But the most remarkable feature of this giant is the opening frond, which
looks like the coiled trunk of a baby elephant. Botanists call this 'fiddlehead'
way of unfolding, which most ferns indulge in, 'circinate vernation'.

Even more spectacular is *Platycerium grande*—the stag's horn or elk's
horn fern. This vegetable monster, grown pendant or lodged in a stout piece

[1] E. J. H. Corner, *The Life of Plants*, Weidenfeld and Nicolson, 1964, pp. 164–65.

of wood, thrusts its infertile fronds upwards, while huge fertile antlers loll downwards. So ferocious does it look that one is thankful to realise that it is immobile.[1] These are the giants; but there is marvellous delicacy and infinite variety to be found in humble species such as the maidenhair fern. Ronald King writes well and fully about them in *The World of Kew*.

Until quite recently the temperamental filmy ferns were also to be found in the Conservatory Range, but such is their sensitivity to draughts that they were not allowed to receive visitors. Now they have been accorded a little 'double-skin' house of their own, tucked away behind the Orangery and approached by a gloomy shrubbery path such as elsewhere in the Gardens tends to lead to a lavatory. I must confess that I am not really much of a pteridophilist; some time passed, therefore, before I got round to calling on them in their new home. Finally, however, curiosity overcame me; but it seems to overcome few others, and the only human being I encountered in the Filmy Fern House was an elderly gentleman failing to find what I think he was in search of.[2]

Why do filmy ferns have to be so cosseted? I gather that they have, like the haemophiliac, as it were a skin too few: leaves for the most part only one cell thick, which demand what in a hospital would be called an 'intensive care unit'. You enter the building to find yourself inside a greenhouse yet also *outside* one, for the ferns are further boxed in behind sheets of glass where they can be maintained in total shade and controlled low temperatures, and by frequent spraying provided with the high humidity they need. They come chiefly from New Zealand, America and Europe — even from Ireland — where they batten on the spray of obliging waterfalls. As in the Wood Museum, you have to be something of a specialist to find much entertainment here.

'Who loves a garden loves a greenhouse too', wrote William Cowper. I do not see that this necessarily follows: as well write, 'Who loves a deer-park also loves a zoo'. However, what cannot be in any doubt is that of all the Houses at Kew in which plants are 'cabin'd, cribb'd, confin'd', the Conservatory is by far the most popular; for it is the botanists' concession to the mere horticulturist, its contents being for the most part chosen so as to provide a perpetual brave show of colour and rich harvest of scent. Quite

---

[1] The mere names of some ferns — for example, *Elaphoglossum, Helminthostachys* or *Didymochlaena* — are frightening enough, and the editor of a horticultural journal is said to have kept tramps away by a notice reading BEWARE OF THE SCOLOPENDRIUMS (hart's-tongue ferns).

[2] But it would appear that sometimes the building is more frequented, for a member of the Kew staff informs me that he was once approached by a whole bevy of schoolgirls asking the way to the 'Filthy Fern House'.

vulgar plants are brought here, just as their first buds begin to open, from reserve greenhouses hidden from public view, and returned to store as soon as they are over. In short, the Conservatory is like the smartest Mayfair florist's—except that there are no cut flowers and that nothing is for sale.

The Conservatory is relatively small and chiefly devoted to potted plants. Now there is at the Royal Horticultural Society's Gardens at Wisley a superb new 'Display House'—ten thousand square feet of it, which is twice the size of Kew's Conservatory. The main section (the temperate) has a pool and is beautifully landscaped, while round the edge of the building are ledges with pot-plants. The general impression is of a glorious garden such as one might expect to find in, say, Madeira, not of an expensive flowershop; and many of the plants are of more than mere horticultural interest. How I wish that Kew had something similar! Its vast Temperate House is a jungle under glass rather than an indoor garden, with flowers too few and far too far between.

There are four greenhouses at Kew that contain succulents—those fleshy plants which, camel-like, store up moisture against a non-rainy day. Three of these Houses are in the T-Range,[1] the fourth (No. 5) in the Conservatory Range.

House No. 5, which is long and narrow, was rebuilt in 1958 and contains at least one spectacular inmate: *Agave americana*. I know that it is more fashionable today to sing the praises of almost invisible rock-plants, but I find this Mexican giant, which has taken so kindly to the shores of the Mediterranean, strangely exciting: as majestic as its animal equivalent, the giraffe. Agaves are what is called 'monocarpic'; that is to say, they take many years—sometimes more than seventy—to flower, and then, as if exhausted by so prolonged and tedious a preparation, pack up and die. One can hardly blame them.

Agaves occupy so much space that the House contains only three or four of them at any given time, each slowly building up strength for its brief weeks of glory; you have, therefore, to be lucky to catch one of them in flower. And in August 1976 I was lucky, for there was a magnificent specimen whose stem had been skilfully steered through a roof-light so that it could thrust its great golden candelabrum high into the blue world outside. An unforgettable spectacle! It must have been nearly thirty feet tall.

The American agave has been grown in English conservatories for more than three hundred years, and a Hoxton gardener named John Cowell, a great lover of succulents, describes his tribulations when at long last his 72-year-old twenty-footer finally flowered in 1729.[2] A French correspondent

---

[1] See chapter 23.
[2] *The Curious and Profitable Gardener*, 1730.

had informed him that the opening of his own flower 'faisait un grand bruit' ('created a great stir'); but Cowell misunderstood him, and the crowds which flocked to Hoxton awaited in vain the expected 'big bang'. Among the spectators were three men 'habited like Gentlemen' who suddenly and savagely attacked the plant, and Cowell's servant when he tried to protect it. Cowell rushed to his aid, was kicked on the head, pulled by the legs, and so badly wounded in the neck with a sword-thrust that he was in hospital for many weeks. Within a year, Cowell and his agave were both dead: the latter as nature had ordained, the former either from his wounds or from his disappointment at thus losing 'the fairest Prospect of possessing an easy Fortune for my Life'. Possibly he had been under the misapprehension that his agave, having once acquired the knack of flowering, would repeat its profitable performance annually.

Agave americana. *Drawn and engraved by William Daniel, 1807*

'Agave' (Greek *agauos*) means 'illustrious', 'noble'. But in classical mythology Agave was an unpleasant Queen Mother who in a Bacchic frenzy mistook her son Pentheus for a wild beast and tore him to pieces. As one looks at the agave's vicious, saw-like leaves, the latter derivation seems equally reasonable.

Should the agave not be flowering, what else is there to see in House 5? There are species of *Echinopsis, Echinocactus, Trichocereus* . . . consult Turrill for the rest; what happens to be performing depends on the season, and in any case plants are constantly being added or subtracted. At the time the agave was flowering, a tree called *Uncarina grandidieri*, a member of the Pedaliaceae, with masses of showy yellow blossoms, was the only other eye-catching exhibit.

*   *   *

This is perhaps a convenient place to mention the Alpine House and the Rock Garden, though they are in fact several hundred yards from the Conservatory Range. Indeed, the Alpine House is so tucked away behind the (now closed) Reference Museum that the hurried visitor may easily miss it. This would be a pity; for though it is a good deal smaller than its counterpart at Wisley it is no less choice and well kept. I understand that a fine new Alpine House, incorporating refinements such as 'chilling pipes' which will make it possible to grow certain very awkward customers, is to be opened in the near future.

Between the Alpine House and the T-Range lies the Rock Garden, dating in its present form from the days of Joseph Hooker (1882). One of its predecessors was made of lava fragments brought back from Iceland as ship's ballast by Joseph Banks in 1772; it served principally for mosses.[1] The current one was built of Westmorland limestone, but this has now been replaced by the more porous Sussex sandstone. Wisley is lucky with its Rock Garden, which clings to the side of a steepish hill provided by nature; in pancake-flat Kew the ground had to be excavated 'in order to give an illusion of height, the main path representing the river in an alpine valley'. It does not really succeed; though Kew's plants are no less interesting than Wisley's, the overall effect is flat indeed.

[1] This lava was also used for a similar purpose in the Apothecaries' Garden at Chelsea.

21

Joseph Hooker

S IR W ILLIAM and Lady Hooker had two sons and three daughters. The elder boy, William Dawson Hooker ('Willie'), a year older and a good deal less precocious than his brother Joseph, qualified as a doctor and at the age of twenty-three made a runaway marriage disapproved of by both families. Almost immediately after the wedding he was found to be consumptive and in due course sent—without his young wife, who had meanwhile become pregnant—to Jamaica for the sake of the climate. On 11 October 1839, in his first letter home, he told his father that he was looking forward to studying tropical diseases, particularly yellow fever; within three months he had died of it. The following year William's youngest daughter, Mary Harriet, had also died—of consumption; she was only fifteen. These two personal tragedies clouded William's early months at Kew.

But Joseph had gone from strength to strength. He, too, had taken a medical degree at Glasgow, and in 1839 joined an expedition to the Antarctic that kept him abroad for more than four years. He sailed, as assistant surgeon and unofficial botanist, under Captain James Ross in the 378-ton *Erebus*, which was accompanied by the slightly smaller *Terror*, both fitted out for magnetic and geographical discovery. One successfully-accomplished objective of the voyage was the location of the south magnetic pole, Ross and his uncle having already found its northern counterpart in 1831.[1] The three southern winters were spent in Tasmania, New Zealand and the Falkland Islands, where Joseph was able to accumulate the material for his *The Botany of the Antarctic Voyage of H.M. Discovery Ships Erebus and Terror . . .* This comprises three separate works, each in two quarto volumes: *Flora Antarctica* (1847), *Flora Novae-Zelandiae* (1853–55) and *Flora Tasmaniae* (1855–59)—the whole illustrated with more than five hundred hand-coloured plates, many of them from drawings by the author lithographed by Fitch.

The story of this adventurous journey is told by Ross in his *A Voyage of Discovery . . .* (1847) for which Joseph provided the botanical notes; Mea Allan[2] gives an excellent summary of it. Joseph never lost his interest in

---

[1] This expedition was financed by Felix Booth, the famous distiller. Its discovery earned him a baronetcy and some names on the map such as the delightful 'continent of Boothia Felix', which sounds like the paradise of gin-drinkers.

[2] *Op. cit.*, pp. 112–37.

Antarctic exploration, and as a nonagenarian eagerly followed the early stages of Captain Scott's last and ill-fated expedition in 1910.

After his return, Joseph was variously and endlessly occupied. For a time he was assistant to Robert Graham, the aged Professor of Botany in Edinburgh; but in spite of a hundred dazzling testimonials he failed, thanks to local intrigue, to be appointed Graham's successor on his death in 1845. For the next two years he was botanist to the Geological Survey of Great Britain, at the same time helping his father in many ways. But the preparation for the press of the scientific results of his voyage was ever uppermost in his mind.

While in Tierra del Fuego he had observed many plants—the common dandelion, for example—that were also natives of the British Isles. This turned his thoughts to the problem of plant distribution in general, a matter he was to discuss later in the important introductory essay to *Flora Tasmaniae*. His friend Darwin was deeply impressed by his findings; 'I know,' he exclaimed, 'I shall live to see you the first authority in Europe on that grand subject, that almost keystone of the laws of creation, Geographical Distribution.' Indeed, Joseph's work was of immense value to the author of *The Origin of Species*, who shortly before its publication in 1859 wrote to him, 'Believe that I never forget even for a minute how much assistance I have received from you'.

Joseph had been able to send back plants, especially from Tierra del Fuego, in Wardian cases, and Lady Hooker mentions in a letter to her father that '2 new kinds of Beech and the Winter's Bark Tree (of the latter only one specimen was in the Kingdom before) are growing beautifully'. But since the death of Banks in 1820, only one collector had been sent abroad by Kew: a certain George Barclay, who had gone to South America and the Pacific islands in 1836. Sir William Hooker, soon after his appointment to Kew, persuaded the Duke of Northumberland and Lord Derby to join forces with him to finance two expeditions: William Purdie, a Kew gardener, was sent to tropical America in 1842, and Joseph Burke a year later to north-west America.

Other collectors followed during the next twenty years, the last officially sponsored by Kew being the unhappy Richard Oldham, sent to Japan in 1861. Sir William, says Alice Coats, 'seems to have treated [Oldham] with quite unmerited severity. Inexperienced, underpaid, and, as it turned out, not constitutionally robust, he was pitchforked into the Orient at the age of twenty-three, and died there three years later.' Oldham admitted that 'through inexperience and ignorance' he had failed to advise Sir William by the first mail of 'certain Bills which I drew'; but he apologised abjectly, and was at a loss to understand the 'harsh and unfavourable tone' of Sir William's reply in which he 'makes no allowances for the troubles I have had all along to encounter'. Oldham, who was to send '13,000 excellently prepared plant specimens, including about ninety new species' to Kew, did not deserve such unkindness.

But the greatest collector sent out by Kew in William Hooker's time was beyond question his son Joseph. Having familiarised himself with the flora of the Antarctic, Joseph very naturally wanted to be able to compare it with that of a tropical country. India was his choice; yet on the advice of two friends he decided to make a particular study of Sikkim, in the eastern Himalaya—territory at that time almost unknown to Westerners, but with a climate for the most part anything but tropical. The Treasury rather unexpectedly came up on Kew's behalf with the offer of a salary of £400 a year for two years, and in November 1847, after taking sad leave of his young fiancée Frances Henslow, daughter of the botanist the Rev. John Henslow, Joseph sailed for India in the suite of Lord Dalhousie, the newly-appointed Governor-General. In April 1848, after spending three months principally in the plain of the Ganges, Joseph reached Darjeeling, that delightful former summer station of the British Raj which lies only a few miles to the south of the borders of Sikkim.

Sikkim is a tiny, roughly rectangular state wedged between Tibet on the north, Nepal on the west, Bhutan on the east and India (Bengal) on the south; it is roughly the size of Lincolnshire, to which in all other respects it bears little resemblance. It contains what was at that time believed to be the highest mountain in the world—Kanchenjunga (28,146 ft.)—and a remarkably rich and varied flora ranging from sub-tropical through temperate to glacial: orchids in endless profusion; primulas, bamboos and ferns and, above all, rhododendrons of a splendour hitherto undreamed of, and only to be surpassed when the treasures of China became known.

The difficulty of describing, in such a way as either to enlighten or to entertain the general reader, long and complicated journeys through a country of which he presumably has no previous knowledge and which he has no intention of visiting, is one that confronts every travel writer. It helps such a reader little to be told that Joseph proceeded 'from Lachung through Yeumtong to Momay' or that, on reaching 'the Tamur river, a tributary of the Arun, he turned upstream and went north to Chingtam and Mywa Guola' (Alice Coats). True, Miss Coats reproduces Joseph's own elaborate relief map[1] of Sikkim; but on this scale most of the names on it are illegible and the reader who really feels the need to follow each stage of the journey would have been better served by a simple one clearly marking the route. For those who are not prepared to wade through the two stout volumes of Joseph's own *Himalayan Journals* I recommend Mea Allan's book (though it, too, is rather name-ridden and has an unhelpful map), or the eminently

---

[1] A map of the greatest importance, which was published by the Survey of India.

Magnolia campbellii. *Hand-coloured lithograph by Walter Fitch after a field sketch by Joseph Hooker*

readable if brief account in Madeleine Bingham's slim little *The Making of Kew*—from which, however, one learns with surprise that Joseph, who was 'nothing if not exact', measured '300 inches or 65 feet of rain' in the hills of Assam.

Sikkim was, in theory, pro-British, her Rajah having been re-instated by our intervention after he had been driven from his throne by the Nepalese.

But that was thirty years back, and the ancient princeling was now a mere puppet in the hands of his powerful, violently anti-European and utterly unscrupulous Dewan (Prime Minister)—a Tibetan by birth and, according to Joseph, 'unsurpassed for insolence and arrogance'. Meanwhile (Sir) Jung Bahadur, virtual ruler of neighbouring Nepal since 1846, was strongly pro-British. So Joseph, having been refused a permit to enter Sikkim from Darjeeling, began his two years of Himalayan exploration by going to eastern Nepal, from where he hoped to sneak unobserved across the border into Sikkim.

Various Englishmen befriended Joseph—among them Dr Archibald Campbell, the British political agent responsible for maintaining relations with the Rajah of Sikkim. Joseph had left Darjeeling at the end of October 1848, and after successfully crossing into Sikkim joined forces with Campbell. In December they were accorded an audience by the Rajah, who had presumably come to accept the *fait accompli* of Joseph's unauthorised presence in his country; the Dewan, crafty as ever, was biding his time. Joseph returned alone to Darjeeling in January, from where he despatched a consignment of sixty loads of plants and geological specimens to Calcutta for shipment to England. His second expedition began in the following May and lasted for seven months. During it he crossed briefly into Tibet, ascended a frontier peak to a height of 19,300 feet—at that time the greatest altitude ever attained by man—and had an unpleasant adventure of the kind that every armchair reader enjoys experiencing vicariously.

It occurred on 7 November 1849, in a stone hovel in Sikkim not far from the Tibetan border where Joseph and Campbell were awaiting a summons to appear before the Rajah—a summons perpetually postponed by the machinations of his Dewan. 'The night was very cold,' wrote Joseph; 'the people crowded into the hut where Campbell and I were waiting. He had scarcely left when I heard him call loudly: "Hooker! Hooker!! the savages are murdering me!"' Joseph tried to go to his assistance, but was seized and held by eight soldiers.

Campbell, says Mea Allan, 'was kicked and tortured, but these were the least of his worries, for at Darjeeling his wife was expecting a baby'. Joseph was unhurt; but the two men were held prisoners for six weeks and made as uncomfortable as possible. However, the Dewan had badly miscalculated. He had hoped to use his hostages to obtain various concessions from the British; instead, the news of a punitive force rushed to Darjeeling scared the Rajah into ordering his minister to free the two prisoners and then sacking him. The incident provided the welcome pretext for our annexation of a desirable slice of Sikkim. These were the good old days of the British Raj.

Joseph had been sending home drawings and descriptions of his rhododendrons, which his father immediately set about preparing for publication in his absence. Work went ahead so rapidly that the first

Joseph Hooker in the Himalaya.
After an oil painting by F. Stone

fascicule—a folio with text by Sir William and ten superb hand-coloured lithographs by Fitch after Joseph's field sketches—reached Darjeeling at the beginning of 1850. 'All the Indian world,' wrote the young man proudly, 'is in love with my Rhododendron book.' Descriptions and plates of twenty further rhododendrons followed in due course, and the equally splendid *Illustrations to Himalayan Plants* was published in 1855.

Finally came an extensive journey through Assam, which produced fewer novelties since it had already been visited by other botanists. Seven men's loads of *Vanda caerulea* were despatched to England, where this lovely blue orchid had become a status symbol for rich plantsmen; indeed, so extensive was the pillaging that the local authorities were soon obliged to prohibit the plant's export to prevent its total extermination. It would seem that in those days the word 'conservation' was not in the vocabulary of collectors. To make matters worse, of Joseph's huge consignment hardly a plant survived the journey. He himself reached Kew on 26 March 1851, having been away for more than three years, and in July was married to his patiently-waiting Frances.

Joseph had endured many hardships and dangers, especially of course during his time in the Himalaya. We read of him at 13,000 feet, reaching up to pluck with frozen fingers the seeds of a very desirable rhododendron; of his monotonous, starvation diet for days, even weeks on end; of his sufferings from mountain sickness, cold, torrential rains and a variety of other torments:

> In the densely wooded Terai, the only safe way of botanising is by pushing through the jungle on elephants; an uncomfortable method, for the quantities of ants and insects which drop from the foliage above, and from the risk of disturbing the pendulous bees' and ants' nests . . . If your shins were as bruised as mine tearing through the interminable Rhododendron scrub at 10,000 to 13,000 feet you would be as sick of these glories as I am . . . I think the leeches are worst; my legs are, I assure you, daily clotted with blood, and I pull my stockings off quite full of leeches; they get into the hair and all over the body . . .

But when he remembered the rich harvest of plants and seeds he had garnered—and, hardly less important, his topographical survey of Sikkim—he knew it had all been worthwhile. In particular, he had discovered twenty-eight new species of *Rhododendron*, many of which were to prove hardy in the milder parts of Britain.[1] Rhododendron Dell at Kew— a little winding valley that had been artificially created in 1773 by a company

[1] Seed of the first Himalayan rhododendron to reach Britain, *Rh. arboreum*, had been sent from Nepal in 1818 by Wallich to Kew and Edinburgh. Kew overheated its seedlings and lost them, but Edinburgh was successful.

of the Staffordshire Militia under the direction of Capability Brown—was the recipient of seedlings of his hardier species; it remains to this day a memorial to Joseph, who started a craze for the rhododendron which seems to gain momentum with every passing year. God may forgive me— horticulturists certainly will not—for still loving best the despised old *Rh. ponticum* ('England's worst weed') of many childhood memories, and the little Alpine Roses (*Rhh. ferrugineum* and *hirsutum*) smuggled back in a sponge-bag from Swiss holidays with such high hopes but only to perish in a Surrey garden.

Joseph was never to lose the *wanderlust*. In the autumn of 1860 he went with a friend to the Levant, arriving on 4 October in Damascus where (he told his wife) the Syrians had the previous day massacred five thousand[1] Christians. A visit was paid to the Lebanon cedars, and near Hebron Joseph had the satisfaction of establishing that the famous oak in the garden of the Russian Hospice, in whose shade Abraham was reputed to have pitched his tent, was obviously less than three hundred years old.

While I have Joseph on the move, I will deal with his two other principal botanical excursions in foreign parts. In the spring of 1871 he went to Morocco with John Ball, George Maw, and a young Kew gardener named Crump who blotted his copybook at the start by forgetting to pack the barometers. He went, Joseph told Darwin, 'partly to try to bake out my rheumatism, partly in faint hopes of connecting the Atlantic Flora with the African and (perhaps most of all) to taste the delights of savagery again'. Savagery he certainly found; for the interior of Morocco was at that time largely unexplored, and their journey proved as uncomfortable as even he could have wished. They suffered in due course from filthy lodgings teeming with obnoxious insects; from equally obnoxious interpreters, suspicious and hostile natives, corrupt officials, and importunate snake-charmers; from revolting food, excessive heat, excessive cold, and endless obstructionism and intrigue. One would like to have been a fly on the wall on the occasion when Joseph was 'assailed with extraordinary vehemence by a Negress'.

At Mogador, and with considerable reluctance, they all donned *jellabias* and tried to pass themselves off as natives; but under the *jellabias* their heavy European boots, which they refused to discard, protruded only too conspicuously, while the muslin they tied round their sola topees signally failed to transform these into turbans. They must have looked very odd indeed.

Maw, in his capacity of geologist, had the worst job, for in a primitive

---

[1] An improbable figure. The major massacre, in which 3,000 adult Christians lost their lives, had taken place in July.

country every collector of stones is believed to be prospecting for gold or searching for buried treasure; but the botanists also found some difficulty in convincing the natives of their innocuousness. Joseph thought he was not unduly stretching the truth by putting it about that his Queen had sent her doctors to bring home plants of medicinal value. This theme was embroidered by the interpreter, and (wrote Ball)

> there is no doubt that the current belief among our own followers was that the Sultana of England had heard that there was somewhere in Marocco a plant that would make her live for ever, and that she had sent her own *hakim* to find it for her. When, in the course of our journey, it was seen that our botanical pursuits entailed rather severe labour, the commentary was: 'The Sultana of England is a severe woman, and she has threatened to give them the stick (the bastinado) if they do not find the herb she wants!'

The fruits of this journey—Hooker and Ball's *Journal of a Tour in Marocco and the Great Atlas...*, published in 1878—was in the main the work of Ball, for Joseph, on his return to England, was almost immediately fully occupied with what came to be known as the 'Ayrton Affair'.[1]

Joseph was sixty when in July 1877 he set out on his last trip—to the Rocky Mountains of Colorado and Utah in the company of General (Sir) Richard Strachey (Lytton's father), Professor Asa Gray, and their wives. It proved very exhausting for a man of Joseph's age, for they climbed the 14,500-foot Sierra Blanca and had to sleep rough at thirteen thousand feet. He was not sorry to be back at Kew by October, bringing with him more than a thousand herbarium specimens.

*   *   *

For ten years—from 1855 until Sir William's death in 1865—Joseph had been Assistant to his father. These years saw the publication of Darwin's great and controversial *Origin of Species*, and also of many important works and papers of which Joseph was either the author or the initiator. Among them was his famous monograph on the *Welwitschia*, which appeared in the *Transactions* of the Linnean Society in 1863.[2]

Joseph seems to have developed a 'vegetable love' for this extraordinary, ugly south-west African which was unlike any other plant on earth, and of which he received specimens from Angola from the Austrian botanist Dr Friedrich Welwitsch. This 'giant turnip', 'octopus of the desert' or 'plant coelacanth' really defies non-botanical description; but we may perhaps

[1] See chapter 22.
[2] See also *Botanical Magazine*, Vol. 89, 5368–9 (1863).

'Welwitschia mirabilis' (W. bainesii) *after a sketch by its discoverer. The plant in the middle distance appears to have four leaves; in fact there are normally two, which become tattered as they age. From Kerner von Marilaun's* The Natural History of Plants

visualise it as a sort of circular wooden table 'cracked like a burnt crust of a loaf of bread' and supported on a short, stout, inverted cone from whose base protrude two broad strap-like leaves up to twenty-five feet long, that become tattered and broken. It is believed to live for some hundreds of years, and it certainly looks as though it might. Some fine specimens used to be on show in an annexe to the Orangery, but they have long since vanished from sight.

On succeeding his father in 1865 Joseph found himself inevitably involved in endless administrative duties and also in various battles soon to be described; yet such was the almost superhuman energy of the man that he found time for everything: for presiding at scientific gatherings all over the country; for writing and editing and lecturing and, of course, for the making of innumerable improvements in the Gardens:

> The Pinetum was entirely his creation. The valley near the Flagstaff, known as the Berberis Dell, was brought to its present condition between 1869 and 1872. The Rockery or Alpine Garden was created in 1882. Numerous avenues, grassed drives and gravel paths were opened out or planted during his Directorship, especially in the Arboretum. To mention only a few of these, the Thorn Avenue was planted in 1868, that

of Atlas Cedars was planted in 1871, the Holly Walk in 1874, the Sweet Chestnut Avenue in 1880 . . .

The range of plant-houses known as the T-range was erected in 1868–9; the Jodrell Laboratory was added to the institution in 1876; a new hall, added to the Herbarium building, was completed in 1877; a wing was added to No. 1 Museum in 1881, and the North Gallery was completed and opened to the public in 1882.[1]

These were some of Joseph Hooker's more important achievements at Kew; it is sad that so brilliant a man could, as we shall see, at times be wholly unreasonable.

[1] *Kew Bulletin*, No. I, 1912.

22

Joseph Hooker at War

JOSEPH HOOKER'S reign of twenty years at Kew was embittered by two wars: the Ayrton War—described euphemistically by Thiselton-Dyer as 'protracted differences'—at the beginning of the 1870s, and the lengthy Earlier-Opening War which was at its height towards the end of the same decade. Mea Allan writes admirably and for the most part impartially about the former, in which Hooker's cause was just; about the latter, which was entirely the result of Hooker's obstinacy, she naturally prefers to remain silent. There was also the running battle of the Wall.

Sir Joseph Hooker. Photograph by Julia Margaret Cameron, c. 1870

The control of Kew Gardens had been transferred in 1850 from the relatively generous Commissioners of Woods and Forests to the unsympathetic Commissioners of the Board of Works. In 1869 Gladstone had appointed a certain Acton Smee Ayrton (1816–86) First Commissioner of the latter — possibly, as Miss Allan suggests, to prevent him from being a greater nuisance elsewhere. Ayrton had made himself unpopular in 1866 by openly attacking the widowed Queen for withdrawing from public life; but Miss Allan has unearthed another and a glorious story which really tells us almost all we need to know about what she calls this 'repulsive blunt-mouthed creature':

> [Ayrton] was present at a grand ball given at Stafford House in honour of the Shah's visit to London in 1873, and the Shah desiring to meet Mr Ayrton a messenger was despatched to find him. Ayrton was in the supper room and on being invited to come forthwith and be presented to the Shah, he retorted through a mouthful of chicken: 'I'll see the old nigger in Jericho first!'

Ayrton was determined to cut down the cost of running his department — which was, of course, very right and proper; but, unluckily for Hooker, he intended to economise principally in the fields of science and the arts. His first target was Kew, which he hoped to reduce to a kind of suburban Hyde Park, and to destroy Kew as a scientific institution he had to begin by destroying Hooker; he therefore inaugurated a campaign of harassment and humiliation intended to force him to resign. *The Dictionary of National Biography*[1] mentions that Ayrton was born at Kew; is it possible that he had crossed swords with Hooker in earlier days and was now taking his revenge?

As is well known, a problem arises when an irresistible force encounters an immovable object; in this case it was unfortunate for the latter (Hooker) that the former (Ayrton) happened to be his boss. Ayrton, wrote Ray Desmond, 'constantly interfered in the internal administration of the Gardens; estimates were drawn up without the Director being consulted; an official report on Kew and its management was published without prior submission to the Director for comment; and unknown to Sir Joseph, an attempt was made to persuade the Curator, John Smith II, to transfer to Hyde Park.' And there was more of the same kind: so much, indeed, that for a moment it seemed as though the immovable object might be about to yield to irresistible pressure. To George Bentham, his friend and collaborator in the immortal *Handbook of the British Flora*, Hooker wrote in abject misery in February 1872: 'My life has become utterly detestable and I do *long* to throw up the Directorship. What can be more *humiliating* than two years of wrangling with such a creature!'

[1] First Supplement.

The major part of the scientific world rushed to Hooker's defence. A letter signed by such distinguished men as Darwin, Huxley, Lyell, Tyndall, and Bentham was laid before Parliament by Sir John Lubbock (afterwards Lord Avebury), representing science in the Commons, which invited the Prime Minister 'respectfully' to decide

> whether Kew Gardens are, or are not, to lose the supervision of a man of whose scientific labours any nation might be proud . . . a man honoured for his integrity, beloved for his courtesy and kindliness of heart; and who has spent in the public service not only a stainless but an illustrious life. The resignation of Dr Hooker under the circumstances here set forth would, we declare, be a calamity to English science and a scandal to the English Government. With the power to avert this in your hands, we appeal to your justice to do so.

The matter was debated in both the Lords and the Commons. In the latter it was discussed during the third reading of the Appropriation Bill, which took place on 8 August 1872. Miss Allan writes:

> The most unpardonable feature of the Return laid before the House was the publication of an official report on Kew and its management which had not been submitted to the Director for answer or comment. Ayrton had caused it to be written by Professor Richard Owen who was notoriously hostile to Kew, and Owen had employed all his great dexterity in belittling Kew and delivering a personal attack on both Sir William Hooker and his son, sneering at the Herbarium whose 'net result' was 'attaching barbarous binomials to dried foreign weeds' . . .

This is misleading. These words were not Owen's but, as he clearly stated, those of 'a great wit and original thinker'. He continued, 'an estimable naturalist has given a better and fitter opinion of the subject; he writes:— "The objection to [herbarium] botany is, that it exercises the memory without improving the mind or advancing any real knowledge . . ." '[1]

During this debate, Ayrton adopted a new pose: that of injured innocence. 'All of a sudden we are treated to a startling transformation scene, and Mr AYRTON presents himself to our astonished gaze as the weak and helpless victim of a scientific tyrant.'[2] In Miss Allan's opinion, Gladstone had all along 'slithered away from responsibility'; certainly he now forced Hooker to apologise for an entirely understandable but rash verbal attack he had made on his superior. This Hooker 'magnanimously' did.

[1] Cf. Dr Johnson on listening to music: 'A method of employing the mind without the labour of thinking at all . . .'
[2] *Saturday Review*, 10 August 1872.

'*Jack in Office*'. *Caricature of
Acton Smee Ayrton, 1872*

But was Ayrton *wholly* to blame? As *The Times* said, he had an 'unfortunate tendency to carry out what he thinks right in as unpleasant a manner as possible'. In the *Recollections* of (Sir) Algernon West, Gladstone's Private Secretary at the time, is a passage from which the *Dictionary of National Biography* sees fit to quote but of which Miss Allan makes no mention: 'I was also concerned in some very complicated negotiations between Mr Hooker, the Director of Kew Gardens, and Mr Ayrton, the First Commissioner of Works, who had quarrelled. Ayrton had an evil tongue, but I confess that I thought him the more reasonable man of the two.' So, one suspects, did Gladstone.

However, in August 1873 Ayrton was very sensibly transferred to another department, and after the fall of the government in the following March he twice failed to get himself re-elected to Parliament. As Ayrton's star sank, Hooker's continued to rise; indeed, his victory over his powerful adversary may have played some part in his now achieving the highest ambition of a man of science in this country — that of the Presidency of the Royal Society.

Ayrton died unlamented in 1886, and as a tail-piece to this regrettable episode I will add the curious obituary notice that appeared in the *Gardeners' Chronicle* on 4 December of that year:

MR. AYRTON.—The death is announced of this gentleman, best known to readers of this journal for his conduct towards the then Director of Kew, and towards men of science and art generally. *De mortuis nil nisi bonum.* It is sufficient to say that Mr. AYRTON's motives were laudable, and that his attacks upon Kew and its management really contributed very much indeed to raise the establishment and its staff in public estimation.

What does this mean? That the management of the Gardens needed a shake-up? That the sympathy that Ayrton's bullying earned for Joseph, and the publicity that the affair gave to Kew, were worth the blood that had been shed? Or was it simply that subsequently (as we shall see) Joseph had made himself so unpopular that in retrospect even Ayrton had become something of a hero for having stood up to him?

*   *   *

Throughout the Ayrton War, public opinion had been on Hooker's side; in the prolonged campaign to force the authorities to open Kew Gardens in the mornings, almost the whole world was against him. But let us first dispose of that little matter of the Wall.

The wall in question is that which runs the whole length of the eastern side of the Gardens. It is now ten or twelve feet high, and a curious account of the use to which it was put in Regency days may be read in Sir Richard Phillips's *A Morning's Walk from London to Kew* (1817):

> As I quitted the lane, I beheld, on my left, the long boundary-wall of Kew-Gardens; on which a disabled sailor has drawn in chalk the effigies of the whole British navy, and over each representation appears the name of the vessel, and the number of her guns. He has in this way depicted about 800 vessels, each five or six feet long, and extending, with intervening distances, above a mile and a half. As the labour of one man, the whole is an extraordinary performance; and I was told the decrepit draughtsman derives a competency from passing travellers.

This giant mural, mentioned also by other authors of the day, had vanished without trace when in 1844 the Vestrymen of Richmond appealed to Sir William Hooker for the wall to be lowered to two feet and topped by iron railings on the score that it would be 'safer and more interesting—and the Gardens benefited by a freer current of air and have the advantage of light from gas'. Against this, Sir William had written, 'informed that it cannot be entertained'.

Nothing further seems to have happened until 1877, by which time the war over morning opening was at its height and Joseph Hooker at the helm. But Joseph, always angered by criticisms or suggestions of any kind made by

Cartoon from Funny Folks, *25 May 1878*

the vulgar public, proved as unyielding as his father had been. When approached about the wall, he alleged that to lower it would let in draught, dust and litter, and that 'the damage to the vegetation would be incalculable'.[1] His father's whips having failed to silence the rebellious Kewites he now turned to scorpions, and on the pretext of preventing thefts spitefully heightened most of the wall by another three feet! It remains thus to this day, except for a few yards near the North Gallery where at one time there was to have been another entrance.

The grievance over the closure of Kew Gardens until 1 p.m., which was principally ventilated in the horticultural journals of the day, was also of very long standing. The author of an article in the *Florist* of 1849, while expressing himself as not ungrateful to Sir William Hooker for persuading the Commissioner of Woods and Forests to sanction the daily opening of the Gardens, nonetheless felt his 'danders rising' when he thought of all those frequenters of pot-houses and skittle-alleys in 'London's dirty, crowded, pestiferous courts' who might otherwise be passing their mornings in Kew's 'perfect paradise':

> 'Tis to tempt them away from the gin-palace, the public house, and the beer-shop, that we would have these delightful Gardens opened at nine o'clock; ay, and we would have in the beautifully kept ladies' cloak-room a building, where they would have an opportunity of partaking of any refreshments they might bring. As to misconduct, there are plenty of ways to prevent that . . .

[1] J. C. Loudon had already replaced the high wall on the north side of Kensington Gardens by railings, thus to this day adding greatly to the pleasure of those who use the Bayswater Road yet without apparent damage to the plants.

How very odd!

The first campaign to get the Gardens open in the mornings began in 1866, soon after Joseph Hooker had become Director, but the authorities remained deaf to all entreaties. They claimed at one time that no one would come, and that therefore the additional cost of staffing the Gardens could not be justified; at another, that so great would be the crowds that bona fide students, admitted in the mornings, would not be able to get on with their work. One student maintained that if he were seen climbing about the rocks in the Rock Garden, hundreds of visitors would believe themselves entitled to do the same.

In 1877 the *Kew Gardens Public Rights Defence Association* was formed — a body determined 'by Hooker or by Crooker' (as a journalist wrote) to see justice done—and the following year open war was declared on Joseph. A horticultural periodical, the *Garden*, played a prominent part in it week after week for many months, and eventually Sir Trevor Lawrence, M.P., raised the matter in the Commons. Some rather dirty linen was very publicly washed, and in that wash some odd facts came to light.

It was undoubtedly Joseph Hooker himself, not the Commissioners, who so stubbornly refused to budge. It horrified him that the funds of a scientific institution were increasingly being used to provide mere pleasure for thousands of Londoners who could not tell, and did not even want to be able to tell, a dicotyledon from a monocotyledon, but who came simply to enjoy the trees and the flowers and the fresh air. In a memorandum dated 23 January 1878, he wrote:

> About 1856, when the decoration of the Gardens was commenced, the tendency to regard the Gardens as a resort for pleasure seekers was developed, and it has rapidly increased. To meet popular demands larger sums were spent on making flower beds, on the purchase of vases and ornamental work and on building Lodge Gates and conveniences all which have attracted crowds to the Gardens and necessitated a larger outlay on Police Patrols, Gatekeepers and on daily labour devoted to attractions, until now fully three-fourths of the expenditure of the establishment may be put down to other than its primary objects. This tendency to encroach on the legitimate objects of the institution has increased till the strain upon its staff is excessive and there is great risk of its scientific character being if not suppressed at least subordinated to the popular.[1]

---

[1] Joseph Hooker, in a letter to the Treasury on 17 October 1873, deplored 'the modern rage for gaudy flower-beds, consisting of but few, and those easily cultivated plants, which year after year fill the beds at one season and the houses during the other three, to the exclusion from both of plants of interest, beauty and utility, which afford that intellectual gratification which once was and still should be, one main object of a garden.'

In his Annual Report on the Gardens for 1877, which was not in fact published until August 1878, Sir Joseph (he had just been knighted) complained that a fern had been damaged by a visitor, and expressed 'an apprehension that it may eventually prove impossible to admit the public on exceptionally crowded days to visit certain collections, at any rate except in restricted numbers, which must be eventually exterminated in the process'. Apparently Hooker, like so many scientists, found English a harder language to master than Latin. Who or what might be exterminated remained in doubt; what was not in doubt was Hooker's obstinate determination to fight to the last ditch.

For it was not so much the ferns as the Hookers who would suffer by the Gardens being made more accessible to the public. As 'Examiner' wrote in the *Garden* (21 September 1878):

> Sir Joseph's private objections are intelligible. For years Kew Gardens have formed a snug little preserve—a sort of happy hunting ground for the scientifically inclined members of the Hooker family. It is, doubtless, a little hard that the privileges so long enjoyed by the latter should have to give way, as they must, to public rights and convenience.

To Hooker's allegation that scientific work of the greatest importance would be rendered 'nugatory' if the public had access to the Gardens in the mornings, the *Garden* riposted:

> 'Science', we are told, requires that Kew Gardens be closed to the public for half the day. Up to about luncheon-time the authorities inside the walls, whoever they may be, are supposed to be in a 'brown study'— absorbed in abstruse speculations on such subjects as the accumulation of water in the stoke-holes, the manuring of the flower-beds, and the spelling of plant names. If we could look over the walls we should no doubt see a multitude of students and philosophers walking to and fro in the grounds during the forenoon. About noon the *savants* betake themselves to their cells to ruminate upon their morning's experiences, and in order also that they may not be contaminated by contact with the ignorant public, who are then permitted to invade their sacred haunts. Seriously, we do not suppose anybody believes for a moment in the plea of 'science' put forth by the Kew authorities. . .[1]

Sir Trevor Lawrence, when he saw the Report, was equally sceptical:

> I could hardly have believed that it could be seriously argued that mowing, sweeping and rolling, which is really all the work to be done in the 'pleasure grounds', would be interfered with if they were opened at 10 a.m. The 'constant improvement and development,' the 'laying out'

[1] The *Garden*, 13 April 1878.

and 'planting new collections', the 'verification, examination and rearrangement of old ones', form a string of phrases intended to create an impression that a great scientific work is being constantly carried on in the 'pleasure grounds'.

In his opinion, all this was rubbish.

Some of the correspondents resorted to satire. 'Figaro' for example, claimed that, disguised as a German *savant*, he had obtained one of the special 'morning' permits issued at the Curator's office to bona fide botanists armed with testimonials from 'two respectable householders',[1] and entered the Gardens, where he had observed

in all forty-one individuals—of whom thirteen were gardeners, or labourers, merely weeding or bedding out . . . Of the rest, no less than nine were favoured young ladies—perhaps relations of the director and his staff—who were most comfortably ensconced on snug seats, reading novels from Mudies. . . . The number mentioned also included five aged gentlemen, who may have been botanists, but who were most certainly fast asleep in garden chairs; eleven other gentlemen not aged and not asleep, but all apparently engaged in testing the effect of cigar smoke on open-air evergreens; and three foreign *savans* [sic], sitting in solemn silence round a small shrub, and examining its buds in turn with a magnifying glass . . .

He concluded:

The assumption that perfect privacy is necessary to enable certain old dry-as-dust professors to watch the Grass grow, or to study the habits of polyandrous Polyanthuses, is simply absurd. If those old boys must botanise alone, let them be locked up in the glass-house with their specimens, and the public even forbidden to stop to stare at them as they pursue their particular task. But to say that thousands of visitors, eager for fresh air, and the pretty sights of the gardens, would interfere with the progress of botany as a science, by quietly walking about on the gravel paths and gazing at the beauties of the scene, is ridiculous.[2]

Various odd facts came to light. A French botanist wrote to complain that he had been stopped by a gardener from making 'written notes' on the plants, the gardener himself confessing that this was 'the most stupid order I ever received, but as it is my duty, I must see that it is observed'. Then a Member of Parliament named Noel alleged on behalf of the Hookerites that 'no institution in this country is so freely open to the public as Kew'—a statement so blatantly untrue that it seemed hardly worth refuting. Two

[1] Such permits were in theory available, but getting one was often made very difficult.
[2] *Funny Folks*, 25 May 1878.

*The Kew Gardens Question. 'Observe the Privileged Few at Their Studies in the
Gardens, and the Public, "who are really Satisfied with Present Arrangements,"
Outside.' Cartoon from* Funny Folks, *25 May 1878*

former employees of Kew testified that the presence of the public in the
mornings would make no difference whatever, since such scientific work as
was done in the Gardens (and it was little enough) was carried out in the
propagating pits and other places in any case closed to the public. There was
much talk of lectures given for students in the Houses being impeded by
visitors, some of whom, 'from a desire to be informed', might even attach
themselves to a party and—terrible thought!—overhear what was being
said. In any case, a gardener with twenty years' experience at Kew
maintained that there were 'hardly any lectures'.

A 'deputation of gentlemen, including the clergy, coming mostly from
Richmond and Kew', waited upon Mr Noel and afterwards on the First
Commissioner, but were accorded no more than placebos. The Hookerites
also acted, collecting signatures and delivering a memorial to the First
Commissioner. Finally, on 15 March 1879 there was a full debate in the
Commons, the principal speaker for the motion in favour of morning
opening being Sir Trevor Lawrence, against it Mr Noel; it was defeated by
196 votes to 94.

However, slowly but surely commonsense prevailed. Even during the height of the campaign Hooker had been obliged to make a gesture by allowing morning opening on Bank Holidays. Then in 1882 daily opening was advanced from 1 p.m. to midday, and in 1898 it was agreed that the Gardens should open daily at 10 a.m. during the six summer months. But it was not until 1921 that this concession was granted for the winter months also. So ended in total victory, after more than half a century, what the *Kew Guild Journal* had once dismissed as no more than 'an agitation . . . fostered chiefly by local malcontents'.

Finally, there is correspondence at Kew about the use of the Gardens by those unable for various reasons to tour them on foot. Though in early times entry was said to have been forbidden to 'Dogs and Footmen', no objection seems ever to have been taken to the admission of bath-chairs, for which a charge was made; and as has already been said, in Victorian days members of the royal family were entitled to ride or drive (sensibly) anywhere. But when in 1909 a visitor asked to be allowed to bring a perambulator into the Gardens, she was informed that this 'would not be conducive either to the pleasure of the general public or to the utility of the gardens as a scientific institution'. A Question was asked in the House, and the *Star* was among those papers which had some fun at the expense of the authorities:

> O, Mr Barrie, what shall I do?
> I want to study botany, but prams are barred in Kew.

Five years later, a crippled architectural student applied for permission to use a bicycle. This was granted, on condition 'that the bicycle be not ridden independently [sic] or at a greater speed than two miles an hour'—the latter a restriction calculated to unseat and possibly cripple for life many a sound rider in no time at all. Then there was a Mr W. M. Nelson with his 'self propelling hand tricycle', who was similarly treated. A precedent having thus been created, soon, no doubt, there were bicycles and tricycles everywhere, and after the First World War there were also sadly many limbless soldiers in wheel-chairs from the Star and Garter Home at Richmond.

But Kew Gardens are very large, and the elderly, even if they are not disabled, find the various Houses and other attractions scattered inconveniently far and wide. Now at Whipsnade there is a charming little train with open carriages, the Umfolozi Railway, which puffs its leisurely way round the Zoo and is vastly appreciated by both young and old; and even Alton Towers[1] has its Towers Express, whose 'skilfully designed facsimilies of steam railway locomotives' drag visitors round in twenty-four-

[1] See p. 35.

seater luxury coaches ceaselessly disgorging 'soft taped stereo music'. God preserve Kew from luxury coaches and potted music! but is there any valid reason why it should not provide something similar to the Umfolozi? Engine and carriages could be camouflaged with rambler roses by some impecunious art student, or even festooned in summer with swags of live flowers; and as for the noise—it would hardly be heard against the perpetual roar of the aeroplanes.

23

T-Range

THERE IS an agglomeration of heated glasshouses at Kew called rather mysteriously the T-Range, thus misleadingly entertaining hopes of light refreshments. The original structure, erected in 1868–9 at the beginning of Joseph Hooker's reign, was in fact the shape of this letter, but subsequent additions have disguised it. Since there is usually some sort of rearrangement going on in these Houses, there seems to be little point in my attempting to describe precisely what happens to be where at the moment of writing (summer 1976); in general, one is likely to find orchids, carnivorous plants, succulents and heaths, and in the heart of the complex is the House that always contains the giant waterlily, *Victoria amazonica*.

In *Scribner's Magazine* for April 1875 there appeared an anonymous poem whose first verse runs:

> What's this I hear,
> My Molly dear,
>   About the new Carnivora?
> Can little plants
> Eat bugs and ants,
> And gnats and flies
> Who is the wise,
>   Who is the great 'diskiverer'?

One relatively cool house in the T-Range is devoted to the majority of these insectivorous (or, more correctly, carnivorous) plants, the tropical nepenthes being housed more snugly elsewhere in the same block. Here Kew approaches its nearest to Regent's Park; but the visitor must not imagine that he will find vegetables roaring after their prey or gorging like the Zoo's lions at feeding time. There are no Triffids, no Wellsian vegetable assassins; and if a screen separates man from plant, it is there only for the protection of the latter from the molesting or thieving fingers of the former.

Carnivorous plants display various kinds of diabolical ingenuity to entice and capture their prey,[1] and may roughly be divided into three groups:

---

[1] For this, in palatable form, see vol I, pp. 119–58, of my favourite book, *The Natural History of Plants* by Anton Kerner von Marilaun (English translation by F. W. Oliver, 1896)—out of

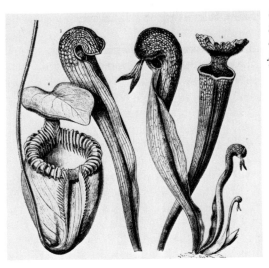

Carnivorous Plants:
Sarracenias, Darlingtonia
and Nepenthes,
from Kerner von Marilaun's
The Natural History of Plants

trappers, snappers and stickers; but it is always a case of ' "Will you walk into my parlour?" said a spider to a fly.' There is the bait: the honey or nectar, to which attention is directed by bright, sinister colour or attractive (to us often repulsive) smell; then each plant uses its own particular technique to restrain, murder, and slowly swallow and *digest* its victim.

Trappers make no movement. The little insect enters the throat of the 'chamber' of the plant; but when it attempts to leave, it either slips and slithers downwards into the gastric juices at the base or, finding itself unable to climb back past a battery of downward-pointing bristles, eventually falls to its death. *Facilis descensus Averno!* The little aquatic bladderworts (*Utricularia* spp.), 'like so many stomachs digesting and assimilating animals' food', come very near to animals; but they are too tiny for effective public display, and all that the visitor can see is what looks like a green sponge in a small tank. So at Kew this group is more happily represented by pitcher-plants such as the sarracenias and darlingtonias from the bogs of North America, and by the fantastic nepenthes, looking like hot-water jugs with lids, from the steaming jungles of Indo-Malaya and Madagascar. Certain other plants—our lords-and-ladies (*Arum maculatum*), for example—also capture insects in this way in a kind of lobster-pot; but their intentions are benign: as soon as the prisoners have done their job, which is

---

date, no doubt, but a mine of fascinating information—or Anthony Huxley's equally delight-ful *Plant and Planet*, Allen Lane, 1974. A brilliant film on the subject, made in the Oxford Botanic Gardens and entitled *The Tender Trap*, has been shown more than once on television.

to pollinate the plant, the confining bristles become limp and the captives can escape.

Snappers are known in Britain by the butterworts (*Pinguicula* spp.) and sundews (*Drosera* spp.). Here are plants that are actively aggressive. Stickiness restrains the victim until the tentacles of the leaves curl over to engulf and suffocate it. Their cunning is incredible: try to fool a sundew with a drop of water or a grain of sand and it does not budge; but any *animal* matter—even a tiny particle of human hair weighing no more than one thirty-millionth of an ounce—will lead to the activation of glands which produce an enzyme that digests it.

Snappers have fared badly at the hands of botanists, some of whom, were there an R.S.P.C.P., would soon find themselves in the courts for cruelty to plants. A Mrs Hughes-Gibb, holidaying at Chagford, described the experiments she made to find out what sundews—'small ruddy plants' she calls them—are capable of enduring in the way of torture, potting one and feeding it successively with red wine, whisky and methylated spirits. By this time it was looking 'very unhealthy' and therefore, in her opinion, in urgent need of Devonshire cream. The plant vomited, rolled over and died. She considered the results of her experiments 'rather inconclusive'.

But the snapper *par excellence* is the Venus' fly-trap or tippitiwitchet, *Dionaea muscipula*, of North Carolina—described by Darwin as 'the most wonderful plant in the world'.[1] Its leaves terminate in what look like the empty shells of the fruit of the Spanish chestnut, and these, when the alarm is correctly triggered, close like a rat-trap. But the miraculous thing about the Venus' fly-trap is that it, alone among plants, can count! There are three hairs on each leaf:

> These hairs are triggers. If only one is moved, which happens if a raindrop strikes it, nothing happens; but if two hairs are touched, or one hair is touched more than once, the leaf lobes move swiftly and silently together (in about a quarter of a second), the bristles on the edge interlocking like fingers of a hand, fatally clamping in any fly which has landed on the lobes. At first the lobes are concave on closing, but once they have locked together they flatten, crushing any soft body within to pulp. . . .
>
> Not only can this plant count the necessary stimuli before its trap operates, but it has a built-in timing device: not less than one and a half and not more than twenty seconds must elapse between the stimuli . . .[2]

Digestion of the victim is very leisurely—at least a fortnight for a fly, more than three weeks for a woodlouse—and, as with human beings, over-

[1] *Insectivorous Plants*, 1875. Joseph Hooker addressed the British Association on the subject of *Dionaea* at Belfast in 1874.
[2] Anthony Huxley, *op. cit.*

*Venus' Fly-trap (*Dionaea muscipula*) from Kerner von Marilaun's* The Natural History of Plants

indulgence leads to the equivalent of apoplexy. Mrs Mary Trent, of New Jersey, noted (in 1873) that 'several leaves [of *Dionaea*] caught successively three insects each; but most of them, not able to digest the third fly, died in the attempt'.

A typical 'sticker' is the Portuguese sundew, *Drosophyllum lusitanicum*, also found in southern Spain and Morocco. Unlike the Droseras, the Drosophyllum makes no movement to catch its prey: they also get served who only stand and wait. It is a highly efficient vegetable fly-paper—indeed used as such round Oporto, where the villagers call it 'fly-catcher'; but flies and other small insects which are rash enough to alight on the glittering drops of mucilage covering the plant's bootlace-like leaves are digested in the usual way. The Portuguese sundew differs from most other carnivorous plants in that it grows in arid places, not in bogs. Its yellow flowers are rather like those of a large buttercup.

*   *   *

'As for the scientific names of Plants,' wrote Southey, 'if Apollo had not lost all power he would have elongated the ears of Tournefort and Linnaeus, and all their followers, as deservedly as he did those of Midas.' Apollo might really have begun with Theophrastus, who about 300 B.C. gave the name *orchis* ('testicles') to a little Grecian wildflower because its rootstock consisted of two ovoid tubers. Thus, thanks to Linnaeus, we now have a family, the Orchidaceae,[1] perpetuating an invisible and indelicate resemblance to be found in only relatively few of its hundreds of genera and thousands of species.

Of course Theophrastus knew only the humble terrestrial orchids of the Levant, not their spectacular, celestial, mostly epiphytic[2] brothers of the tropics. Yet even so, surely he might have coined a more imaginative name for these Mediterranean weeds that Jakob Breyne described so vividly:

> If nature ever showed her playfulness in the formation of plants, this is visible in the most striking way among orchids. . . . [Their flowers] take the form of little birds, of lizards, of insects. They look like a man, a woman, sometimes like an austere, sinister fighter, sometimes like a clown who excites our laughter. They represent the image of a lazy tortoise, a melancholy toad, an agile, ever chattering monkey. Nature has formed orchid flowers in such a way that, unless they make us laugh, they surely excite our greatest admiration. The causes of their marvellous variety are (at least in my opinion) hidden by nature under a sacred veil. . .[3]

But not entirely: that vegetable prostitute the bee orchid (*Ophrys apifera*), for instance, so perfectly imitates the posterior of a female bumble-bee that it arouses the male bee to a pseudo-copulation. Yet the mystery deepens, for the bee orchid, unlike other *Ophrys* species, is self-pollinated and no longer needs the services of the lustful bee. Perhaps the required sort of bee went out of business.

It is the fantastic tropical orchids, in all their infinite variety and ingenuity, that the visitor to Kew will find in the T-range. The first of these to reach England, *Bletia verecunda*, came to Kew from Jamaica in 1731. By 1789 the number of exotic species had risen to fifteen, and by 1813 to eighty-four; but at first their requirements were little understood and it was not until some twenty years later that the cult of this astonishing family began in earnest. In 1843 the Duke of Bedford presented the famous Woburn collection of orchids to the Queen, who passed it on to Kew; this necessitated the building of a new hothouse, which by the end of the decade

---

[1] *Orchis* is now a genus, 'orchid' a member of the family Orchidaceae. A similar convenient distinction is not to be found with most families—and here, surely, the botanists might come to our aid. And why, incidentally, did they make Orchis *feminine*, when the Greek word, and what it stands for, are masculine? *Orchis mascula* is surely grotesque!

[2] Growing on a plant but not deriving nourishment from it—as opposed to parasitic.

[3] *Exoticarum Plantarum Centuria Prima*, Danzig, 1678, transl. Oakes Ames.

could boast of more than eight hundred species. The disease that John Blowers[1] calls 'orchiditis' (the word 'orchitis' having already been snapped up by the medical profession for a different, more painful and less infectious complaint) was soon to become an epidemic in millionaire circles; today one has to be almost a billionaire to keep a tropical orchid house heated.

Nature has provided man with some thirty-five thousand species of orchids, but man considered that there was still room for improvement. In 1852 an English surgeon named Harris conceived the idea that orchids might be interbred by hand pollination, and four years later, with the assistance of an expert grower, Mr J. Dominy, the first hybrid thus raised was flowered. Today there are probably no fewer than fifty thousand named hybrids, many of them far more spectacular than the species; and when Dr Lindley prophesied that hybridisation would drive the botanists mad, even he can hardly have foreseen the magnitude of the nomenclatural headache to come.

By crossing *Laelia* with *Cattleya* was produced the bigeneric × *Laeliocattleya*. This in its turn was interbred with *Brassavola* giving × *Brassolaeliocattleya*; but when, in 1922, × *Brassolaeliocattleya* 'Ena' was crossed with × *Sophrolaeliocattleya* 'Marathon' even the botanists recognised that × *Brassosophrolaeliocattleya* was too much of a mouthful and that a fresh start had to be made. So this handsome hybrid was christened × *Potinara*, after M. Potin, President of the Paris Orchid Society. The wisdom of this decision, which might well have been taken in time to spare us × *Brassolaeliocattleya*, becomes even more apparent when we realise that some modern hybrids have more than a dozen different strains in their ancestry.

But all of this has little or nothing to do with Kew, where in due season you will find, admirably displayed, earthbound or suspended species of these 'bosom orchids' (as they have been called): the ever-popular cymbidiums, the aristocratic cypripediums flaunting their Habsburg jowls and handle-bar moustachios, the oncidiums and odontoglossums with their arching sprays of blossoms, the miltonias whose faces are like pansies, and the large, promiscuous cattleyas clamouring to mate with almost any of their innumerable cousins. Their variety is infinite: the 'column' (combined male and female sexual organs) of *Peristeria elata*, the Holy Ghost flower, is dovelike, that of *Cynoches chlorochilum* swan-like; and the flowers of oncidiums seem to hover like butterflies over their arching sprays. You will find every colour except purest blue, even *Vanda caerulea*[2] being no more than an approximation of it. And perhaps it may be forgiven of a family of

---

[1] *Orchids*, Garden Book Club, 1962. In what follows I have made some use of this handy little book.
[2] See p. 155.

'*Odontoglossum bluntii*' (*O.* crispum *var.* bluntii) *drawing by John Day, December 1866*

flowers so beautiful that one genus only, *Vanilla*, works for its living—or did so work until it was found that vanilla flavouring could be produced more cheaply synthetically.

But there are three south American orchids that I do not recall ever having seen at Kew—three in which I take a particular interest: *Cattleya bluntii* (now considered as merely a variety of *C. mendelii*), *Miltonia × bluntii*—a natural hybrid between *M. clowesii* and *M. spectabilis*, and, most especially, *Odontoglossum bluntii*—now 'referred to *O. crispum*'. This Blunt was a certain Henry Blunt, who collected orchids in Colombia and thereabouts in the mid-1860s for Messrs Hugh Low & Co., married a Brazilian lady, and spent the latter part of his life in Brazil as a coffee planter; a photograph in the *Gardeners' Chronicle*[1] shows him in a morning coat, handsome and very dashing.

The chief claim to fame of Cousin Henry (for such, though I cannot locate him in the family arboretum, he must surely be) was his successful introduction into England in 1865 of *O. crispum*, favourite of the Edwardian orchidophiles. It was first named *O. bluntii* in his honour by the great Heinrich Gustav Reichenbach, but subsequently found to be merely a variety of that extremely variable species, *O. crispum*; nonetheless, his was

[1] Series 3, 26: 432–33 (1924).

the first plant of this spectacular species to flower (in December 1866) in this country. There are four or five drawings of '*O. bluntii*' at Kew by John Day (1824–88), a skilful artist and successful cultivator of orchids.

*   *   *

House 7A in the T-range was the gift to Kew in 1931 of a Mrs Sherman Hoyt of Pasadena, California, and contains, basically, the American cacti and other succulents which she had exhibited at Chelsea two years earlier. I do not know who she was, or why she was so generous, but I can well understand that she may have been reluctant to lug all those prickly plants back to California, where there are plenty of them already; however, to throw in the building as well was kind indeed.

The chief feature of the House is a set piece: an agglomeration of red rocks (actually for the most part Somerset Old Red Sandstone), bristling with cacti and backed by an apse painted by Perry McNeely to represent the Mojave Desert, near Los Angeles. This kind of panorama was fashionable in Victorian times, and I still find it rather fun; as one sits on the well-positioned bench it is almost possible, with half-closed eyes, to imagine oneself back in that exciting landscape. What one most misses—other, of course, than the sense of the wide open spaces—are all the exquisite, plucky

'*The Mojave Desert*'. *Living plants set against a painted back-cloth, in the building presented by Mrs Sherman Hoyt*

little annuals—the 'desert snow' (*Limnanthes*), the infant lupins, the innumerable bright-eyed daisies—which star that semi-desert after a shower of rain. There is a wonderful Walt Disney film, 'The Living Desert', which gives a vivid picture of this sudden blossoming, and to see American succulents in captivity one should go to the Huntington Gardens near Los Angeles.

Alongside House 7A is House 7B, containing South African succulents, many of which we knew as mesembryanthemums until the genus was split into a hundred pieces. One of these is *Lithops*, plants that pretend to be stones and in some cases even (it is alleged) take a hint from the chameleon and adjust their colour to match the stones they find themselves among. I rather doubt whether you will want to linger here unless you are an addict.

There is much else in the T-Range. One House is devoted to pelargoniums—the 'geraniums' of the common man—another to ericas (heaths); most of these come from South Africa, and Francis Masson (1741–1805 or 1806), who was responsible for the introduction of so many species of them, made the two genera immensely popular. House 12 is the home of the pineapple family (Bromeliaceae), almost all natives of tropical or sub-tropical America and many of them epiphytes. What more is to be seen in this labyrinth of hothouses and warmhouses (if I may coin a word) the visitor must discover for himself.

Close to the T-Range is a mound covering the old ice-house. In 1945 the eastern side of it was covered with chalk and planted with hardy 'calcicoles'; but 'the white man's grave' (as it soon came to be called) never flourished and was later dismantled. Some scree-beds have recently been made nearby.

24

'*Aunt Pop*' and other matters

SIGNPOSTS IN various parts of the Gardens direct the visitor to the North Gallery. These worry Mea Allan, and possibly others also: 'Correct', she writes, '—but misleading. One expects also a South Gallery and perhaps East and West ones.' They point, of course, to the Gallery presented to Kew in 1882 by Miss Marianne North to house her remarkable collection of 848 oil-paintings, mostly of flowers.

The Victorian age, we all know, had more than its fair share of parent-ridden, unfulfilled spinsters too dutiful, too timid or too poor to defy their families and flout public opinion by breaking free from the fetters that bound them. Those relatively few who did were therefore not commonplace women merely bored by domesticity, not 'women's-libbers' out to prove they were as good as or better than men, but for the most part courageous women deaf to ridicule but very alert to a call so clarion that it could not remain unanswered. Some were missionaries, others nurses, yet others travellers or explorers; but however important their achievements, most learned societies either refused to admit them or made admission as difficult as possible. The Royal Geographical Society briefly set its doors ajar but soon closed them again—to the great satisfaction of *Punch*:

> A lady an explorer? A traveller in skirts?
>   The notion's just a trifle too seraphic:
> Let them stay and mind the babies, or hem our ragged shirts;
>   But they mustn't, can't, and shan't be geographic. . . .

Marianne North did not abandon home; it might rather be said that home abandoned her, in that on the death of her beloved father, a widower whom she had looked after since her mother's death, she suddenly found herself alone, and therefore free, as also rich enough, to do what she had always longed to do—travel all over the world painting flowers. She was now nearly forty; Mary Kingsley, whose circumstances were in many respects comparable to her own, had been similarly liberated at the age of thirty, only to die within eight years.

Marianne was born in 1830 at Hastings, where her father, who came from a distinguished and well-to-do Norfolk family, was intermittently its representative in Parliament. The girl, artistic and musical, was given the best teachers, and since Mr North had the *wanderlust* she had the good fortune to travel with him all over Europe and on one occasion as far as Syria and Egypt. These journeys with 'the one idol and friend of my life' lasted either for a few weeks or for many months, depending upon whether her father was seated or unseated at the time. When in London, she wrote,

> We rode often to the Chiswick Gardens [belonging to the Royal Horticultural Society] and got specimen flowers to paint; were also often at Kew, and once when there Sir William Hooker gave me a hanging bunch of the *Amherstia nobilis*, one of the grandest flowers in existence. It was the first that had bloomed in England,[1] and made me long more and more to see the tropics. We often talked of going, if ever my father had a holiday long enough.

Marianne's account of her travels was published, soon after her death in 1890, by her sister Janet, the wife of John Addington Symonds. First came *Recollections of a Happy Life* (2 vols., 1892), covering the years from 1871 to 1885 during which she travelled extensively, sometimes dangerously, usually alone, in Canada, the United States, South America, the West Indies, South Africa, the Canaries and the Seychelles, India and Ceylon, Japan, Java and Borneo, Australia, New Zealand and Tasmania. The book's immediate success led a year later to a sequel, *Further Recollections of a Happy Life*—a single volume dealing with earlier journeys made in the company of her father. Together the text runs to more than a thousand unhurried pages of enjoyable and often witty reading—for example, of a visit to Rome:

> One day we saw a grand mass in St Peter's, during which the poor old Pope [Pius IX] in vain tried to get a pinch of snuff; no sooner had he got his fingers on his box than he was violently seized, and put into some gorgeous new raiment and had to hide it again: he never to the end succeeded, though he was infallible . . .

Or this, of a Nubian woman:

> She was sitting on the steps of a sakkiah or native machine for raising water, flogging the beasts who turned it, and her baby was seated near her on the sand, a perfect lump of black flies, and so completely hidden by them that one could only discover it was a baby by its general shape and happy childish noises. . . . I very nearly bought one one day at the mother's wish in return for two empty reels of cotton and a button, to my father's intense horror, not decreased when he was told I wished to hang it up to the cabin ceiling to act as a fly-trap.

---

[1] Not quite true. This spectacular Indian tree had been first flowered in England in 1849 by Mrs Lawrence, of Ealing Park, who presented a raceme to the Queen.

Marianne North. Oil painting of New Zealand Flowers and Fruit, 1881. The spherical plant in the foreground is a small specimen of Raoulia eximia, *the '*Vegetable Sheep*', big plants of which are often mistaken at a distance by New Zealand shepherds for a strayed animal*

Marianne North. Photographed in Ceylon by Julia Margaret Cameron, 1876

Or of the polished Turkish Governor of Safed, who 'examined our sketches, and though he held most of them upside-down his compliments were without stint, and given with that air of sincerity which can never fail to be gratifying'.

In Ceylon in 1876 Marianne met a woman at least as remarkable as herself—Julia Margaret Cameron. Mrs Cameron, though much pre-occupied with a series of photographs of the 'absolutely superb back' of a native gardener, interrupted this labour of love to record for posterity her distinguished visitor, who wrote:

> She dressed me up in flowing draperies of cashmere wool, let down my hair, and made me stand with spiky cocoa-nut branches running into my head, the noonday sun's rays dodging my eyes between the leaves as the slight breeze moved them, and told me to look perfectly natural (with a thermometer standing at 96°)! Then she tried me with a background of breadfruit leaves and fruit, nailed flat against a window shutter, and told *them* to look natural, but both failed . . .

There are also, of course, innumerable descriptions of the plants she found and painted, which included a new genus in the Seychelles that Joseph Hooker named *Northea* in her honour; she is further commemorated in a very striking nepenthes from Borneo—*N. northiana*.

In the summer of 1880, Marianne, though still far from the end of her travels, offered to build a Gallery in Kew Gardens at her own expense, and at the same time presented her paintings to the nation. The gifts were accepted, and two years later the Gallery opened its doors to the public.

The architect was her old friend the versatile James Fergusson,[1] who gave his services free. He happened at that moment to be much concerned with the subject of the lighting of classical buildings, and I suppose that 'Pompeian' would best describe the interior of the North Gallery which, according to the *D.N.B.*, 'is generally admitted to be one of the most successful picture galleries as regards light in the kingdom'. Externally the building is red-brick and commonplace, with a veranda added subsequently to afford shelter to a custodian in charge of 'wet umbrellas and ladies' clogs'; there were also seats, but these were later pinched by William Dallimore[2] for use in his Temperate House.

Now I know that I have somewhat viciously attacked the obsolete method of display adopted in the museums at Kew, and that all that I wrote of them really applies equally to the North Gallery. Nothing could be more outmoded, more absurd, than to squeeze upwards of eight hundred paintings into a couple of rooms which might reasonably have housed a hundred, jamming them so close together that the walls look like a gigantic botanical postage-stamp album. But the North Gallery is not so much a museum as a museum-piece: something as whimsical, as extraordinary, as 'period' and as precious as the Albert Memorial or the Watts Mortuary Chapel at Compton, and it must never, *never* be touched.

---

[1] James Fergusson (1808–1886), indigo merchant, antiquarian, orientalist, architectural writer and much else besides. See the *D.N.B.*

[2] See Chapter 25.

The Marianne North Gallery

The paintings themselves, which for the most part show exotic plants in their natural surroundings, are of the greatest botanical interest; artistically, however, they are rather marred by the curiously dry and unattractive quality of the paint. They are grouped according to the country of their origin, and since Miss North, like Nature, abhorred a vacuum, yet further flowers scramble up the door-posts and across the lintels. The result is very odd indeed—and absolutely fascinating.

An excellent and detailed catalogue, published at the time of the opening of the Gallery, sold some seven thousand copies in the first year. Kew kindly presented me with one of the enlarged sixth edition (1914, 162 pages, price sixpence); today there is nothing available beyond a very short leaflet, and I suppose that a new edition of the book would have to cost a couple of pounds at the very least.

Marianne set out in November 1884 on what was to prove her last journey— her destination Chile, her main objective to paint the monkey-puzzle, the only one of the world's great trees that had so far eluded her; she was already a sick and weary woman. Back in England, she put the finishing touches to her Gallery and then withdrew to an old Cotswold-stone house at Alderley, in Gloucestershire. Soon she was a complete invalid; but she still adored her flowers, and in the last letter to her sister, written in June 1890 only a couple of months before her death, she told her:

> My peonies are a grand sight, and the iris and poppies and tree-lupins, rhododendrons and gaillardias; the great pink and white eremurus from the Himalaya have flowered for the first time in the rose garden, but I only managed to get there twice. Bleeding comes on if I walk much, and I fear I do not get stronger, in spite of turtle soup. . .

Her niece, Dame Katharine Furse—mother of Admiral Paul Furse, the distinguished botanist and botanical draughtsman—told me that she was always known in the family as 'Aunt Pop'.[1]

*   *   *

Standing beside the North Gallery, probably hardly even noticed by those who have come to Kew for flowers or fresh air, is a little lodge with a towering chimney-stack. This building, which is of considerable architectural interest, was designed in 1866 by William Eden Nesfield (1835–88), the Wykehamist landscape-gardener's Etonian son—an architect at one time in partnership with Norman Shaw. Nesfield developed, almost a decade before Shaw, a style based on the red-brick, sash-windowed architecture of late seventeenth- and early eighteenth-century England. Yet 'Shaw's posthumous reputation swallowed up Nesfield's'[2]—in part, perhaps, because Nesfield designed no public buildings. His *magnum opus* was Kinmel in Denbighshire, now the Clarendon School for Girls, whose entrance lodge (1868) is a sumptuous version of the humble little building at Kew.

*   *   *

Since we are within a stone's throw of the Flagstaff I had better deal with it now.

This vegetable monster, erected in 1959, is the fourth spar of the Douglas Fir (recently renamed *Pseudotsuga menziesii*, I see) to reach Kew from its homeland, British Columbia. For convenience I will refer to them as 'A', 'B', 'C' and 'D'.

'A', presented in 1856 by a Rotherhithe timber merchant named Edward Stamp, was fated from the start, for while being towed up the Thames it was cut in two by a tug. On reaching Kew it was spliced and hoisting begun; but

---

[1] I also gratefully acknowledge help and information given me by two other members of her family: Mrs Roger North and Mrs Louis Morgan.
[2] 'Kinmel, Denbighshire—II' by Mark Girouard, *Country Life*, 11 September 1969.

the tree and tackle blew over, and the spar, now broken into three pieces, had to be abandoned. Mr Stamp immediately presented another and yet larger one ('B'), which was successfully erected in 1861 on Victory Hill, where Chambers's Temple of Minden had once stood. Its height above ground was 159 feet, and it was surmounted by a glittering star. Princess Mary Adelaide wrote in her Journal on 2 May 1861 that immediately after breakfast she 'hurried to the Pleasure-grounds to see the flagstaff set up by sailors and shipwrights before the delighted eyes of the frantically excited Hookey, the astonished eyes of Kewites of all classes, and the disapproving eyes of our party who considered it highly tea-gardeny!'

In 1913, 'B' was discovered to be suffering from dry rot and condemned. Then came the War, and it was not until October 1919 that it was replaced by 'C', the gift of the Government of British Columbia and 214 feet high. But in 1956 this was found to be harbouring a wood-rotting fungus (which it had presumably brought with it), was lopped by 78 feet and soon afterwards taken down.

'D', the gift of the British Columbia Loggers Association and other bodies, was larger still—225 feet—and a full and illustrated account of the felling, transport and erection at Kew in 1959 by Sappers of this giant from Vancouver Island may be read in the *Kew Guild Journal*.[1] Barney Feeney, the principal truck-driver responsible for getting the spar the 25 miles from the interior of the Island to the coast, wrote, 'I've been hauling logs for 20 years both by locie and diesel truck, and I said to myself if they hadn't shortened this pole by 50 feet I would never have got round some of those bends in the canyon. Some day I hope to get over to Kew and say hello to this old fir again.'

[1] 1958, pp. 578–79 and 1959, pp. 678–81.

25

Dyer and Dallimore

SIR JOSEPH Hooker's first wife had died in 1874, and eighteen months later he had married *en secondes noces* a widow, the well-named Hyacinth Jardine (*née* Symonds), with whom, on his retirement from Kew in 1885, he had settled on lime-free soil at Sunningdale in a house that was soon to be engulfed in Himalayan rhododendrons. His doctors, diagnosing 'arterial degeneration in the vessel of the brain', had given him two years to live; God, more generous, allotted him a full twenty-five.

Age had mellowed Joseph, and if he was now known familiarly as 'Lion' it was because of his shaggy appearance rather than for any ferocity; his days of snarling and biting were over. True, at children's parties he would hide under the dining-room table to emerge sensationally roaring; but it was the roar of a very tame lion, calculated to amuse rather than to alarm the youngest infant present. Then there was his star turn, his 'eyebrow act', which Julian Huxley remembered witnessing as a child. The children 'watched him as he drew down his very long eyebrows, crossed them and anchored the ends between his lips. Then came the Moment. Suddenly he opened his mouth and the hairy coils sprang back to their normal position!'[1] It must surely have been the benign nonagenarian that Mrs Massingham had in mind when she applied to Joseph Hooker the improbable epithet 'gentle'.[2]

At the age of ninety-four Joseph was still working with undiminished zeal on the balsam family (*Impatiens*): apparently a botanist's nightmare— 'worse than orchids', he said despairingly. But his time had almost run out. He died on 10 December 1911, and having rejected an advance offer of burial in Westminster Abbey was laid beside his father in Kew churchyard. A memorial plaque in Wedgwood jasper ware, designed by Matilda Smith and placed in the church, shows him in profile, surrounded by some of his special flowers; the famous eyebrows are so in evidence that it looks almost as if a large butterfly had alighted on his brow.

Joseph's name is immortalised in a genus rather mysteriously called 'Sirhookera O.K. (Josephia) Wight'; I am not familiar with it. He is more unhappily remembered by an unloved alien that has now found its way into

---

[1] Mea Allan, *op. cit.*, p. 241.
[2] Betty Massingham, *Miss Jekyll*, David & Charles, 1966.

recent British floras as 'Joey Hooker's Weed'. This is *Galinsoga parviflora*,[1] a devilish sort of South American groundsel which was introduced in his day into the Herbaceous Ground (near the Cumberland Gate), from where it jumped the high wall to become in Surrey gardens a vegetable pest the equivalent of the grey squirrel in the animal world. It was kind of Matilda Smith not to include it in her memorial plaque.

*   *   *

A certain Professor Dyer had been appointed Assistant Director in 1875. Two years later he married Joseph's eldest daughter,[2] and was thus as well poised as he was well qualified to succeed his father-in-law on the latter's retirement. In 1891 Dyer increased his self-esteem by hyphenating his final Christian name to his surname; in 1899 he eagerly accepted a knighthood, and so, nearly thirty years later, was able to make an impressive exit from this world as 'Sir William Turner Thiselton-Dyer, K.C.M.G., C.I.E., F.R.S., F.L.S., etc., etc.' He may best be regarded as the last lap of the age of the Hookers, thus making their joint reign (from 1841 to 1905) as long as, and almost coincidental with that of Queen Victoria.

No one can deny that Thiselton-Dyer did a great deal for Kew during his thirty years there. He was a born administrator, an able organiser, and—in his own words—a 'botanical pope'; he seems also to have been a man of some taste. But he was more respected and feared than loved; his obituary in *The Times* described him as an autocrat who suffered fools impatiently, and Dr Turrill, not normally uncharitable, wrote of him:

> He was direct in speech and incisive in style and disliked ambiguity and any compromise with principles. It was unfortunate that he often wounded the susceptibilities of many whose views he did not accept. In many ways he was an autocrat and even a martinet, and many stories of his treatment of the staff at the Royal Botanic Gardens have been told to the writer by old Kewites. Thus, once when members of the Herbarium staff approached him with a request that he would support an application for an increase in their then very low salaries he replied that there was nothing valid to support the request. The cost of suits, among other things, was pointed out to him, and his answer was to visit a second-hand shop in Richmond, to purchase a suit for 7/6, and to parade the

---

[1] Also called Kew Weed, and Gallant Soldier by some who have trouble with its generic name.

[2] On his wedding day he received a postcard from a friend inscribed with the following riddle:
'What is closer than a hook and eye?'
'A hooker and eyer.'

Memorial tablet to Sir Joseph Hooker, designed by Matilda Smith, in Kew Church. The plants shown are Aristolochia mannii, Nepenthes albomarginata, Cinchona calisaya, Rhododendron thomsonii *and* Celmisia vernicosa

Herbarium dressed in it and proclaiming how cheap was the cost of living. There are many taller stories than this and probably they have lost nothing in the telling—and some of them are best forgotten.

Is it conceivable, one feels inclined to ask, that on some occasion the ancient Thiselton-Dyer, revisiting Kew, gave young Turrill a taste of his brusqueness? And, indeed, was it perhaps Turrill who wrote that obituary in *The Times*?

The great Sir William Thiselton-Dyer might not have cared to find himself sharing a chapter—and, indeed, getting a rather poor share of it—with William Dallimore, a youth of twenty who came to Kew in 1891 as a student gardener. But Dallimore deserves the fuller treatment, for he has left such a splendid account of the day-to-day life of a young Kew gardener in late Victorian times. His manuscript is in the Library at Kew, but extracts from it were published many years later in the *Journal*[1] of the Kew Guild, a society of Old Kewites which he was largely responsible for founding, with Dyer's encouragement, soon after his arrival there. These *Journals* — 'school magazines', as it were — contain a lot of interesting material about the doings of 'Old Boys' all over the world and of those still 'at school' (there is always a section entitled 'Wedding Bells'); but possibly the most valuable articles are those in which veterans such as Dallimore recall a distant past.

Dallimore arrived at Kew at the end of January, and having deposited his few belongings in the depressing lodging-house a friend had found for him he set out for his first sight of the Gardens whose praises his mother had often sung:

> It was a dull, damp, messy kind of a day, and everything looked dirty and dismal. The Aroid House — the first seen — was not inspiring; it looked as though it was covered with slates instead of glass, but it was not until I saw the Ferneries, Greenhouse, Succulent House and T-Range that I fully appreciated the dirt. The glass had not been washed after the fog and it was black with filth. To make things worse the Ferneries were wholly, and some of the other houses partly, glazed with green glass,[2] and most of them needed rebuilding. I did not know then what a harmful effect London fog has on plant life, and was not prepared for the many leafless and flowerless plants that should have been in first rate condition. Neither did I know of the scheme of reorganisation that was to transform the whole face of the establishment within the next few years . . .

He found the work he was put to in the Palm House — it consisted mainly of a perpetual war on mealy bugs — monotonous, the hours (6 a.m. to 6 p.m., six days a week, in summer) long, and the pay (seventeen shillings a week) not over-generous. His first sight of Thiselton-Dyer occurred one day as he was leaving the Palm House with several other student gardeners for the lunch break:

> We were walking together, some talking, others smoking, when suddenly pipes were thrust into pockets and conversation hushed. I very naturally asked the reason for such strange behaviour, and was told, *sotto voce*, to 'Shut up'. Presently we passed a rather slender, bearded man wearing riding breeches, brown velvet jacket, tweed waistcoat and Tyrolese hat,

---

[1] 1933, pp. 263–72; 1937, pp. 665–68; 1955, pp. 228–43; 1956, pp. 381–86; 1957, pp. 479–83; 1958, pp. 580–82, and obituary, 1959, pp. 702–03.
[2] The Palm House and Temperate House were initially glazed with green glass, but this was eventually replaced.

and smoking a cigarette. He took little notice of us, but after he had passed I was informed that he was the Director, that I must be very careful what I did when he was about, and that he rarely spoke to a young gardener. Moreover, he was the only member of the Staff who was allowed to smoke in the Gardens.

The Director contributed a rather patronising article to the first number of the *Kew Guild Journal* (1893) in which he explained the attitude adopted by Kew towards its student gardeners, of whom there were then about seventy:

> As you know, we do not 'coddle'.[1] We treat our young men as 'men' and expect them to work out their own salvation. We wish them to be manly, self-respecting and strenuous. We put, with the help of the Government, what help we can in their way, and leave them to make an intelligent use of it.

That, agreed Dallimore, was 'exactly how I found the place operating in my early days, except that men were not always encouraged to "work out their own salvation" if their salvation did not conform to some other person's interests, neither was it possible to get beyond a certain point in working out one's own salvation'.

Space does not admit of the relation of much that is of considerable interest, and an enterprising publisher, taking advantage of the present craze for everything Victorian, might do far worse than produce a condensed version of Dallimore's 800-page typescript. It was soon clear that the 'Boy'—as the beardless youngster was for a time always called—would go far, and his rapid promotions inevitably aroused jealousies. He proved himself particularly skilful as a propagator of difficult plants, and this brought him into contact with several distinguished collectors. Indeed, eventually, through his successful raising of some disa hybrids (disas are terrestrial orchids, chiefly natives of Africa) he actually met the Director, who brought that great orchid enthusiast, his friend Jo Chamberlain, to see them.

In 1896 Dallimore was put in charge of the Temperate House, where once again insect pests were his chief headache. Fumigation, using real tobacco confiscated by excise officers and treated to make it (allegedly) unfit for smoking, had been tried with success in the Palm House, but it had been believed that certain plants in the Temperate House would react

---

[1] In 1875, the year that Dyer came to Kew as Assistant Director, a young gardener named David Judd described the initiation ceremony to which he had been subjected on his arrival. He was 'chained up before the bothy fire' and 'branded with the letters K.G.—Kew Gardens, while a constable of the garden read over the rules to be observed . . .' (*Gardeners' Chronicle*, 19 June 1875).

unfavourably to it. Dallimore thought otherwise, and obtained permission to make the experiment:

> One wet afternoon in November, when the atmosphere was heavy, I collected about $1\frac{3}{4}$ cwts. of tobacco from the stores, got together all the fumigating pots I could find, borrowed two braziers from the Clerk of Works and a portable forge from the men who were building the new wing, with two labourers from the Arboretum to help. . . . The men were employed on the job, and in order to see that no tobacco was allowed to blaze I walked about from point to point damping the tobacco when necessary. The forge was the most effective unit for we got a volume of smoke from it almost like that from a factory chimney.
>
> After the first hour the atmosphere became unpleasant, and after $1\frac{1}{2}$ hours the first casualties occurred, some of the young gardeners having to leave the house. It took $2\frac{1}{2}$ hours to use all the tobacco, and by that time the smoke was very dense. At the conclusion there were only two labourers, the stoker, and one young gardener to leave the house; I was still about but very unhappy. . . .

The two labourers and the stoker did not turn a hair and, though warned of the risk, smoked the tainted tobacco throughout.

The experiment, repeated at intervals, was extremely successful in curing the infestation; incidentally, it also cured Dallimore of smoking for life.

In 1901 Dallimore was made foreman of the Arboretum, which involved, amongst other things, keeping an eye on workers scattered over a very large area. Here, wrote one of his subordinates, he earned a new nickname: 'We call Mr Dallimore De Wet because we never know where he is. He comes to look over our work, stays a short time, then goes away. We watch him off and think we are all right for a couple of hours, but after a short time we may look round and find him coming again from quite a different direction.' De Wet was, of course, the Boer general whose ubiquity was proving so disconcerting to the British troops in South Africa.

Dallimore makes it plain that he was still finding Thiselton-Dyer very tiresome. The Director hated seeing leaves on the paths, but if a man was caught sweeping them up he was told that he ought to be better employed than 'tickling three or four leaves about with a broom'. Then there was trouble with Lady Thiselton-Dyer, who had put herself in charge of the waterfowl in the Gardens although there was a man already doing the job, and with Miss Thiselton-Dyer, 'looked upon as a horsewoman', who created all sorts of difficulties in the stables. 'We could not understand,' wrote Dallimore, 'why the Director allowed his womenfolk to interfere in garden matters.' He was, of course, still the innocent bachelor.

While admitting that it was 'an education' to serve under Thiselton-

*Sir William Thiselton-Dyer and his Constables, c. 1905.
In the background, King William's Temple*

Dyer, and that his garden-planning — for example, the opening up of vistas and the planting of great drifts of snowdrops and daffodils — was admirable, Dallimore could not conceal his dislike of the man. He described the Director as 'a very exalted and unapproachable person, very efficient but out of sympathy with his subordinates', who 'acted as though he was the owner of the place rather than its custodian' and who enjoyed humiliating his principal officers in the presence of their underlings.

He had a passion for uniforms, getting himself appointed Inspector of Constables so that, even though it involved the removal of his beard,[1] he could strut about the Gardens in peacock splendour. In fact, everybody was ordered to wear a uniform — the stokers, for example, 'blue uniforms, piped with red'. Alone the firemen rebelled, and were left to do their grimy and dangerous job in clothes more suitable.

It may not be generally known that after the Boer War there was, though obviously to a far lesser extent, an outbreak of discontent among soldiers returning to civilian life of the kind so familiar after the two World Wars.

[1] Or so it was said; yet in the photograph he appears to be bearded.

The hours of the junior gardeners at Kew were intolerably long, their pay wretched; and there was no way in which they could air their grievances, all complaints being rejected outright by Dyer. But in 1903 two men, one of them named William Purdom, came to Kew and decided to fight for better conditions. In 1905 a Meeting of the United Government Workers' Federation was held on Kew Green, at which two Labour Members of Parliament were present and Purdom and his friend much in evidence. News of this reached Dyer—some accounts say that he actually attended it—and next day the two rebellious gardeners were sacked.

But Dyer had acted rashly. The Members of Parliament made representations to the President of the Board of Agriculture and Dyer was ordered to reinstate the men. Before the year was out, he resigned the Directorship of Kew; he was only sixty-two. He seems to have made a gracious exit. All the higher staff were presented with signed photographs, being given the choice between one showing him in riding-breeches, velvet jacket and tweed cap, and another in which he was wearing his uniform as Inspector of Constables. 'Most of us,' wrote Dallimore, 'chose the former, and he was quite disappointed. He was very proud of his uniform.'

It is hard to feel much affection for Dyer, but he was a scientist and a scholar of considerable distinction who did much for Kew and for the Colonies. He worked with his friend Joseph Chamberlain, who was at the Colonial Office from 1895 to 1903, to develop economic botany and colonial agriculture. He enlarged the Library and the Herbarium building, started the *Kew Bulletin*, and while Assistant Director helped to make the Jodrell Laboratory 'the best botanical laboratory in Europe'. And above all, he added greatly to the beauty of the Gardens. He was succeeded by Lieutenant-Colonel (later Sir David) Prain.

In 1909, Dallimore, who was now nearly forty, joined the Museum staff and was largely responsible for the formation of the Wood Museum—an appropriate task since his work in the Arboretum had made him a leading authority in this country on trees and shrubs and their cultivation; *A Handbook of Coniferae*, which he wrote in conjunction with A. B. Jackson, has remained a standard work. Later he took charge of the Museums of Economic Botany. He retired in 1936 to a small house near Tunbridge Wells which he renamed 'Kew Cottage'. The day before his death, in his eighty-ninth year, he had been planting a batch of new rose-trees that had just arrived.

'. . . and only man is vile'

A CAREFUL AND EARNEST NOTICE
This garden earnestly requests that visitors will spit betle
outside the railing, and knock the ashes of pipes also outside.
(Notice in Howqua's famous garden at Canton)

AT KEW, almost every prospect pleases, and only relatively few of the visitors are vile.

There is an entertaining correspondence file in the Herbarium Library which tells sad stories of those who when visiting Kew have been caught either breaking the law of the land or transgressing against the regulations of the Gardens. Sinners in the first category were for the most part involved in theft or sexual irregularities; lesser offenders mostly damaged plants or made nuisances of themselves in a variety of ways.

Wanton damage is recorded as early as 1771, when one June night 'some villains got into the garden of her Royal Highness the Princess Dowager of Wales, at Kew, and destroyed all the greenhouse plants, which were deemed a very curious collection'.[1] Exactly a century later a Miss Stone was surprised 'knocking off the flowers of Rhododendrons with her Parasol', and when reprimanded immediately broke off a large branch to show how little she cared. Then there was Mr Wright, stopped in 1898 for bringing a 'large bag' into the Gardens. But how large must a bag be to be a *large* bag? Mr Wright maintained that his was only a *small* bag. After five years of careful, prayerful consideration the Board of Agriculture (which had taken over the control of the Gardens in 1903) laid down that any bag bigger than $7'' \times 5'' \times 4''$ would be counted as 'large', and presumed to have been introduced into the Gardens with felonious intent.

Just *what* is forbidden by these Regulations? Obvious things, of course, such as getting drunk in the Gardens, or mistaking them for a fun fair or a pop festival or a brothel. Or a parade ground: in July 1861, a party of two hundred South Middlesex Cadet Volunteers marched, muskets at the slope and preceded by their band, to the main entrance and demanded admission. The Porter, faced with a situation without precedent in his experience, persuaded the band to deposit its instruments at the gate, but allowed the soldiers to enter and drill in the Gardens. However, soon afterwards a new

[1] *Gentleman's Magazine*, 1771, *41*, p. 284.

Regulation was added—to the effect that 'No unauthorised person shall drill, or practise military evolutions, or use arms, or play any game or music, or practise gymnastics . . . in these gardens and grounds'. In the 1870s came a further Regulation which read, 'As these gardens are for instruction and recreation, smoking, idle sports, and play are forbidden.'

So, very reasonably, one cannot play a trombone or a transistor in the Orchid House. But Regulation 16, as now worded, makes the use, or even the possession of a hearing-aid equally reprehensible in that it is technically 'an apparatus . . . for the reproduction by electrical or mechanical means of sound'. Regulation 23 prohibits you from delivering a public address in the Gardens, and Mr G. Jacobs was not telling the whole truth when he wrote to the Director:

> Sir—I shall esteem it a favour if you will kindly let me know, if you instructed keepers at the Gardens VR13, VR15, also a man in plain clothes to force me out, because I had a parrot on my shoulder, they laid old [sic] of me in such force that caused me to fall down and the bird flew on the tree, the man in plain clothes refused to give me his name. . . .

For Constable H. Fitzwater had a different and well substantiated version of the story. Noticing a large crowd, he went to investigate and 'saw the man with the parrot giving a sort of performance, showing tricks with his bird, and giving a regular lecture to the people about Lloyd George . . .'

So what is there left to do at Kew? Well—you can stretch your legs (but not too wide: see Regulation 18). Or—if all else fails—you could even, perhaps, look at the flowers.

There were other complaints made by visitors about the staff. In 1910, a Mr Long maintained that Goodridge, the foreman of the Palm House, had deliberately turned his hose on him and his sister, thus 'considerably spotting his sister's dress'; but the foreman claimed that he had merely misjudged the force of the jet, and Mr Long was told not to be silly. In 1920, Miss Mollard alleged that she had surrendered (as was then the rule) her magnificent and expensive camera at the entrance, only to be fobbed off on leaving with a very inferior one in its place; we are not informed of the outcome. Even the plants were sometimes accused of aggressive behaviour: 'One of the attendants at Kew Gardens told the writer that he was once severely rated by a lady who had been struck in the face by the pollinium of *Catasetum saccatum*,[1] and had come to him with the disc yet sticking to her cheek! Such experiences are not uncommon.' In the Munich Botanic Garden the poison ivy (*Rhus toxicodendron*) is kept caged like a lion.

---

[1] An epiphytic orchid from Demerara; the 'writer' was either A. E. Knight or Edward Step, joint authors of *Hutchinson's Popular Botany*. The pollinium is an agglomeration of pollen.

Kew has never attempted to emulate Howqua's garden at Canton, in which a label attached to a fruit-tree near the Library of Verdant Purity (i.e., the summerhouse) bore the inscription, 'Ramblers here *will be excused plucking the fruit.*' We hear as early as 1772 of a certain Tom Rolls, apprehended for 'cutting ten brace of melons from the Royal Gardens at Kew,' and the *cause célèbre* also dates from the time when Kew was still royal property. In 1824, Robert Sweet,[1] a very distinguished and highly respected nurseryman, author of a number of important botanical and horticultural works, was indicted for 'feloniously receiving . . . Seven Plants, value £7; and Seven Garden Pots, value 6d. the Goods of our Lord the King; which, on the night previous, had been stolen [from Kew Gardens], he well knowing them to have been stolen'. The case came up before Mr Justice Best at the Old Bailey, and after evidence had been heard from men with such improbable names as Mr Wacey Whiskey, and much testimony given of the defendant's high reputation and unblemished record, Sweet was acquitted.

Inevitably, dubious sexual behaviour and bawdy talk were fairly frequent causes of complaint. One has little sympathy for Albert Newcombe of Ealing, in trouble on 16 August 1911, for using 'filthy and obscene language' to five girls aged between eleven and fourteen who had shared a seat with him near the foot of the Pagoda. But just when did the behaviour of courting couples overstep the permitted bounds? Poor David Prain became involved in this difficult problem when in December 1921 he received a letter from a certain Mr John Batten. It was, alleged Mr Batten, quite impossible to walk in the remoter parts of the Gardens (even, apparently, in mid-winter) without coming upon scenes which filled him with shame, embarrassment and revulsion, and he insisted that Sir David should take immediate and drastic action.

Sir David sought legal advice from the Office of Works. 'It is a fine point,' he wrote, 'as to whether a "lovers' embrace" can be held to be an "act in violation of public decency". When such embraces are accompanied by exposure of the person our Constables in the past have always interfered . . .' He himself saw no objection to what he coyly and rather vaguely termed 'amorous dalliance'.

The legal adviser studied the Regulations and replied that where 'amorous dalliance' was concerned, 'If it means a man kissing a girl (or vice versa) in an ordinary and usual manner', then clearly no exception could be taken. But he was a man of the world: 'There are, however, different ways of kissing. . . .' In his opinion the Regulations were not well drafted: 'I believe that the words "to the annoyance of the persons using a Park" allude to the use of "profane, indecent or obscene language" and not to the commission

[1] See *The Trial of Robert Sweet*, London, 1824.

of "any act in violation of Public decency". It is quite possible that the latter instead of causing annoyance might cause pleasure or amusement.' He postulated various 'positions' that couples might be likely to assume, and gave his opinion on their acceptibility or otherwise:

'(a). A man and girl lying together in close embrace, the man lying upon the girl as if in the act of connection.' This was clearly indecent.

'(b). A man and a woman lying *parallel* to one another in close embrace. In such a case as this, unless the man accompanies it by throwing his legs across the girl, or has his hand upon her person either from beneath her skirts, or through her blouse, I do not consider it anything more than a lack of taste and modesty. If, however. . . .'

Prain studied the letter and replied, 'But what is quite as common as (b) and what does offend visitors is the practice the woman of a pair has of reclining upon the man and tickling his neck or nose with a feather or a spike of grass. . .' He himself would not be shocked by such behaviour, yet he felt that some visitors to the Gardens might be.

But Mr Batten was determined that 'lying on the grass', however innocently, must be altogether forbidden, and he insisted that Prain should write to this effect to the Minister of Agriculture. Why Prain did not simply tell him to go to hell is not clear; though a soldier, he does not appear to have been a very forceful character. He wrote as requested; but he added a caution that in his opinion such a regulation 'might arouse the ridicule of the Press'—a thing always to be dreaded. The Minister heartily agreed: 'Mr Batten's suggestion,' he replied, 'is a foolish one and, even if adopted, it could not be carried out properly. . . .'

Poor Mr Batten! Let us trust that he never went to the Istanbul Public Gardens where, I am told, there is a 'lovers' corner' labelled 'Flirtation permitted here'; and I also hope that he never chanced to visit Kew when *Amorphophallus titanum* was in flower, or he might have felt obliged to protest to Dame Nature herself.

Even the sight of a bare limb was at one time considered as shocking in the Gardens as it used to be in Roman Catholic churches. In 1884, a correspondent wrote to the Director to protest that people were being admitted to Kew 'in déshabille, and not infrequently to the extent of exposing their lower limbs', with the result that the Curator received instructions to exclude 'men with bare legs'.

The problem of dress arose again about 1895 when Thiselton-Dyer courageously decided to employ three young women as gardeners. The following appeared in the *Daily Telegraph* on 23 January 1896:

The innovation of employing female gardeners at Kew appears to have landed the authorities in an amusing difficulty. Sir Trevor Lawrence,

*The First Lady Gardeners at
Kew (photograph c. 1895)*
'*They gardened in bloomers the
   newspapers said,
So to Kew without waiting all
   Londoners sped ;
From the tops of the buses they
   had a fine view,
Of the ladies in bloomers who
   gardened at Kew.*'

distributing prizes on Saturday at Kingston, said that when three ladies were engaged at Kew Gardens the first difficulty that arose was as to the costume they should wear. They were asked what dress they preferred, and the bloomer costume was suggested, but the result was not satisfactory. . . . People used to get on the tops of omnibuses to see the young ladies at work. The Director of the Gardens said that would not do, and told the young ladies that they must wear a dress similar to that of the ordinary gardeners. They accordingly, Sir Trevor added, appeared in 'suitable costume'.

The Times pointed out that these ladies were at all events much more decently arrayed than was 'the first gardeneress, Eve', and a religious journal seized the opportunity to remind its readers that 'when sex ceases to be emphasised in dress, the baser passions will have less stimulus'. The dress ultimately ordained for '*Horticultrix kewensis*' was 'brown bloomers, thick woollen stockings and ordinary brown peaked caps', and she was further enjoined to wear long macintoshes on her way to and from work. As Thiselton-Dyer put it, he was not going to encourage any 'sweethearting'.

It was the opinion of Bishop Heber, unworried about sex discrimination, that in beautiful surroundings only *man* was vile; but where Kew was concerned, certain women were to prove themselves even viler. In the early hours of the morning of 8 February 1913, suffragettes broke into the Gardens and ran amok in the Orchid House, leaving behind them a note to the effect that orchids were destructible 'but not women's honour'. They got away; but a fortnight later 'two voteless women', calling for 'Peace on earth and good will towards men *when women get the vote*', burnt down the Refreshment Pavilion and were caught. The building ('in the Swiss chalet style') was replaced in 1915 by another whose appearance, in the opinion of the *Kew Guild Journal*, 'leaves much to be desired'; if this is the present one, I find it pleasant enough.

Thirty years later another vandal, Adolf Hitler, dropped more than thirty high explosive bombs and 'thousands' of incendiaries on the Gardens, breaking a fair amount of glass but killing no one, and doing far less damage then the suffragettes or, indeed, nature herself, whose great hailstorm of 3 August 1879 broke nearly 40,000 panes weighing eighteen tons.

By far the most extraordinary and persistent trouble-maker at Kew was a certain Mr Austin Farmar, a septuagenarian who haunted the place and pestered the staff for seven whole years (from 1917 to 1924) before Sir Arthur Hill, who succeeded Prain as Director in 1922, finally took him to court and had him permanently barred from the Gardens.

Farmar was a well-informed but mentally unstable amateur botanist whose chief complaint was that more than three thousand plants in the Gardens and Houses were misnamed, and that the staff were a set of ignorant fools; that he was not wholly mistaken about the labels is confirmed by Prain's private admission that Farmar's corrections 'did serve a useful purpose'.

Farmar's favourite technique was to attach himself to visitors and 'show them round'. Many of these, mistaking him for an official of the Gardens, were flattered by this attention and impressed by his knowledge; but his pomposity and melodramatic gesticulations sometimes provoked mirth, and on one occasion he wrote angrily to Prain to complain of a young gardener in the Palm House who 'mocked my actions as I described the growth of the "stem" in the Musa [banana]'. There were constant scenes, for Farmar never missed an opportunity of loudly denouncing the incompetence of a foreman, especially if he happened to be within earshot. Some 'accidentally' turned the hose on him; but Mr Raffill, of the Mexican House, overhearing himself described as 'a scoundrel, a liar and a scamp', a man who '*thinks* he knows Latin', fetched a constable. Farmar shouted to Raffill, 'Come outside! You're in your own dung-heap here!' and unpleasantness inevitably ensued.

There was another fracas in 1920, with a foreman named Van Houtten, that ended in a brawl during which Farmar alleged he was hosed, knocked down, and his shoulder so badly dislocated that he had to have hospital treatment under an anaesthetic. Prain established to his satisfaction that Farmar had been the aggressor; but, weakly, he still took no action beyond requesting the Ministry to provide him with a plain-clothes female detective. (Why *female*?) He also asked whether he was empowered to prevent this menace from entering the Gardens; but Farmar had a season ticket with six months still to run, and the legal adviser to the Ministry said that this could not be revoked, even if the money was refunded.

In January 1921, when Farmar applied for a new season ticket, his request was refused and his money returned. However, it made no difference; he simply paid his penny each day at the turnstile and continued his visits as before. Then came some unpleasantness over a small girl; but it cannot have been very serious, and since the father refused to allow his daughter to give evidence in court it could not be followed up. The legal adviser wrote, 'I think we must get rid of this horrible old man, even at some risk of trouble'; but still nothing was done

Three years passed, and Farmar was being as awful as ever. In March 1924, after another scene, a new line of action was tried: Sir Arthur Hill, now in the driving seat, wrote to Mrs Farmar begging her to use her influence to stop her husband visiting the Gardens. He received a pathetic reply: she was in hospital undergoing a serious operation; the day on which the last scene had occurred was the anniversary of the death of her husband's beloved first wife. For the past ten years she had done all she could for the poor old man, who was now eighty. Why could not Kew stop persecuting him?

At last, after yet another row in the Temperate House, a summons was applied for, and in spite of the evidence of a Twickenham magistrate that in his opinion the defendant 'knew more about the plants in Kew Gardens than all the officials put together', Farmar was found guilty of 'wilfully annoying persons lawfully using the Gardens', fined £2 with ten shillings costs and ordered to keep away. When, six weeks later, he attempted to slip through the turnstiles, he was prevented from entering. Kew never saw him again.

27

Kew—Yesterday, Today and Tomorrow

THIS MUST be a chapter of loose ends: of things that lack of space have elbowed out, and of more recent happenings—for though the overall pattern of Kew was established once and for all by the Hookers and Thiselton-Dyer, there has been continual progress.

Dr Turrill's book on Kew deals amost exclusively with the botanical and scientific aspects of the Gardens, whereas I have deliberately chosen to stress the historical. It may, however, be useful if I mention here those attractions that each season regularly provides in various parts of the Gardens, though notices posted at the entrances always list special plants at that moment in flower.

In snowdrop-- and again in bluebell-time there is the obligatory pilgrimage—and what a long way it seems!—to the Queen's Cottage. Daffodils are at their best round the Temple of Aeolus. Between late March and early May there is the marvellous plantation of magnolias[1] to visit, and should you catch a spring when the rose and crimson Himalayan *Magnolia campbellii*[2] has chosen to put on a special show you will hardly be able to fight your way to it through the sea of photographers. Unforgettable, too, are the crab-apples near the Water-lily house and the avenue of Japanese cherries that leads to King William's Temple. Something is almost always happening in spring in Rhododendron Dell; then there are the irises near Cambridge Cottage; and here and there enough *Syringa* spp. to justify Alfred Noyes's recommendation to 'go down to Kew in lilac-time' and, if you feel so disposed, 'wander hand in hand [which the authorities permit] with love in summer's wonderland'.

Now the roses: the bloated modern cultivars with names like 'Ma Perkins' or 'Mrs Potter Palmer' near the Palm House, and the wide-eyed species chiefly to be found between the Temperate House and Moss Hill. The hardy heaths, too—and, incidentally, how long will it be before we have *Erica* 'Ted'? So summer gives way at last to autumn, trees turn to gold, and a million unloved (by me) half-hardy annuals are uprooted from the formal beds and thrown upon the bonfires. Now, and throughout the winter, is the

---

[1] Consult the map in the *Souvenir Guide*.
[2] Named after Joseph Hooker's friend, Dr Archibald Campbell (see p. 153).

time for the energetic to explore the remoter parts of the Gardens—the Lake and the Arboretum. The climate and soil of Kew are inimical to certain trees and shrubs; Kew has therefore acquired two vegetable Whipsnades, as it were—the National Pinetum at Bedgebury in Kent (1923) and Wakehurst Place in Sussex (1968), which are rewarding at all times of the year.

The nearer we get to the present day, the more difficult it becomes to write frankly about those who have controlled the recent destiny of Kew; some indication of what they achieved is to be found *passim* in this book.

Dallimore has something to say about (Sir) Arthur Hill, who became Assistant Director in 1907 and Director in 1922. He found him a tidy, methodical man, sympathetic, and ready to do all that was in his power to improve the working conditions and wages of his subordinates. His only adverse criticism was that Hill, a public school and university man, showed 'a subtle difference in his attitude' towards those who had not had the same advantages as himself; but Edward Hyams adds that his 'good qualities were partially concealed by a pompous manner and a way of making somewhat cynical judgments'.[1] Hill met his death in 1941 while riding in the Old Deer Park. I knew him only very slightly.

Sir Edward Salisbury, Director from 1943 to 1956, is that *rara avis*, a scientist who can express himself in English comprehensible to the layman; he is, as I write, still very much alive at the age of ninety. I took tea with him on several occasions in the early fifties, and was always fascinated by the brilliance and variety of his conversation. One day he told me that he always inspected the trouser turn-ups of guests recently back from abroad, thus sometimes finding seeds of exotic plants imported in all innocence in defiance of the Regulations laid down by the Ministry of Agriculture and Fisheries. On another, he discussed shock treatment of plants with particular reference to a magnolia—I forget the species—in the Temperate House which did not normally flower until about thirty years old. In February 1943, however, bombs destroyed a lot of the glass in this House, thus exposing a ten-year-old specimen to sudden severe cold—with the result that it immediately flowered! Of subsequent Directors I will leave others to speak when the time is ripe.

In the summer of 1910 an important 'Japan-British Exhibition' was held at the White City, Shepherd's Bush. Among the exhibits that attracted particular attention was a copy, four-fifths the actual size, of a famous Buddhist temple gateway in Kyoto known as the Chokushi Mon ('Gate of the Imperial Messenger'), dating from the latter part of the sixteenth century.

[1] *The English Garden*, Thames & Hudson, 1964.

The cost to the organisers of dismantling and returning this bulky copy to the country that already possessed the original may well have seemed hardly to make sense, and I imagine that when the Exhibition closed, the Kyoto Exhibitors' Association looked round for—to put it bluntly—somewhere to dump it. Not being British, it did not qualify to join the model of the Taj Mahal at the Imperial Institute, and possibly the Director of the Victoria and Albert Museum—who was, I believe, approached—begrudged the space it would occupy. So, and not for the first time when a handsome white elephant had to be stabled, somebody thought of Kew—and in my opinion it proved a very happy thought indeed. The offer was accepted and in due course the Gateway was installed on Moss (i.e., Mosque) Hill, a site that at all events already had oriental (though Moslem and bogus) associations.

The Gateway, says Dr Turrill, is 'made of the close-grained wood of *Cupressus obtusa*[1] and is roofed with a thick layer of cedar-bark shingles and sheet lead'; its overall colour is tawny, chocolate-brown and shoe-polish black, enlivened by a few touches of bronze. The figures and animals with which it is decorated are finely carved, and the setting could hardly be bettered. Wisterias bestride the railings that enclose it, Japanese azaleas sprawl at its feet and mature planes and cedars stand guard over it. It may be an oddity to find at Kew—but then, so is the Pagoda; and the Chokushi Mon is at least an example of genuine oriental craftsmanship.

I do not know the precise dimensions of the Chokushi Mon, and, surprisingly enough, neither Dr Turrill nor the author of Murray's *Handbook for Travellers in Japan* (1903 ed.), both gluttons for statistics, have seen fit to enlighten us here; one might perhaps equate the Kew version of it with a haystack or a small pantechnicon. It also seems at first sight strange that the Japanese craftsmen chose to make this small reduction in scale, but it must be remembered that a four-fifths *linear* reduction means that the *volume* is approximately halved.

Murray provides us with a detailed account of the original gateway, which was brought to Kyoto from Hideyoshi's wonderful palace at Fushini and is also known as *Higurashi no Mon* 'because a whole day might be spent in examining it'. I have not seen it, but I am perplexed by Murray's description of its principal carvings:

> The subject on the transverse panels is Kyo-yo (Hsü-yu) a hero of early Chinese legend, who, having rejected the Emperor Yao's proposal to resign the throne to him, is represented washing his ear at a waterfall to get rid of the pollution caused by the ventilation of so preposterous an

[1] Now, I gather, changed to *Chamaecyparis obtusa* ('*chamai*, on the ground, i.e. dwarf, *Kuparissos*, Cypress', says the R.H.S. *Dictionary*). But *C. obtusa* grows to 80 or 90 feet, and *C. lawsoniana* up to 200 feet. Perhaps some botanist can explain why these giants have been so misleadingly renamed.

idea; the owner of the cow opposite is supposed to have quarrelled with him for thus defiling the stream, at which he was watering his beast.

Perplexed—because no such scene is anywhere to be found in the copy: no ear, no waterfall, not even a cow! Dr Turrill, however, exactly describes what is figured on the Gateway at Kew, and I cannot account for the discrepancy:

> The panels ... portray in open carving an ancient Chinese legend illustrating the devotion of a pupil to his master. On the western panel, the master—Kosekko—is seen on horseback crossing a bow-shaped bridge over a river into which he has thrown his left shoe. On the opposite panel, the devoted pupil—Choryo—is shown rising from the water on the back of a dragon (which has come to his aid) and is holding up the recovered shoe with the toe pointing to his mouth.

As I sat on a conveniently-placed bench to study the Gateway, I felt that all that was lacking to complete the picture was a bevy of kimono-clad maidens. This was too much to hope for; but soon there did arrive a little company of schoolgirls which, as is customary today, included a few non-Europeans. Among them were two Asians, and though they were certainly not Japanese they did, I thought, cast a wistful glance at the Chokushi Mon as they passed by.

In October 1971 the Emperor of Japan, Hirohito, planted in Kew Gardens near the main entrance a Japanese cedar (*Cryptomeria japonica*) sent from Tokyo. His visit to England, had, very understandably, met with a certain amount of hostility, and there was no great surprise when next morning the tree was found cut down and sodium chlorate poured on its roots to destroy them. Nearby lay a card inscribed, 'THEY DID NOT DIE IN VAIN' (though one might argue that the cedar had). A man was arrested but later released, and soon afterwards unroyal hands planted a replacement.

Until Prain's day, admission to the Gardens had always been free, but in 1916 a charge of one penny was introduced. This was abolished in 1924, re-introduced in 1926, abolished again in 1929 and once more introduced in 1931; what accounted for all this chopping and changing I do not know. In 1951 there was a correspondence in *The Times* about what was the best pennyworth in London. Sir Sydney Cockerell proposed Kew Gardens, and the entrance charge was immediately raised to threepence. In 1971, with the advent of decimal coinage, this became one new penny—almost the only adjustment I know of where a price was actually, if only marginally, reduced. And 1p it has remained—so that Kew is still 'in for a penny' whereas the Zoo is now 'in for a pound'. It is still the best pennyworth in London; even public lavatories are now twopence, I am told.

I trust that Mr Brenan, the present Director, should he read this, will not forthwith raise the charge to 3p. If so, then let there be a vast outcry; for public protests, though it may take time (remember the war for morning opening!) do usually bring eventual victory. One battle very swiftly won was that which was fought on the outbreak of the Second World War, when the Gardens were immediately closed altogether. Air-raid shelters to accommodate fifty thousand people would, it was alleged, have to be constructed — which was impossible. But was this the real reason? May it not perhaps have seemed a heaven-sent opportunity for restoring, if only for a season, the Gardens to the scientists? Fortunately there was so vociferous a cry of indignation that within a fortnight the authorities had been obliged to relent.

On 27 April 1969 a sinister article appeared in the *Sunday Telegraph* predicting that the Gardens would be closed altogether to the public within the next five years, so that the institution could become 'the centre of a worldwide campaign against food shortage in underdeveloped countries.' An 'official' of Kew informed the reporter that its filing cabinets 'probably contained all the secrets' necessary to avert disaster, but that nothing could be done 'if we go on pretending to be a public park'. Another 'official' informs me that all this research is already being carried out by commercial firms. However, nearly a decade has now passed, and happily there is still no sign of this horrible threat being implemented.

Australia is the only continent, indeed the only country, now to have a whole House to itself at Kew. Until this was built in 1952, most non-hardy Australians (other than orchids and ferns) had to struggle for survival in the overcrowded Temperate House, where there was neither the light nor, since their companions did not care for it, the dryness to which they are accustomed in their homeland. Inside the new Australian House, with glass supported by slim aluminium ribbing, it is so light that one might almost be out of doors, and it can of course be kept as dry as is necessary.

The House was originally stocked from seed of some six hundred plants indigenous to Australia, collected and presented to Kew by a very remarkable and enormously wealthy Scot, Captain Neil McEacharn, whose grandfather had made a fortune in Australian gold mines. He was very kind to me, and since his name is not mentioned either by Dr Turrill or in the Souvenir Guide, I shall digress to pay a small tribute to his memory.

In 1930, while on his way from Venice to London, Neil noticed in *The Times* an advertisement of a property for sale on Lake Maggiore. For the past two years he had been thinking of making a garden in Italy; when, therefore, his train reached Verbania-Pallanza he broke his journey, saw the place, and bought it as casually as you or I might buy a packet of cigarettes. Within twenty-five years, and in spite of the War and the necessity later of dispensing with the services of fifty of his gardeners, he had extended and converted the grounds of the Villa Taranto into the finest botanic garden in Italy. On his death he bequeathed it to the Italian nation to be the country's equivalent of Kew Gardens.[1]

Neil was one of the kindest, simplest, most humble, most generous, most genuine men I have ever known. He had been twice a widower when, some thirty years ago, I first met him, and his second wife, Emma, had been a first cousin of Queen Wilhelmina of the Netherlands. But he was wholly without class-consciousness; consequently, when one stayed in his hospitable, comfortable but rather pretentious house—it had been built in 1875 in continental-baronial style, and Neil himself referred to it in his book as 'a horror'—one might find as fellow guests a princess or two, a duke who owned most of Scotland, and a couple of working gardeners who had, one felt, hung up their spades in the hall. All were made equally welcome, and talk (over the champagne) would be of magnolias, not of grouse moors.

Neil told me something that, though wholly irrelevant, is perhaps worth recording. In the thirties he found himself inexplicably summoned to Rome by Mussolini, who immediately began cross-examining him about his family. How was his sister? Was his aunt still alive? The mystery was soon solved: Mussolini had been having English lessons from the old family nurse, and since Neil and his relations had often provided the material for conversation, his curiosity had been aroused. It was thanks to Mussolini's orders that throughout the War the untenanted Villa Taranto and its garden were left untouched; and Neil, who cared nothing for politics, never found the least embarrassment in speaking later of his gratitude to that monster for this particular kindness.

But to return to Kew. The Australian House is admirably designed, though inevitably it is not big enough, and in particular it is too low: only thirty-three feet at its highest point. There are wattles (*Acacia* to the botanist, mimosas to you and me and the florist) which grow all too quickly to eighty or a hundred feet, and a blue gum (*Eucalyptus amygdalina* var. *regnans*) that in its native land has been known to attain almost the height of our St Paul's Cathedral (365 feet). The House is, however, excellently managed, obstreperous trees being first lopped and finally replaced by youngsters. In the large central bed we can become acquainted with many other characteristic Australian plants such as the banksias, bottlebrushes (*Callistemon*) and that brilliant vegetable ladybird—Sturt's desert pea (*Clianthus formosus*). There is Australia's only rhododendron, *R. lochae*, from Queensland, which was first flowered at Kew in 1939. And then, a reminder of old England, there creeps everywhere a modest little violet not

---

[1] See 'The Villa Taranto: A Scotsman's Garden in Italy' by Neil McEacharn, *Country Life*, 1954.

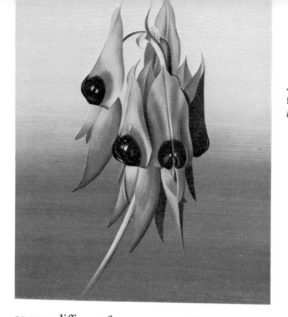

*Sturt's Desert Pea (*Clianthus formosus*). Study in acrylics by Paul Jones*

so very different from our own, *Viola hederacea*. How many emigrants must have looked upon it in Australia and sighed for the motherland!

Dr Turrill mentions one thing that I find fascinating. Certain of these plants from Australia, where their summer is of course our winter, soon adjust themselves to the seasonal change, as the traveller by air adjusts himself to the change of hour. Others, however, accustomed to flower in (say) December, their midsummer, continue to flower in December in England. What creatures of habit these must be!

Between 1956 and 1962, three gifts of sculptures were used to enliven the Pond and its surroundings.

First, from an anonymous donor, came replicas of the ten heraldic animals that James Woodford R.A. designed to mount guard over the Abbey Annexe at the time of the coronation of the present Queen; they have been placed in front of the Palm House, facing the Pond, and frankly I could well manage without them. Far more exciting is the superb pair of stone kylins (Chinese fabulous leonine beasts), bequeathed to Kew in 1958 by Sir John Ramsden, which now recline *à la* Landseer beside the steps on the south side of the Pond. No sinologist seems prepared to say whether these two engaging monsters, which weigh ten tons apiece, date from the Ming or the Ch'ing dynasty.

'This worthy gentleman' (as the *Kew Guild Journal* calls Sir John) also made other handsome bequests to Kew, including a Venetian well-head which has been given a home in a little formal garden behind the Dutch House, made at Sir George Taylor's suggestion in the 1950s and planted with flowers popular in the seventeenth century. The Queen's Garden (as it is called) needs time to mature, and should give even greater pleasure to future visitors to the Palace.

In 1962 a splendid bronze figure of Hercules and Achelous (a river god metamorphosed into a large serpent), which had been purchased by George IV in Paris in 1826 and placed on the East Terrace at Windsor, was presented to Kew by the Queen. It is the work of François-Joseph, baron de Bosio, a Monegasque who was official sculptor successively to Napoleon, Louis XVIII and Charles X; another cast of it can be seen in the Tuileries Gardens in Paris, and the principality of Monaco, proud to claim so distinguished a sculptor as one of its citizens, figured it on a stamp in 1948. The statue, converted into a fountain, now stands in the centre of the Pond, and the siting of it could not possibly have been bettered.

What lies in the future? There has long been talk of a grand new Museum; but I am informed that nothing has been settled. Now that a vast sum of money has been granted for the reconstruction of the Temperate House, it must seem highly improbable that Kew will get yet another costly building in the foreseeable future. But should it ever materialise, let it be intelligently designed and its contents displayed neither in dreary outmoded halls not yet in a labyrinth of trendy black claustrophobic boxes. *Medio tutissimus ibis*.

*   *   *

So—finally—what is Kew?

To the botanist, Kew is a scientific institution, but one whose work is sometimes hindered, and whose funds are excessively squandered, to provide ignorant Londoners with a day in the fresh air among flowers whose names they neither know nor greatly wish to know.

To the average visitor it is, indeed, little more than that. He sees a plant he is fairly sure is lilac, but he finds it labelled '*Syringa* "Souvenir de Louis Späth"', he sees what he thought was syringa, but Kew calls it *Philadelphus*. So he gives up. However, it is all delightful. The sun is shining, the sky is blue, and there are smells that remind him, perhaps, of a distant childhood in the country; there is a nice cafeteria, and the children are enjoying themselves playing what might almost be called 'games' but which yet just escape offending against Regulation 15. He is vaguely aware that someone, somewhere, might be looking at plants through a microscope: he had noticed, near the entrance, a vast complex of buildings labelled 'HERBARIUM. NO ADMITTANCE EXCEPT ON BUSINESS', and in the Gardens something called the Jodrell Laboratory, also out of bounds and more suggestive of telescopes. . . . But Kew is, of course, first and foremost a garden. Then, suddenly, it clouds over, and the wife's feet are beginning to hurt (she ought never to have worn those shoes!).[1] It is time to go back, tired but content, to dirty, noisy London.

[1] See the delightful account of just such a family outing to Kew in Radcliffe Hall's *Adam's Breed*.

There is, however, another though far smaller class of visitor, the practising gardener who has come to Kew armed with some basic horticultural knowledge and with the intention of adding to it. But even he (or, more likely, she) is not really what Kew, in the opinion of the botanists, is there for. He is jotting down the names of shrubs that are making a particularly brave show. He ought really to be at Wisley; but Wisley is so far away and awkward to get to, and in any case the annual subscription of the Royal Horticultural Society is now more than he can afford. Kew still costs only a penny . . .

And finally there is—*rara avis*—the *real* botanist: very likely a foreigner from some continental botanic garden who is making the purest botanical pilgrimage to the Kew Herbarium, the Mecca of his particular faith. He has perhaps come there in order to pursue his work on the reclassification of a genus of obscure weeds whose scientific names will in due course have to be altered in all the textbooks; but in the luncheon break he eagerly enters the famous Gardens. With what emotion, what devotion, he studies in the Palm House *Encephalartos woodii*, grown from a branch of the only plant ever found in the wild, or that weary, crutch-supported *Sophora japonica* near the T-Range—one of five imported from China by James Gordon in 1753 and still capable of producing its panicles of creamy blossoms in late summer. For such treasures, alone, the journey would have been justified.

So Kew has to be a compromise. You and I contribute through taxes to its upkeep; it is therefore only fair that our vulgar tastes should also be catered for. And I think most people will agree that, taken all in all, Kew does its job remarkably well. Each visitor will probably find something to criticise—and no one will accuse me of having pulled my punches; but there is far more to praise than to condemn.

I have seen, at one time or another, a good many botanic gardens in various parts of the world, and obviously there is much in many of them where Kew cannot compete. What, for example, is the Succulent House at Kew by comparison with the Huntington at Los Angeles? What is its Palm House for those who know the Peradeniya Gardens in Sri Lanka (Ceylon)? But where, at the Huntington or Peradeniya, are those sheets of snowdrops and bluebells in spring? And what, incidentally, would many of these gardens have been without the help and advice of men whom Kew trained and sent all over what was once our great empire—and beyond?

In brief, Kew remains not only the greatest botanical institution but also one of the most enchanting gardens in the world.

FLOREAT KEW!

W.J.W.B.
The Watts Gallery, Compton,
June 1977

Index